Over in the Country

A Blue Ridge Mountain Family's Stories

Becky Cannaday Merchant

Over in the Country

A Blue Ridge Mountain Family's Stories

Becky Cannaday Merchant

BUENA VISTA, VIRGINIA

1 3 5 7 9 10 8 6 4 2

Library of Congress Control Number: 2007943729
Over in the Country
A Blue Ridge Mountain Family's Stories
Becky Cannaday Merchant

Includes Bibliographical References

p. cm.
1. Virginia History 1785–1950 2. Genealogy: Kennady/Cannaday family 3. Genealogy: Semmes/Simms family
4. Genealogy Rakes family 5. Appalachian farming, early 20th century 6. Appalachianna
7. Southwest Virginia, early 20th century 8. Moonshine recipe
I. Merchant, Becky Cannaday, 1941— II. Title.

ISBN 13: 978-0-9800077-2-5 (softcover : alk. paper)

ISBN 10: 0-9800077-0-6

Front cover painting of the Simms farm house by Elva Simms Cannaday.
Back cover photograph of Paul and Eula Simms on their wedding day, 1905.

Book Design by Patricia Gibson
Cover Design by Christopher Johnson
Creative Director Patty Williams

Mariner Publishing
A division of
Mariner Companies, Inc.
131 West 21st Street
Buena Vista, VA 24416
Tel: 540-264-0021
http://www.marinermedia.com

Printed in the United States of America

This book is printed on acid-free paper
meeting the requirements of the American Standard for Permanence of
Paper for Printed Library Materials.

Over in the Country

A Blue Ridge Mountain Family's Stories

Becky Cannaday Merchant

BUENA VISTA, VIRGINIA

1 3 5 7 9 10 8 6 4 2

Library of Congress Control Number: 2007943729
Over in the Country
A Blue Ridge Mountain Family's Stories
Becky Cannaday Merchant

Includes Bibliographical References

p. cm.
1. Virginia History 1785–1950 2. Genealogy: Kennady/Cannaday family 3. Genealogy: Semmes/Simms family
4. Genealogy Rakes family 5. Appalachian farming, early 20th century 6. Appalachianna
7. Southwest Virginia, early 20th century 8. Moonshine recipe
I. Merchant, Becky Cannaday, 1941— II. Title.

ISBN 13: 978-0-9800077-2-5 (softcover : alk. paper)

ISBN 10: 0-9800077-0-6

Front cover painting of the Simms farm house by Elva Simms Cannaday.
Back cover photograph of Paul and Eula Simms on their wedding day, 1905.

Book Design by Patricia Gibson
Cover Design by Christopher Johnson
Creative Director Patty Williams

Mariner Publishing
A division of
Mariner Companies, Inc.
131 West 21st Street
Buena Vista, VA 24416
Tel: 540-264-0021
http://www.marinermedia.com

Printed in the United States of America

This book is printed on acid-free paper
meeting the requirements of the American Standard for Permanence of
Paper for Printed Library Materials.

Dedicated to

Paul and Eula Rakes Simms,
my Grandparents

and

Elva Simms Cannaday,
my Mother

Table of Contents

Opening Note

When I was a little girl I used to feel sorry for my friends who didn't have grandparents like mine, with a farm like theirs to wander and play on and to let my imagination run free. I was only ten years old when they sold their country home and moved away, but I remember that farm and that house well and with remarkable detail fifty-five years later.

I could not give my own children or grandchildren such a place, but I can give them, my cousins and their children and grandchildren, and any other relative or friend a piece of the past – a part of American History through the Simms' family's stories.

This memoir centers around Paul and Eula Simms, their children – Earl, Elva, Edsel and Betty, and their home in the Virginia foothills of the Blue Ridge Mountains during the first half of the twentieth century.

The protagonist of this drama, Paul Simms, was a self-sufficient farmer who prospered in a place where most didn't, thanks to hard work, determination, imagination and good business sense. He had a creative, perverse side that I credit to family tradition and an inherited twist in one of his chromosomes. Eula Rakes Simms, unlike her husband, wasn't interested in modern inventions or wandering too far from her home. She was, nevertheless, a compliment to Paul, working beside him and supporting him in his many endeavors; she was a woman who could rise on any occasion to any challenge. The two of them were the mainstays of their community on Hurd's Branch in the Endicott area of Franklin County.

Paul and Eula did not live their lives in isolation or spring up without a past of their own. Stories of the first family members to settle along Runnett Bag Creek in Franklin County have always been part of family lore, and I have included them in this memoir. I followed the genealogical and migration records of the Cannadays, (Paul's mother's family), the Simmses, (Paul's father's family) and the Rakeses, (Eula's father's family), from as far back as I could "reach" until they found their way to the Blue Ridge Mountains in Franklin County. The Cannadays were among the earliest people to settle in that valley and, at one time, claimed as much as five square miles along Runnett Bag Creek. The Rakeses, Columbus McGruder and his wife Ophelia, moved from Patrick County to their "plantation" on Otter Creek in the 1890s. The arrival of the first of our Simms' kin in Franklin County is a long and fascinating story that began in 1640.

I have heard "William Ignatius Marmaduke Simms," a blend of names, run together like a line of poetry repeated all my life. I will never forget the day I found a large white roll of paper in my office at the Stonewall Jackson House Museum and planned to throw the cumbersome, unknown and unwanted "junk" in the trash. Before I did, I thought I ought to have a look at it. So I unrolled the document, which turned out to be a genealogy, and was struck by the first names on the list: Marmaduke Semmes (1640-1693) married in 1668 to Fortune Medford Semmes (d.1701). There were our original ancestors, our Simms' Adam and Eve, at least in America. The chart was handsomely inscribed with hundreds of names (including William and Ignatius), lineage lines, and dozens of biographical notations. It had been researched and prepared by Tom Corse, another Semmes descendent, who had given this copy to our curator some years before, even though it had no relevance to Stonewall Jackson. It had plenty for me and my family. This document added important historical information to the other Simms genealogy that I had inherited.

I conducted additional research at courthouses in Rocky Mount, Stuart and Martinsville, as well as at the Library of Virginia, digging for information about the three families, looking for deeds and land grants and any other evidence I could discover about their past. I only scratched the surface in my courthouse work and know that there is much more to do. My chief purpose, after all, has been to save the family's stories and to honor my grandparents.

The Simms' homeplace was a modest farm tucked into a remote Virginia valley, like thousands of other similar places. And like those other farms, this one is gone, burned to the ground by the careless next owners.

It is hard to go back over in the country and visit the site of my grandparents' farm or to even look at the land where that cherished place once stood – without the white frame house and the smell of wood smoke, the chopping block and the mowed fields, the carefully planted vegetable garden, the snowball bush in the corner of the yard, the hillside swing, the slamming screen door, and people working the farm. It seems so unlike itself, so small, but, by the lay of the land, the through road, the branch and the spring, the upper house and granary which are still standing, I know it is the same place.

My grandparents' vacant, weedy, abandoned fallow farm reminds me of the death mask of Stonewall Jackson which was a great curiosity on display at his home in Lexington — the clay image of a once vibrant, outstanding general now diminished to an alarmingly small life-less shell.

The farmhouse and my grandparents have left us. All that remain are the stories.

1
Settling the Ancestors

This first chapter settles the Simms, Rakes, and Cannaday families, who were the ancestors of Paul and Eula Simms, in southwest Franklin County. It seems likely that two of the families migrated from central Virginia and one from the Eastern shore of Maryland; all three arrived—the Cannadays in Franklin County, the Simms and Rakes in nearby Patrick County—just before or just after the American Revolutionary War.

In writing this essay I have relied on handed-down stories, courthouse documents, and the genealogical research which previous family historians have carried out. There remain significant gaps in the stories of our pioneer kinsmen and women, and plenty more courthouse research to do, but perhaps we have enough information to add a bit of flesh to their skeletons, to give life to the begats, who, without the stories, become a mere list of names.

Our families, like most early Americans of English and Irish descent, had dozens of children, and they bequeathed to them the same first names, generation after generation. All the Williams and James and Ignatius and Marmadukes, Elizabeths and Janes can cause confusion without a genealogical chart at hand while reading about the family pioneers—especially the Kennady/Cannaday clan. Consequently I have provided family genealogies as a guide for this chapter.

Because this is a memoir of Paul and Eula Simms and the land that supported them and their family, we start with them before going back in time.

The Cannadays

...granted by the said Commonwealth unto William Kennady Senior a certain tract... containing five hundred and fifty one acres by survey... November 1785, being in the County of Henry on head branches of Runnet Creek.

William Kennady/Cannady, Sr. b. c1715 d. c1805	m	Biddy
William Kennady/Cannaday, Jr. b. c1735 d. 1801	m	Nancy
James Cannaday, Sr. b. c1755 d. 1817	m 1775	Elizabeth Rakes b. c1756 d. c1853
James Cannnaday, II b. c1783 d. 1861	m 1813	Sarah Young b. c1797 d. 1861
Caroline Y. Cannaday b. 1820 d. 1899	m 1841	Ignatius Andrew Jackson Simms b. 1816 d. 1855
James Robert Simms b. 1844 d. 1928	m 1872	(1) Lucinda Elizabeth Cannaday b. 1851 d. 1886
Paul Simms b. 1878 d. 1964	m 1905	Eula Rakes b. 1886 d. 1982

See Appendix A for a more complete Cannaday genealogy.[1]

What did Paul Simms see more than a century ago when he surveyed his newly acquired land, 100 acres of uncultivated potential? I want to think that he saw his future and that it made him happy. Not that he would have ever said or even thought such nonsense. At 25 he was experienced with farm work and knew that years of hard manual labor lay ahead. But he was a man determined that his farm would be the best, the most productive, the most successful anywhere around, and that he and his family would thrive and prosper.

In 1903 Paul purchased "a certain tract or parcell [*sic*] of land lying on the waters of Running [*sic*] Bag Creek in Franklin County known as the Martin land containing one hundred acres more or less..." from his father, James Robert Simms, for what was surely the favorable price of $2 an acre.[2] The land was a small portion of a huge grant made to three Irish immigrant brothers by the name of Kennedy/Cannaday around the time of the American Revolutionary War, land which was inherited and divided and sold by the children, grandchildren and great grandchildren over the next 125 years. The grant stretched from the Blue Ridge Mountains (near the current landmark "Smartview" on the Blue Ridge Parkway) down the slope of the mountain as far east as the Smith River, about five square miles. Or that is what we always thought, the way the story passed from dinner table to family gathering, from memory to memory.

It is not easy to let go of comfortable family myths, told and retold over the years, stories that connect us to a particular and much loved place, stories of pioneer ancestors—unless the reality of hard evidence requires it. There are only a few official documents before 1800 to anchor our family history, and plenty of room for speculation and lore to fill in the gaps. But they are there and we have to respect them.

One of the first anchors of evidence is, indeed, a land grant, actually a warrant—or official permission—issued by the Commonwealth of Virginia in 1782 and signed by the Lieutenant Governor, Beverly Randolph, to William Kennady Sr. in 1787 for 551 acres "lying and being in the County of Henry on the head branches of Runnet Creek."[3] It appears that the family legend of a land grant is accurate. What with literacy problems of the day, the name Kennady for Cannaday and various other spellings, which clerks wrote according to sound or custom, is easily explained. The surname Kennady is near enough to Cannaday, the place name Runnet Creek (known to us as Runnett Bag Creek) as familiar to our family's ears as the James River is to eastern settlers, and the location in Henry, soon to be Franklin County, are convincing evidence that William Sr. was among our earliest ancestors to settle on land in that part of Virginia. The size of the land grant, as land grants went in those days, was puny, much smaller than we thought, and it appears to have been made to only one man, not three brothers.

Warrants for land grants of this time period were complicated and used for various purposes. They were given to soldiers for Revolutionary War service or to farmers who assisted in the war; they were often purchased outright and then exchanged or sold by the original recipient, like script, to someone else.

Virginia had more land than cash, and the young government often paid men for service in the French and Indian or the American Revolutionary Wars with awards of land. Considering the date of the Cannaday land grant, 1782—squarely at the end of the Revolutionary War—it is easy to assume that it was payment for military service or for supplies such as horses, mules, grain, food or other goods furnished by the Senior Kennady/Cannaday, who, by my best guess would have been sixty at the start of the war, to the American troops fighting for Independence.

The one problem with that scenario for our family is that the land Virginia designated for veterans of the American Revolutionary War was generally located in what were the far reaches of the Commonwealth—current day Kentucky and Ohio. But that was not always the case.

Other land grants, which came from the Crown of England, usually to impoverished younger sons of aristocrats, were not at all likely to have been awarded to our Irish ancestors, who repeatedly took up arms against the hated British monarchy.

Another road to acquiring a land grant was to purchase one from the Commonwealth.[4] A man, say William Kennady Sr., could have purchased a warrant for a specific amount of land (or he could have bought it from another warrant holder), 551 acres from Griffith Dickerson, perhaps. Then Mr. Kennady/Cannaday Sr. would locate unclaimed state land—in Henry/Franklin County, maybe—have it surveyed (possibly paying the surveyor off with a portion of the property), present his warrant along with the description of the newly surveyed land for registration at the courthouse in Rocky Mount, the county seat of his claim. After at least six months (in this case, several years) or time enough to make sure the claim was uncontested and thus legitimate, the new landowner, Mr. Kennady/Cannaday Senior, went to Richmond to have his land grant verified and signed by the Governor, or his agent, the Lieutenant Governor.

The land grant document to our kinsman read:

> *Know ye that by virtue and in consideration of part of a land office Treasury Warrant number twelve thousand five hundred and eighty-two (#12,582) is granted by the said Commonwealth unto William Kennady Senior a certain tract or parcel of land containing five hundred and fifty one acres by survey bearing date the fifth day of November 1785, being in the County of Henry on head branches of Runnet Creek*

The description of the surveyed parcel followed. It was signed by Lieutenant Governor Beverly Randolph and dated June 21, 1787.[5]

Original Cannaday homestead, c1780.

That important document provides much useful information about acquisition of land in early America by our ancestors. It took a total of five years from the date of purchase or award of the land grant in June 1782, to the time it was surveyed and posted in Franklin County Courthouse in November 1785, to the final registration with the Commonwealth in 1787. The document stated that the parcel of 551 acres was a part or portion of the land warrant, and it clearly identified the recipient as William Kennady Sr.[6]

In the 1780s William Cannaday Sr. and his wife Biddy found their way to the foothills of the Blue Ridge Mountains, to a wilderness not easily accessible even today with modern roads and gasoline-powered automobiles. The river and creek beds, the animal tracks and Indian trails must have been essential pathways to homesteads for them, and for even earlier pioneers. But once there, they found the most agreeable, available land they could, and had it surveyed and registered in the county seat. The area they staked out for themselves was a long, narrow, generally flat stretch of land in a pleasant valley along the banks of Runnett Bag Creek, surrounded by hills and hollows that soon rolled up into mountain peaks. Their homestead was well supplied with two essential resources, copious woods and plentiful fresh water. They took possession of their land in the foothills of the Blue Ridge; they cleared as many acres as they needed for farming and used the wood for fencing, for fuel, and for building a home. One of our more precious "heirlooms" from the William Cannaday family was the log cabin they built on the rise of a hill, nestled near a flowing spring, just above Runnett Bag Creek. It sat there for over 200 years, but sadly, in 2004, the old log house collapsed from lack of attention and use, a truly unfortunate loss.

William Cannaday Sr. was not the only Cannaday who settled along Runnett Bag Creek. Early courthouse documents confirm that at least two more families of Cannadays lived there. Besides William Sr. and his wife Biddy, there were William Jr., his wife Nancy, and their son James and his wife Elizabeth, all of whom settled in the same valley around the same time. It was not long before there were many more Cannadays in the valley and much more land in their hands.

For over 150 years descendents of William and Biddy Cannaday Sr., their son William Cannaday Jr. and his wife Nancy lived, married, multiplied, and prospered in this remote, beautiful, but unlikely place where they had first established a foothold. Some, of course, moved on, but many, including those important to us, remained. During the early years of settlement, the Cannadays took possession of land in Franklin County along Runnett Bag Creek. The deeds on record at the courthouse in Rocky Mount indicate that the Cannaday families were intent on purchasing a continuous stretch of land along this small, distinctive waterway. The creek was the one identifiable and constant feature in the descriptions of the deeds, called indentures, on file, beginning in the late 18th century, about the time that Franklin County was "born" from Henry and several other counties.[7]

Multiple deeds from 1786-1804, both purchase and sale by Cannadays are on file at the Rocky Mount Courthouse, and provide evidence of this drive for land. During that time, four Cannadays bought and sold property along Runnett Bag Creek. I am convinced that they were related but, without a more thorough genealogical study, I am unsure of the nature of their kinship.

The late 18th century was a favorable time for land acquisition in this part of Virginia, and all over the South. Victory at Yorktown meant that the British were no longer around to incite the Indian attacks against the colonists which had discouraged western expansion and settlement; the vast new country was open for settlement. In an agrarian society like that of early southern America, ownership of farm land was essential for survival, at least 100 well-situated acres were necessary for a self-sufficient farmer to have a chance at success. The Cannadays had certainly mastered that lesson and went about buying or acquiring large quantities of land. William Sr. by grant and purchase accumulated over 1,000 acres between 1785 and 1790. He paid 59 pounds for 450 acres (and an unknown amount for the other 550 acres, which may have been a land exchange with Griffith Dickerson). In 1792, probably because of his advanced age—he was an old man in his 80s, he began to sell off his property, in most cases to relatives.[8]

His son and our kinsman William Cannaday Jr. (c1735-1801) acquired 360 acres in 1792 and 1793. Interestingly, 128 of those acres came from "cashing" in a portion of the same land grant (warrant #12582) issued to or acquired by his father.[9] The document on file in the Rocky Mount courthouse and at the Library of Virginia indicates that the warrant was originally issued to Griffith Dickerson, who must have sold the grant to Cannaday or exchanged it for other property.[10]

In 1801 William Jr. died, about four years before his father, the long-lived William Sr. Soon after his son's death William Cannaday Sr. purchased ten acres of inherited land from each of William Cannaday Jr.'s heirs—his wife Nancy, their five children and spouses, for ten pounds each. I assume that the grandfather wanted to help out his daughter-in-law and his grandchildren by providing them with a sum of money for a rather small amount of land, 110 pounds for 110 acres.[11]

Besides the Williams, there were two other Cannadays, John and James, who bought and sold property during those years. Without more information, I am not sure of their relationship to the Williams. The names John and James were as common then as they are today, and often passed from generation to generation. Those Cannaday "boys" could have been William Sr.'s brothers or his sons, but I believe they were his grandsons. We know that William Cannaday Jr. and Nancy had sons named John and James, and by the 1790s those two men were in their thirties, married and in need of land.

John Cannaday must have struggled to make ends meet. In 1789 he purchased a house and 75 acres for 50 pounds. Only three years later in

1792, he sold the same property for 45 pounds, five less than he paid originally.[12] In 1801 he bought 30 acres from his grandfather William Sr. for 15 pounds, the same year that William Sr. paid John 10 pounds for his 10 inherited acres. James Cannaday, on the other hand, appears to have prospered. If my supposition that James is William Cannaday Sr.'s grandson is correct, then this James Cannaday was our kinsman whom I write about in some detail later in this chapter.

When William Cannaday Jr. died in 1801 at age 69 (only 19 years after settling the land with his father and son), he left all that he had to his widow, Nancy, to his five children, and their spouses.[13]

I am keenly interested in all of William Jr. and Nancy Cannaday's children and want to know what became of them. Did they leave the area? Where did they settle? What share, if any, of the original property became theirs? I have not yet found records that provide answers to those questions.

We do, however, have a few documents that provide information about James I (c1755-1817), William Jr. and Nancy's oldest child, the man from whom our family story and line continue. These documents include property deeds, his will, and his record of military service during the American Revolutionary War.[14]

James Cannaday was about 21 on October 8, 1776 when he enlisted as a private in the 3rd Virginia Regiment and fought under General Nathaniel Greene. He served continuously until March 1, 1777 and perhaps longer—but that is all we know for sure.[15]

According to Hughes Cannaday (b. c1868), a teacher, early family historian, and a great grandson of James and Elizabeth, his great grandparents, James I and Elizabeth, along with James I's widowed mother Nancy lived in the family's original log house.[16] James continued to acquire land; in fact by 1804 he had at least 700 acres and probably much more.[17] James and Elizabeth farmed their land and improved the house by adding porches and rooms. They were fruitful and multiplied; they had at least eight children, and may have had as many as a dozen.

Persistent legends surround James I's wife Elizabeth Raikes (or Rakes)—stories that she was related to Sir Robert Raikes, an Englishman who founded Sunday Schools to educate poor children. It was said that she was a child bride of 14-years of age who played with her dolls while her husband worked in the fields and fought in the war, that, after she became a widow, divided her house down the middle because she couldn't get along with her mother-in-law and, finally, that she lived to the remarkable old age of 105.

Once again the documents suggest that we must make some alterations of those myths. There is no evidence, other than the similarity of names and maybe some wishful thinking, that she and Sir Robert Raikes were related. There is little doubt that Elizabeth lived a long life. According to notes made by her grandson Isaac Young Cannaday (1817-1861) in the *Record of Deaths* on file at the Rocky Mount courthouse dated September 1, 1854, Elizabeth Rakes Cannaday (1756-1853), his grandmother, was born in Buckingham County, Virginia and lived to be 97-years old.[18] If Isaac was correct about the dates, Elizabeth must have been in her 30s when she and her husband James I began acquiring land and settled in Franklin County. Perhaps they met and married in Buckingham County before moving West. It is probable that the entire Cannaday/Kennady clan migrated from Buckingham County, which was (and still is) in the middle of the state, before homesteading in Franklin County. The Rakes' family records (perhaps Elizabeth's relatives) suggest that a branch of that family also left Buckingham County for Patrick County, in western Virginia, around 1787.

As to the myth that Elizabeth was living in disharmony with a relative, there is indeed evidence that she fought pitched battles with someone with whom she was forced to live—perhaps it was her mother-in-law Nancy Cannaday. In 1830 the Court at Rocky Mount ordered that "Elizabeth Cannaday widow of James Cannaday" be allotted 100 acres with a line drawn "straight to the middle of the dwelling house and... out the kitchen..."[19]

At the time of his death in 1817, James I owned six slaves and, according to the inventory of his estate, other assets valued at almost $2000, plus a significant amount of land. In a slight twist to the normal written will, James' was verbal, recorded and attested to in court by his executors, sons James II and William. They followed their father's wishes concerning the distribution of his estate, making sure that the youngest son Pleasant, who was 16 at the time of their father's death, legally received 369 acres, the "lands he [James I] lived on himself and two hundred dollars."[20] No doubt he expected Pleasant to remain in the original Cannaday homestead and take care of his mother, James I's widow, the long-lived Elizabeth. In addition James II and William made sure that their brother John received 200 acres and William, 30 acres, as James I promised. With those exceptions, he put "them all on an equal footing."[21] It is difficult to know how much land James I actually owned. I suspect that the deeds on file at Rocky Mount, which indicate that he purchased 750 acres, do not tell the whole story.

James' I son, James II, did not inherit the homeplace, nor any specified parcel or tract of land from his father, but that did not deter him from acquiring sizeable amounts of property during his life-time; perhaps it even inspired him.[22]

James Cannaday II was 34 and married to Sarah Young at the time of his father's death in 1817. They had three or four of the dozen children they eventually raised to adulthood. By this time he was well along on the road to prosperity. He owned at least 278 acres on Runnett Bag Creek and had cash enough to buy one of his father's slaves, Archer, for $750. Two years later, in 1819, he purchased his brother William and sister-in-law Martha's home and 140 acre farm for $800. William and Martha had decided to move to Patrick County. Thus began James II's great land grab. In almost 50 years (1812-1861) he made 30 trips to the country seat in Rocky Mount to register new land purchases and an occasional land sale. During that period he accumulated over 3,000 acres, the most significant of which was the Hairston Estate (1200 acres) and a mansion known as the Runnett Bag Plantation. This property, which he bought in 1841 for $5,400 from Malinda and John Hairston of Mississippi, was at the confluence of Otter and Runnett Bag Creeks. Toward the end of his 78 years, James II began selling some of his estate to his sons: 247 acres to Isaac in 1851 for $500, 300 acres to James B. in 1859 for $3000 ($1000 in cash and $2000 as a gift—by this time inflation had hit the South) and 442 acres with premises to John Treadwell for $5000 in 1860. John was his youngest child and only 27 at the time of this significant purchase, which was probably a portion of the Hairston estate.[23]

Some of James II's success can be attributed to his work as a surveyor, a particularly useful skill in the early days of the country's settlement, which often resulted in acquisition of land as payment for work provided.

According to Frieda Cannaday, a tireless researcher into the Cannaday family (the family into which she married) courthouse records indicate that James II was appointed "surveyor of the Road from the fork of Otter Creek to the ford of Runnett Bag in place of Charles Cannaday resigned with the allotment of (?) lands filed" in August 1823, assigned "to view way for road from Patrick to Franklin and report" in June 1832. He was appointed as "surveyor of the Road from the ford of Otter Creek to Cannady's Mill on Runnett bag with the last of the (?) lands filed" in July 1833.[24] Maybe we should think of him as the George Washington of Franklin County.

One of James II's contributions to the welfare of the community was a road he built, known as Cannaday's Gap—a steep, unpaved two to three mile incline, straight up the side of the Blue Ridge Mountains to the juncture of Franklin County with Floyd County. The road, perilous as it was, provided access to another portion of the state and was a boon to that remote section of Virginia.[25]

According to his grandson Hughes Cannaday's written account, James II owned all of the land along Runnett Bag Creek (and on both sides, says Frieda) for five miles from the Blue Ridge Mountains to the Smith River, and he owned as many as 50 slaves at some time during his lifetime. Hughes Cannaday said that his grandparents, James II and Sarah Cannaday, lived on a farm along Runnett Bag Creek, about a mile east of the original log cabin, in a house with two stories and a double porch that sat in the curve of the road. This is the house that eventually belonged to Matt Spencer.

James II owned a mill and a farm located at Endicott on current Route 40, both of which James' grandson, I.T. Cannaday later purchased. He also owned the previously mentioned Runnett Bag Plantation (known as the Hairston Estate and Mansion) at the juncture of Runnett Bag and Otter Creeks which served as quarters for his Negroes. A significant portion of this plantation, 442 acres and the premises (the mansion, I assume), John Treadwell Cannaday, James II's youngest son, purchased from his father in 1860 for $5,000. Apparently in the settlement of the estate James II's executors decided that John should receive another 400 acres as his share. John Treadwell Cannaday subsequently bequeathed this land to his son Hughes Dillard Cannaday who said that it consisted of 859 acres.[26]

More than family lore support the claims that James Cannaday II was a wealthy man. His will and land deals verify it.[27] In the summer and fall of 1861 typhoid fever or an epidemic of another sort took the lives of several members of the James Cannaday II family, as well as a number of their slaves. Son Isaac died in August 1861, and James' wife Sarah two months later on October 18, 1861. In the opening paragraph of his will, which he drew up October 29, 1861, James II said, "knowing the uncertainty of life and being bodily afflicated [*sic*]" he wished to dispose of his estate as he provided in his will. He died of the dreaded disease six days later, November 4, 1861.

At the time of James' death, his wife, three of their 12 children, a son-in-law and an unknown number of his slaves were dead. He felt particularly responsible for several widows: one was his daughter Caroline, a woman of 41; the other was Mary, widow of Isaac, who had recently died. His ten remaining slaves he left to his daughters, except Caroline to whom he left land. To a favored grandson, seven-year old William James Byrd whose mother had died, he left a "likely Negro boy" and $1000. He stated that he considered all his children equal, but he made exceptions: to Mary, Isaac's widow, he left 300 acres less the 42 that he had previously sold to Isaac; to Stephen he left the tract of land on which he lived less the land he willed to Isaac's widow; and to Caroline he bequeathed several tracts of land, one containing 280 acres lying on the waters of Runnett Bag, another containing 235 acres, a parcel of 32 acres on Runnett Bag Creek, and a tract lying on Buttermilk and Runnett Bag Creek (several miles south of Endicott). In his will James stated specifically that Caroline could hold the Buttermilk tract in fee simple, which meant that she could sell the land without restrictions. He did not make that notation about any of the other land which she, or any of his other children inherited. In addition to the property, he left her $500. James valued Caroline's inheritance of land at $1800 and Stephen's at $3000. Obviously concerned for her welfare, he further provided that if she fell into debt, "I desire that she shall not be required to refund or pay back any portion to my heirs." In addition, he provided that "if his remaining estate amounted to more than that given to Caroline, she was to be made equal with all of my children..."

And so we come to Caroline Young Cannaday, Paul Simms' "Grandma," who was born in 1820 and married to Ignatius Andrew (Andy) Jackson Simms in 1841.

With the Cannaday ancestors well-established along Runnett Bag Creek in southwest Franklin County, we will leave them and try to work out how the Simms family found its way to this same place.

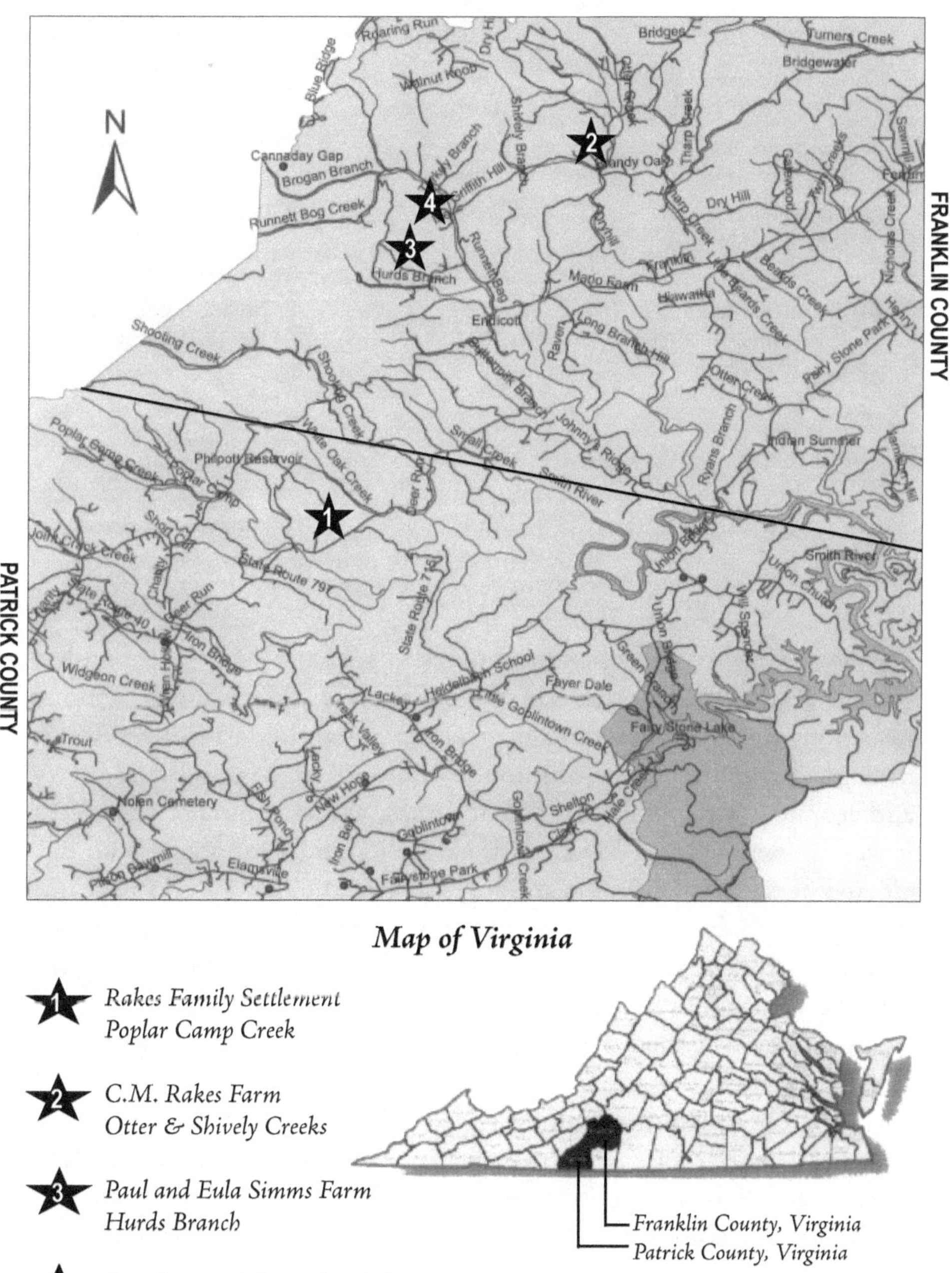

The Simms Family

"If only Grandma hadn't sold that land, we'd all be millionaires."

Marmaduke Semmes b. c1635 d. 1692	m 1668	Fortune Mitford b. c1647 d. 1701
Marmaduke Semmes II b. c1675 d. 1717	m 1707	Elizabeth Clarkson b. c1679 d. c1736
Francis Semmes b. c1711 d. 1171	m 1733	Lucretia Chapman
Ignatius Semmes/Simms b. 1745 d. 1819	m (1)c1772 (2)1790	(1) Sabret Hobart d. 1788 (2) Jane Nance
Ignatius Andrew Jackson Simms b. 1816 d. 1855	m 1841	Caroline Y. Cannaday b. 1820 d. 1899
James Robert Simms b. 1844 d. 1928	m 1872	(1) Lucinda Elizabeth Cannaday b. 1851 d. 1886
Paul Simms b. 1878 d. 1964	m 1905	Eula Rakes b. 1886 d. 1982

See Appendix A for more complete genealogy of Simms' family

According to well-documented records in the Maryland archives, Ignatius Andrew "Andy" Jackson Simms' ancestor, Marmaduke Semmes, was among the first immigrants to arrive in America. Marmaduke, Andy's great-great grandfather, sailed into the harbor of St. Mary's Island, Maryland around 1660.[28] That settlement on the western shore of the Chesapeake Bay was a haven for English Catholics and Protestants who had suffered persecution at home and had come to the New World in search of religious freedom. We have reason to believe that Marmaduke Semmes, his wife Fortune, and many of their descendents were Catholics.[29] By the time the future Simmses found their way to Franklin County, Virginia, however, they had shed their past religious affiliation and become members of other denominations, Methodists, many of them.

When Marmaduke Semmes arrived in Maryland, which had received its colonial charter only 30 years earlier in 1632, he enjoyed several advantages, a head-right and political connections.[30] The head-right meant that he, like anyone else who had paid his own passage across the ocean, was entitled to 50 acres of land as an inducement to help settle the new country. His political connections earned him the position of Door Keeper of the Upper House of the Maryland Assembly in 1662. In the early days of the Colony, its governmental body met on St. Mary's Island. Door Keeper of the state's elected assembly was a political appointee and served as a Sergeant-at-arms who maintained order during meetings of the assembly and kept the riff-raff out.

In 1668 Marmaduke (wonder if his friends called him "Duke"?) Semmes married Fortune Watson Medford, an educated, gentle lady.[31] She had arrived in Maryland in 1664 with her husband, Bulmar Medford (or Mitford), who died in 1665 at the young age of 21. Many new settlers from the cool climates of England perished from illnesses such as malaria, which were prevalent in the warmer climates of the American colonies, or other diseases that they had never been exposed to previously. He left her a warrant for a 250 acre land grant which she received in 1666[32] and a baby boy she named Thomas.[33]

Fortune and Marmaduke Semmes were a part of the local landed gentry. Over the next 25 years they acquired by both purchase and grant, three estates. The largest of these was a 836 acre parcel of land which they called St. George's. It was in St. Mary's or nearby St. Charles County and was the estate they made their home.[34] The second parcel, "Middle Plantation," which Semmes bought in February, 1674, was a 300 acre woodland farm located in Cecil County, many miles north of St. Mary's, at the northernmost point of the Chesapeake Bay at the confluence of the Elk and the Susquehanna Rivers.[35] In 1684 he received from Lord Baltimore a 400 acre grant which came to be known as "Semmes Forest," also in faraway Cecil County.[36]

The only practical way to travel from St. Mary's to Cecil County in those days was by water. Considering his life in St. Mary's and at St. Georges, which was probably on the Potomac River, Marmaduke must have owned a boat or a ship and been a seafarer, or he may have hired boats to make the trip.[37]

Fortune and Marmaduke Semmes acquired more than 1500 acres, abundant land on which to raise their five sons (one of whom was Thomas Medford, Bulmer Medford's child) and to insure their futures.[38] Death came very early to our seventeenth century grandparents, or so it seems to us, but their contemporaries would have considered them long-lived. Marmaduke was about 58 when he died and Fortune about 54.

When Marmaduke drew up his will in 1690, he stated:

> *In the name of God aman I Marmaduk Simms of St. Mary's County in The Province of Maryland plantor being sick and weake ...doe make ordaine and appoint this my last will and testament..."*

To his son, Anthony he left 200 acres from the St. George's Plantation and the 400 acre Semmes Forest in Cecil County; to son James he left Middle Plantation in Cecil County. The remaining land around St. George's Plantation and their home he left to Fortune for her life-time, to be distributed to sons John and Marmaduke after her death, with John having first choice of the land. In a memorandum he added that Anthony was not to receive the house or any money. Marmaduke Semmes died three years later in 1693.[39]

Fortune remained at St. Georges until her death eight years later in 1701. In her will she followed her husband's wishes by providing for her sons John and Marmaduke. To John she left 319 acres, half the remaining acreage of St. Georges Plantation, to Marmaduke, 319 acres, the other half "which said part belongs to the plantation I now live upon with the housing and all the appurtenances thereunto belonging after my decease unto him the said Marmaduke." She left a small sum, 20 shillings, to her son from her first marriage, Thomas Medford (who was about 35 years old at the time of her death). Perhaps when he came of age, Thomas inherited the original 250 acres of land granted to his father. To her grandson, also named Thomas Medford, she left a two-year old heifer and to another grandson Marmaduke, son of Anthony, she left a mare colt.[40]

The fourth and youngest son of Marmaduke I and Fortune Semmes was named for his father. In fact, during the early Colonial period many of the children and grandchildren of this first Semmes in America named their boy babies Marmaduke in honor of the family patriarch. Marmaduke II, the son of Marmaduke I, was our ancestor (and the one that matters most, of course). He was born around 1675 and married Elizabeth Clarkson in 1707. This was Elizabeth's second marriage. She was born around 1679 and married her first husband, William Smith, in 1692 when she was quite young, 13 or 14-years old. Marriage at such a tender age would be a shocking event today but was quite common then, in part because there was little opportunity for schooling of any sort for girls and young women. Apparently Elizabeth and William Smith had no children; she was a widow by the time of her wedding to Marmaduke II, 15 years later.

From Fortune's will we know that her son Marmaduke inherited a sizeable portion of St. George's plantation, as well as the plantation house. It seems safe to assume that Marmaduke II and Elizabeth Semmes resided at St. George's with their three children, Ruth the oldest, born in 1708, Francis, the only son, born in 1711, and Elleanor, a second daughter, born in 1714. The year 1717 proved fateful for Marmaduke and Elizabeth Semmes. Early in that year, or perhaps at the end of 1716, they lost an infant girl whom they had named Elizabeth. They countered that tragedy when Elizabeth became pregnant. Before spring, however, Marmaduke must have fallen ill and suspected that he would soon die. He drew up a will in which he mentioned his wife, his three children, the unborn child and a Catholic priest, James Haddock, verifying my supposition that the first American Semmes were Catholics. On May 11, 1717, at the age of 45, Marmaduke Semmes II died.[41] Later that year, his widow Elizabeth Semmes gave birth to a baby girl in Bryantown Hundred, St. Charles, Maryland. She called her newborn Elizabeth, both to preserve her own name and as a memory of the first baby Elizabeth, who had died.

The next Semmes ancestor in our line was Francis Semmes, born in 1711, the second child and only son of Elizabeth and Marmaduke II. Francis married Lucretia Chapman in 1733, and the couple had ten children. Like their parents and grandparents, they lived in Maryland on the border of St. Charles and St. Mary's Counties in the Newport Hundred.

Over the next 34 years Francis Semmes bought, traded and sold property, most of it adjacent to St. Georges. In 1736, three years after his marriage to Lucretia, Francis sold a tract of land called "Stoney Hill," which he had inherited from his mother Elizabeth Clarkson Semmes. That property, in Prince George's County, was purchased by William Clarkson (a relative, perhaps a cousin?). With the sale of Stoney Hall, Francis was in a position to add to his estate and five months later, he purchased 103 acres in the "St. Georges" tract from one of the many Marmaduke Semmes. Both men were listed as "planter" on the deed transfer. It seems likely that this Marmaduke was a cousin who had inherited a portion of the "St. George's" plantation. During the next 30 years Francis continued to buy and sell land. In 1747 he sold 103 acres of "St. George's" to Hudson Wathen, perhaps because he needed money to support his growing family—he had seven children by this time. In 1764 he obtained 100 acres in "Charles Borrough," on the north side of Zachiah Swamp, from Benjamin Fendall,[42] and in 1767 he sold a portion of "St. George's" now referred to as "Simeses (*sic*) Fragment," containing 103 acres, to Bennett Wathen.[43]

By my reckoning Francis Semmes owned a little over 200 acres when he died on Christmas Eve, 1770. His estate was settled seven months later; his goods and chattel valued at 504 pounds, were distributed to his wife and children. How the executors disposed of the land or whether Ignatius, the sixth child and our ancestor, received any of the property, I don't know. The will was very generally written and did not describe the property Francis left to his heirs.[44]

Ignatius Semmes was born in September, 1745, married Sabret Hobart around 1772, and lived his first 30 years in Charles County, Maryland. With the American Revolutionary War brewing in the colonies, he joined the 26th Battalion of the Maryland Militia from Charles County in 1776, and served for a year as a private in Capt. William McPherson's company.[45] In 1777 he made a fateful decision, certainly one important to us. He and Sabret (called Sabrid) left Maryland and moved to Henry County, Virginia, one of the counties from which Patrick and Franklin counties were formed in 1791 and 1786. On December 31, 1777, he took an oath of allegiance to the United States.[46] It is possible that Ignatius Semmes signed up for another tour of duty in the Revolutionary War after he moved to Virginia, but I have found no proof that he did. A second enlistment could explain why he moved to Virginia which had promised to reward volunteers with land for war service. At that time, the western boundary of Virginia was the Ohio River, and the new state government had plenty of land to use to pay its debts. The western boundary of Maryland was its current border, and that state had little available land or money to reward its men for fighting in the war. It is also possible that Semmes had received a cash payment from Maryland for his service in 1776, and moved to a location that offered more opportunity than his home state.

In September 1778, a year after his arrival in Virginia, Ignatius began accumulating his fortune, eventually amassing more than 3,000 acres of land and 27 slaves—property and chattel that would qualify him as a planter. He began with a modest purchase of 177 acres on Beaver Creek in Henry County for which he paid 75 pounds. Two years later, he added 100 acres located at the fork of Beaver and Simms Creek, for which he paid 80 pounds; in 1782 he received 152 acres on Flat Creek in Henry County in payment for survey work. The survey was of 500 acres for Charles Copland, land that had been issued to him by a treasury warrant #12427. Semmes received 30% of Copland's land as payment for his survey. Five years later, in 1787, Ignatius sold the 177 acres on Beaver Creek for 200 pounds, a tidy profit of 125 pounds in just nine years. That was just the beginning. In 1798, he purchased 558 acres on the south side of the Smith River, and in 1802, 295 acres on Bowens Creek—all in Patrick County.[47]

In the meantime, Sabra died in 1788, apparently without producing any children. He did not remain a widower or childless for long. Two years later, in 1790, now 45 years old and spelling his name Simms, Ignatius married Jane Nance. The couple soon began their family of ten children; they did not stop the "proliferation" of Simms babies until 1816 when the tenth and last child, Ignatius Andrew "Andy" Jackson Simms was born on September 22, when his father was 71-years old. (Quite a guy!)[48] One month before Andy's birth, Ignatius purchased over 2100 acres of land on the border of Patrick and Franklin Counties for which he paid Samuel Duval of Logan County, Kentucky, the amazingly small sum of $400. According to descriptions of the land in the deed, Mill Creek and the Smith River crossed and re-crossed his substantial new estate.[49] During the 1790s Ignatius and Jane Simms either moved their family from Henry to Patrick County, or they stayed in the same place while the border of the counties moved. Patrick was formed from Henry in 1791.

Ignatius Simms died in 1819, a wealthy man. In his will, he bequeathed to his "well beloved wife Jannet Simms ... the home tract of land containing 588 acres and also the benefit of the griss [*sic*] mill on Bowins Creek" and household goods and livestock and "everything of that kind on my plantation ... in order that she ... may be enabled to raise my dear infant children;" to all of his children he left slaves, household goods and to some a portion of his real estate—to his daughter Jancee Foster 100 acres (property which adjoined that of Charles Foster, probably her father-in-law); to his son Marmaduke 152 acres near the head of Smith River in Patrick County. In Item 11 of the will, he remembered his two-year old son: "I give and bequeath to my well beloved son Ignatius Andrew Jackson Simms two Negroes called Pallice & Elin also one feather bed and furniture, one horse saddle & bridle, one cow & calf, with the increase of said negroes to him & his heirs forever." In addition he left to his three minor sons, including Ignatius Andrew Jackson "all land not already disposed of." The final appraisal of his estate (excluding 3,000 acres of land) which "included twenty-seven negroes, totaled $11,338."[50]

We do not know where exactly in Patrick County the Ignatius Simms family settled, but we do know that it was at some point on the Smith River, a long waterway that meanders through the northern portion of the county, eventually flowing into the current reservoir of Philpott Dam at the borders of Franklin, Patrick and Henry Counties. According to the deed to his last large land purchase, the 2,000 acres lay on both sides of the Smith River and Mill Creek, both of which traverse the current borders of Franklin and Patrick Counties near the Philpott Dam area. We can probably assume that his final acquisition of land was close to his homestead and other holdings. If so, the Ignatius Simms (d. 1819) plantation was located within ten miles or so of the holdings of James Cannaday II (d. 1861), which eventually expanded to a point on the Smith River that was flooded to create Philpott Dam.

Surely those two prosperous families knew and socialized with each other. No doubt that was how Caroline Young Cannaday came to know Ignatius Andrew Jackson Simms, even though his father was a contemporary of Caroline's grandfather James Cannaday I.

In 1841, 22 years after his father's death, Andy Simms of Patrick County married Caroline Cannaday of Franklin County. He was 25; she was 21. They started their life together in Patrick County where Andy had received a portion of the family homestead. On February 23, 1838, several years before his marriage, Andy, two of his brothers, and their mother Jannet sold 580 acres and the residence to a man named Burnett for $1,400; on that same day Andy purchased a part of 100 acres. Eleven years later in 1849 he and Caroline bought 75 acres in Patrick County from his sister and brother-in-law Jane and Lewis Foster, who had moved to Georgia.[51]

In time Caroline and Andy Simms moved west to Raleigh County, Virginia (later West Virginia), where they invested in a sizeable tract of land. They probably had two or three of their five children when they left

Patrick County, but they may have had all five children and moved as late as 1855. In March of that year, they sold 70 acres and relinquished their rights to another 100 acres in Patrick County. In those deeds they were listed as residents of Raleigh County. Not long afterwards, in a terrible turn of events, Andy Simms died, leaving Caroline a widow at thirty-five with all those young children to care for. She sold the Raleigh County land, an action that may have been as devastating as the death of her husband. Certainly her grandson Paul thought so because coal was later discovered on the property Caroline and Andy had owned. "If only Grandma hadn't sold that land, we'd all be millionaires," Paul used to say, remorsefully.[52]

After the sale of her Raleigh County land Caroline moved her young family—James Robert Simms the oldest child was 11 at the time—back "home" to Franklin County where she knew her well-to-do father James Cannaday II would see that she and her children were safe and secure. Six years later, in 1861, James II died.

Caroline's father made generous bequests to all nine of his living children, as well as to his widowed daughter-in-law, and to a motherless grandson. Even though her father had provided for her financial welfare, Caroline Simms must have thought God had turned His back on her. She now had to manage her family—two teenage boys, one, Jim, who was hankering to run off and join the fight for the Confederacy, Jack, and three younger girls, Julia, Mary, Jenny—and her new land holdings, alone. All without the love and support of her parents, both of whom she lost so quickly to typhoid fever in the fall of 1861. But, as Mary Simms said about her mother-in-law: "Caroline was a tough old thing." She had to be.

I have often wondered how Caroline dealt with the three separate parcels of land she had inherited, all of which were situated along Runnett Bag Creek, and were spread out over several miles. With the exception of a tract at the juncture of Buttermilk and Runnett Bag Creeks on the eastern edge of her father's estate, it is unclear from James II's will where her other property was located. A second parcel, though not explicitly identified in the will, was the J. R. Simms family homeplace located on Runnett Bag Creek and nearby Hurds Branch, two or three miles west of the Buttermilk Creek acreage. In a transaction that proved crucial to our family's history Caroline bought 100 acres adjacent to her second parcel.

In 1863, just two years after James II's death, Caroline paid her brother James B. Cannaday, who was living in Floyd County, $200 for the additional land, which I assume he had inherited from his father. According to the deed, the100 acre parcel bordered her land on Runnett Bag Creek, as well as that of other property owners.[53] Significantly, the deed between Caroline and her brother James was "encumbered by Susan Martin widow of William Martin, deceased, so long as the said Susan Martin shall live." After that time, the property passed to Caroline Cannaday Simms free and clear.

This land was a part of the property Caroline left to her son James Robert Simms when she died in 1899, and which he in turn sold to his son Paul in 1903—l00 acres "known as the Martin land". The Martin encumbrance tells us that this was the tract that became the home of Paul and Eula, their children Earl, Elva, Edsel, and Betty—farm and land at the heart of this memoir. In all likelihood, Caroline and her children lived in the log house "at the bottom of the hill" near the intersection of Runnett Bag Creek and Hurd's Branch, the land which adjoined the Martin-encumbered property. This is the house that by 1899, if not before, became home to her son Jim, daughter-in-law Mary and their family. It was about a quarter mile west of the original homeplace of Caroline's parents, James II and Sarah Cannaday.

Ignatius Andrew Jackson Simms II (Uncle Jack), Caroline's second son, married Blanche Shelton, purchased a house from Sears & Roebuck, and became a successful businessman in Rocky Mount where he owned an entire city block. His most popular establishment was the saloon which stood in the middle of his downtown property.

Julia Simms and her husband Turner Griffith migrated from the wilds of western Virginia to the wilds of the western frontier of America and settled in Missouri.

Julia's sister Mary disappeared, but her youngest sister Virginia or Jenny lived in Roanoke with her husband Lewis Hancock. She was the child who cared for her mother when she gave up housekeeping. Caroline was 79 when she died in 1899.

Her oldest son, James Robert Simms, our colorful grandfather, whose life and antics I write about in the next chapter, can only be described as a wild young man. After running away to fight in the Civil War as a private in the 37th Battalion, Virginia Cavalry and carrying on an impetuous love affair, Jim settled down and married Lucinda Elizabeth, "Betty," Cannaday, his second cousin, in 1872. (Jim and Betty shared a great grandfather, James Cannaday I.) As a result, their five children, including Paul, had a double dose of Cannaday genes.

So at last, the Cannadays and the Simmses are all present and accounted for. They were among the pioneers who settled the part of Franklin County that came to be known as Endicott. I wish we had their complete stories and not just the bare bones information, but we don't, at least for the time being.

Now, we have one more set of ancestors to move into Franklin County, the Rakes family of Eula Mae Rakes Simms, Paul's wife.[54]

Map of Maryland

1 *St. Mary's – 1st settlement in Maryland*

2 *Charles County – location of Marmaduke & Fortune Semmes' estate*

3 *Cecil County – location of Middle Plantation & Semmes Forest*

The Rakes Family

In 1787 Charles Rakes paid 62 pounds for a tract of land in the Counties of Henry and Franklin "lying on Shooting Creek and the branches of Smiths River."

Charles Rakes (c1745-c1838)	m 1827	(1) Jane Rakes (2) Nancy Hall Hubbard
Samuel Jackson Rakes (c1783-1852)	m 1815	Lucinda Nowlin (1801-1865)
Richard Randall Rakes (1827-1905)	m 1854 1892	(1) Sarah Deborah Turner (c1836-1887) (2) Mary (Molly) Dent (1868-?)
Columbus McGruder Rakes (1864-1952)	m 1885	Ophelia Thomas (1867-1920)
Eula Rakes (1886-1982)	m 1905	Paul Simms (1878-1964)

See Appendix A for more complete genealogy of Simms' family

The first name in the big blue "Rakes" genealogy book, our American "Adam," is Charles Rakes, born c1745 in Buckingham County, Virginia. He lived more than 80 years, maybe even 90, married twice, and had 12 children by his first wife Jane. He wed his second wife Nancy Hall Hubbard, a widow, when he was in his late 70s. Not surprisingly, there appear to be no children from this union, but there were plenty from the first. Intriguingly an early family historian said that Jane Rakes was, by tradition, an Indian, but that "there is no proof."[55]

I have gone in search of our Rakes family ancestors, first in Buckingham County where I had no luck, and then in Patrick County where I found a gold mine of Rakes documents. The cache of records included wills and deeds drawn up by clerks and justices of the peace and lawyers—men who had the enviable ability to read and write. Until the arrival of Richard Randall Rakes in 1827, our Rakes forefathers were illiterate and had to trust the important written documents of their lives to the expertise of other men, depending on them to record their marriages, births, deaths, last wills and testaments, as well as to transfer their land.

It must have been on such a day as my trip from Henry County west to Patrick that Charles Rakes and his family (and probably Ignatius Simms who settled in Henry/Patrick County, and maybe even William Cannaday) found their way into that part of western Virginia—a way unmolested by the rigors of mountain crossings and with eastern sunlight shining on low-lying clouds over the Blue Ridge Mountains in the distant horizon—a landscape that would have drawn any pioneer's heart.

Like the Cannadays who settled along Runnett Bag Creek and considered that little stream their own, the Rakes clan adopted the waters of Poplar Camp Creek in far northeastern Patrick County. The Poplar Camp area butted up to the border of what is now Franklin County and the rolling terrain of the Blue Ridge Mountain foothills.

It was around 1778 when Charles and Jane Rakes decided to leave Buckingham County. I have wondered why they would take such a risk. Perhaps they were tobacco farmers whose land, like much of the soil of eastern Virginia, had been depleted from growing that exhausting crop, and were looking for fresh earth and new opportunities, or perhaps they had "caught" the new American adventuring spirit and were lured to the western part of the country. Charles was in his early thirties; he and Jane must have thought that if they were to make a move, that was the time in their lives to take the chance, before they were too old for such a transition. Consequently they sold their home-place in Buckingham and moved with however many children they had at the time (three or four) to a 200 acre farm on the border of Henry (soon to be Patrick) and Franklin Counties.[56] Charles bought this land from William Edwards. According to the deed Charles paid William 62 pounds for a tract of land in the Counties of Henry and Franklin "lying on Shooting Creek and the branches of Smiths [sic] River... to the ridge that divides the waters of Shooting Creek and Turkey Cock..." Significantly the location of this first Rakes home was very near Poplar Camp Creek area, the section of Patrick County which became home to many of Charles Rakes' descendants, including his son Samuel, his grandson Richard Randall, and his great grandson Columbus McGruder.

Six years later, in 1794, Charles increased the size of his farm by 115 acres, purchasing another parcel of land which lay on both sides of Shooting Creek. According to the deed, this property included a house, a garden, an orchard and other buildings, and he got it for what was surely "a song"—ten pounds. A few years later he sold 140 acres of his other property on Shooting Creek to James Pemberton of Franklin County for 60 pounds. Charles conducted several more land deals. In 1806 he bought 70 acres on the north side of Smith River for $120 and, finally, 30 years later he sold 50 acres to his friend Samuel Boyd for $100. This was land which bordered Boyd's other property and through which the Smith River flowed as far west as Shooting Creek.[57]

By 1827 Jane Rakes had died, probably exhausted from hard work and from birthing and caring for a dozen children. I am unsure of the date of her death, but I know that it was before 1827 because in that year Charles married his second wife, Nancy Hall Hubbard, a widow. Men always need women and wives, but never more so than in the early years of the nineteenth century when they were desperate for help with the farm and the family, and to have someone to love, of course, as well as to tend to them in their old age—Charles was close to 80 when he married Nancy. She also needed the protection and security—and love, too—from a man and a marriage. The couple had ten years of marital "bliss"—in the twilight of their lives, certainly in his.

By the time of his death in 1838, Charles Rakes had accumulated a modest estate—two to three hundred acres of land, five slaves and personal belongings valued at $3,750. He had drawn up his will in 1835, stating that he was weak of body but sound of mind, and then laying out his final wishes. He directed that his worldly goods be distributed equally to his wife and children. He requested that they divide up the slaves or work out an agreeable arrangement for their ownership. He must have known that that could have created problems because there were more family members than there were slaves. So he stipulated that if they were unable to settle the matter to everyone's satisfaction, that his executor, Samuel Boyd, sell the Negroes and disburse the money equally among his wife, his children and his grandchildren.[58] After examining the document which recorded the settlement of Charles Rakes' estate, I have concluded that family members did in fact purchase the slaves. It is hard to know for sure because an item in the final accounting states: "By receipt of Samuel Rakes, $375, November 24, 1838," without explaining what exactly Samuel Rakes had bought.[59] That was a significant amount of money for that time, however, and in line with the appraised value of several of the slaves.

Samuel Rakes (c1783—1852), the first born of Charles and Jane Rakes, was in his fifties in 1838 when his "old man" died. He had married Lucinda Nowlin in 1820 and with her had a large family; in fact, with few exceptions, the fertile couple had a baby every other year beginning in 1821 with the birth of Charles and ending in 1846 with the birth of Betsy, number thirteen. Richard Randall, their number five child, born in 1827, was 11 years old when his grandfather Charles died.

Samuel not only loved and acquired children; he loved and acquired land. At age 32, like an expert Monopoly player, he began amassing property and did not stop until 1847 when he turned 64, nor did he sell or dispose of any of his land (or any that I have found evidence of). His first purchase in 1815 was for 300 acres which bordered a Rakes line (probably his father's). In 1831 he added another 100 acres; this parcel adjoined his land and lay on both sides of White Oak Creek. Four years later he acquired a tract from Fleming and Delia Thomas, property they had inherited on Poplar Camp Creek, the Smith River and bordered his land. He paid them $400 for an undisclosed amount of property, perhaps 400 acres. The next year, 1836, he bought two more parcels from estates of deceased owners, both on Poplar Camp Creek and both for an unspecified number of acres, perhaps 200, for which he paid $190. There was more. Over the next ten years he added another 1,000 acres to the approximately 1,000 he already owned. All of the new land joined his property and all of it, except one 200 acre parcel on the Smith River, was on Poplar Camp Creek.[60]

By his death in 1852, Samuel Rakes had accumulated more than 2,000 acres for which he had paid about $1 per acre. The value of his estate, including land ($4,737), nine slaves ($4,041), debts owed to him ($2,422) and the sale of other property ($18,883), came to more than $30,000. Not bad for a man who had inherited less than $400 from his father and signed his name with an "x." Samuel's will was simple.[61]

He left his wife a Negro boy and one third of his estate; he bequeathed to his children equal shares of all that remained. He instructed his executors, Francis Turner and William Hall, to appraise, sell and distribute his estate to his heirs. Thus it appears that it was the practice in those days for the executors to have an estate appraised, then to liquidate the assets and distribute the proceeds to the heirs, according to the wishes of the deceased.

According to the Samuel Rakes' estate records on file in the Patrick County courthouse, family members bought all but one of the slaves. (Interestingly, Samuel and Lucinda's son-in-law, Isaac Y. Cannaday, a cousin of Caroline Cannaday, who was married to their daughter Polly, bought a Negro woman named Ann and her child, Wilson, for $701.) Family members also purchased the real property which Samuel had so carefully amassed over his lifetime. Lucinda retained the home tract, more than 600 acres, for which she paid $2,400, and Richard Randall Rakes purchased the Burnett tract of more than 500 acres along Poplar Camp Creek for which he paid the estate $1,460.[62]

When Samuel died in 1852, his son with the wonderfully alliterative name, Richard Randall Rakes, was 25 years old and still a bachelor. Richard (1827-1905), known as Dick, lived 78 years and had a total of 11 children, eight with his first wife, Sarah Deborah Turner, and three with his second, Mollie Dent. Dick and Sarah Rakes were married for 33 years, from 1854 to 1887, when she died of liver disease at age 51. By that time, most of their children were grown and four were married. Dick was in his 60s in 1890 when he married his second wife Mollie who was 40 years younger than he. Over the next eight years they had three children, the last of them born in 1901, when Dick Rakes was a senior citizen of 74.

Richard Randall Rakes (1827-1905), father of Columbus McGruder Rakes, grandfather of Eula Rakes Simms

It is hard to know what would inspire a 22 year old woman to marry a 64 year old man—money, a shortage of men, desperation. I don't believe it was overwhelming good looks. In his only surviving photograph, which must have been taken toward the end of his life, this grandfather looks remarkably like a "hell and damnation" minister. He is dressed in a black frock-coat and a large brimmed hat, his face is deeply furrowed, his eyes are dark and piercing, he has enormous ears and a scraggly mustache and beard, and his expression is a scowl. So, his big attractions must have been riches and availability.[63]

By the time of his second marriage in 1890, Dick Rakes had acquired quite a spread of land. He had followed his father Samuel's example of amassing property. Beginning in 1852 Dick used his inheritance to invest in 500 acres of the family estate. He eventually expanded his holdings to more than1200 acres, all on or near Poplar Camp Creek.[64] In 1861, still married to Sarah and a relatively young man of 34, Dick Rakes enlisted in the Civil War. Fortunately for us (and for him too), he survived the war, came home and fathered Columbus McGruder Rakes. That baby's birth in 1864, a year before the end of the war, indicates that Dick either did not stay with his unit until the surrender at Appomattox, or that he was home on leave in 1863. If not, Sarah had some 'splainin' to do.

Dick and Sarah gave that son the marvelous name of Columbus McGruder Rakes, lovingly called "Gooder." If his father's picture was accurate, we have to assume that Gooder Rakes inherited his gentle good looks from his mother, Sarah. He was fair-skinned and had reddish-blonde hair and blue eyes. He did have the distinctive high cheek bones of his old man.

While researching records at the Patrick County courthouse, I found a copy of Richard Randall Rakes' will and the accompanying document which indicated that the older children in *Rakes v. Rakes* had contested the will in 1906. The jury found in favor of Mary (Mollie) E. Rakes, the second wife, and against the older children; it recognized the will, called exhibit A, as the legitimate last will and testament of Richard R. Rakes.[65] In the will, written in 1904, a year before his death, R.R. Rakes stated that he had "rewarded his children from his first marriage with $630 each" and $1,300 to Charles M. Rakes, who must have been Columbus McGruder Rakes and was mis-identified by the clerk. R.R. Rakes had a son named Charles Jefferson Rakes, but he had died in 1896, eight years before Dick Rakes wrote his will. He did not "consider his older children entitled to more." If so, he stated, he would give it to them before he died. In addition, he stipulated that if Mary died or remarried before their youngest child reached the age of 21, all his property was "to be held in trust for the benefit of my said children born of Mary E. Rakes." C. M. Rakes was one of his executors, C.P. Nolen, the other.

Thus Gooder Rakes appears to have been a favored and trusted son, which is not surprising, considering his sweet and gentle nature.

Born in 1864 during the last years of the Civil War, C.M. "Gooder" Rakes was the fourth son of Dick and Sarah Rakes. He grew up and lived with his eight siblings in the Poplar Camp area of Patrick County. He remained there for seven years after his marriage to Ophelia Thomas in 1885 and the birth of two of their little girls, Eula and Iva.

Ophelia Thomas Rakes (1867-1920), mother of Eula Rakes Simms

They apparently lived on a 200 acre farm on Poplar Camp Creek, the same stream the Rakes' clan had settled on three generations before.[66] It is interesting that the young couple, perhaps hoping for a quick and easy fortune, sold the mineral rights to 180 acres of their land, as well as the rights to timber to build any necessary structures for the mines, the rights to water use in the mining operations, and the rights to enter and leave their property. For all these privileges, Gooder and Ophelia received one dollar and the guarantee of $.10 per ton of iron or manganese, and 25% of the net profit for any other minerals extracted from their land. The lease, obviously written to the advantage of the mining company, was for 99 years, but would be null and void if the company did not begin operations within ten years of the date of the contract.[67] Whether the company did in fact mine the land and Gooder and Ophelia realized any benefits, I do not know. They did, however, sell this property, which included more than188 acres and their house, just three years later to W.E. Rakes (Gooder's brother) for $1000, the last payment due December 25, 1892.

Three months later on March 21, 1893, C.M. and Ophelia Rakes left Patrick County for good. With the proceeds from the sale of their land on

Poplar Camp Creek and the gift from his father or maybe even a pay-off from the mineral sales, they moved to Franklin County. They paid $1,500 for 150 acres of fertile farm land in southwest Franklin County located at the juncture of Shively and Otter Creeks. Their farm was in a lovely, generally flat valley in the foothills of the Blue Ridge Mountains three miles on the other side of the Griffith Hill from Runnett Bag Creek and the Simms farm.[68] By the time they moved to his "plantation," the affectionate name he gave to his modest home and land, Gooder and Ophelia's little girls, Eula and Iva, were 7 and 5.

We now have at least a bare outline of the story of migration of the three families—Cannaday, Simms, and Rakes—who found their way to the eastern slopes of the Blue Ridge Mountains and were settled in southwest Virginia by the late eighteenth century.

Notes for Chapter I, Settling the Ancestors

The Cannaday Family

1. See Appendix A for complete Cannaday genealogy.

2. Deed Book 52, p. 454, Rocky Mount Courthouse, Franklin County, VA.

3.Treasury Warrant #12582, Library of Virginia, Archives, Richmond, VA.

4. According to the warrant on file at the Library of Virginia, 1000 acres sold for 1600 pounds in 1782. This seems very expensive but currency in the late eighteenth century was unstable and the value of a pound at that time had been grossly devalued because of uncertainties in the country.

5. Frieda Clark Cannaday, *The Cannaday Family of Virginia and West Virginia*, St. Petersburg, FL, 1988, 14.

6. As early as 1779, a William Cannady received a land grant of 108 acres on "Riconnet Bag Creek" in Pittsylvania County (a predecessor of Franklin), and before that in 1772 another or the same William Cannady received 375 acres in Halifax County (a county adjacent to Pittsylvania). Library of Virginia, Land Office Patents B, 1779-1780, p. 10, Reel 43, and Land Office Patents No. 40, 1771-1772, p. 836, Reel 39.

7. A detailed study of the deeds and available land surveys of the property this family acquired in the early days of settlement would be fascinating, in both the broader look at the way that land was acquired and the narrower case of one family's steady accumulation of property in one place over a short period of time, an early American success story.

8. See Appendix B for land transfer records of William Cannaday Sr.

9. See Appendix B for land transfer records of William Cannaday, Jr.

10. Library of Virginia, Land Office Grants No. 34, 1796, p. 446, Reel 100.

11. See Appendix B for land transfer records of William Cannaday, Sr.

12. See Appendix B for land transfer records of John Cannaday.

13. See Frieda Clark Cannaday, *The Cannaday Family of Virginia* and West Virginia, p. 13 for more information on William and Nancy Cannaday's family.

14. John H. Gwathney, *Historical Register of Virginia in the Revolution*, on file at National Archives in DC.

15. In 1997 James Cannaday's descendants gathered at his gravesite on a hillside overlooking Runnett Bag Creek and the family's original log home to place a marker, provided by the DAR, and to pay tribute to our own Revolutionary War veteran. See Appendix D for Dr. Holt Merchant's remarks.

16. See Appendix E for Hughes Cannaday's account of the Cannaday family history.

17. See Appendix B for record of James Cannaday I's land transfers.

18. Isaac Cannaday represented Franklin County in the Virginia Legislature, 1856-7.

19. See Appendix C for reference for James Cannaday Sr.'s will regarding Elizabeth Cannaday.

20. See Appendix C for references for James Cannaday Sr.'s will.

21. Land surveys on record in Franklin County indicate that James I and Elizabeth Cannaday's children held land throughout the county, some as far away as the Smith River. Daughter Mary and her husband Pleasant Thomas settled on Poplar Camp Creek, a tributary of Smith River, in Patrick County; son Charles, who married Mary Ingram, left his four sons about 450 acres each in Patrick County on the south side of the Smith River; and son William, "Patrick Billy," settled on the north side of the Smith River.

22. For more complete genealogy and record of James II and Sarah Cannaday's family, see Clark, *Cannaday Family of Virginia and West Virginia*, p. 25, 36-39.

23. See Appendix B for list of James Cannaday II's land transfers on record at Rocky Mount, VA courthouse.

24. From Clark, *Cannadays*, p. 24. Records in Rocky Mount Courthouse, August 1823 p. 176; page 209, June, 1832; p. 323, July 1833.

25. See Appendix E, Hughes Cannaday's account of Cannaday family history.

26. This estate was situated three miles southeast of Endicott on Route 789. In the early 1950's the federal government purchased a large portion of that land near the Smith River from Hughes Cannaday's heirs; it was flooded when the U. S. Army Corps of Engineers created Philpott Dam.

27. See Appendix C for James Cannaday II will reference.

The Simms Family

28. The genealogical record from http://www.familysearch.com does not say that Marmaduke was born in England; it uses the notation "of" by his name.

29. Leon Wilde's genealogical research website on Francis and Ignatius Semmes.

30. Thomas Corse genealogical chart.

31. According to the Semmes genealogical chart researched and compiled by Thomas S. Corse in 1988, Fortune was literate. This was an unusual accomplishment for a seventeenth century woman and indicated that she was a member of the gentry.

32. See Corse genealogy.

33. See Appendix C for reference to Fortune Semmes' will.

34. As noted in both Fortune and Marmaduke's wills, this was land purchased from Thomas Simpson.

35. See Appendix C for reference to Marmaduke Semmes' will.

36. Land grant from Lord Baltimore noted by Corse genealogy; "Semmes Forest" mentioned in Marmaduke's will.

37. According to the will of Marmaduke I and Fortune Semmes' grandson, Francis, he lived in Charles County on the Newport Hundred. The designation "hundred" indicated sufficient land to support 100 families. There is a small town called Newport on a current map of Maryland, very near the Wicomico River which flows into the Potomac River.

38. Genealogical records on http://www.familysearch.com indicate that Fortune and Marmaduke had six children, two boys who did not live beyond a year, one named Anthony and one named James. It was the custom in those days to give the same name to the next surviving child of the same sex—a custom which they followed—in order to preserve the name.

39. Marmaduke Semmes' will. See Appendix C for reference source.

40. Fortune Semmes' will. See Appendix C for reference source.

41. See Appendix C for reference source of Marmaduke Semmes II's will.

42. There is a Zechiah Swamp very near the town of Newport in modern-day Maryland.

43. See Appendix B for reference sources of Francis Semmes land deals.

44. See Appendix C for will reference.

45. "Revolutionary War, Militia List," p.40, Maryland Historical Society.

46. History of Henry County, Virginia, pp 304-310. "The General Assembly of Virginia, when the United States was in its infancy, passed an Act to oblige all free male inhabitants of the State above sixteen years of age to give assurance of allegiance to the same. The following is a list of those who took the oath from the original record among the files in the Clerk's office... At the time some were away fighting Indians, others hunting and there were a few who refused to take the oath." Ignatius Sims' name is on page 309.

47. See Appendix B for list of Ignatius Simms' land transfers.

48. The practice of naming a son "Andrew Jackson" after the Indian-fighting/English-fighting President was popular among Democrats of this period.

49. See Appendix B for land transfer reference.

50. See Appendix C for Ignatius Simms' will reference.

51. See Appendix B for listing of land transactions for Andrew Jackson Simms.

52. Actually this lost fortune story could have ended in another lost fortune story. After the Civil War, many of the families who owned property in West Virginia were pitifully poor; desperate for cash money, they were easily duped by Yankee scoundrels who bought the mineral rights of land, much of it rich in coal, paying unsuspecting mountain folk very little money for what was black gold for the coal barons; they stripped the land of its coal, without any regard for the safety of the miners or the devastating damage they did to the landscape; other Northern speculators came South, clear-cut the forests, took away the timber, leaving the lands denuded and desolate.

53. See Appendix B for list of land transfers for Caroline Cannaday Simms.

54. I did not follow her mother Ophelia Thomas' ancestry because I knew so little of them.

The Rakes Family

55. The early records of Buckingham County have gone up in smoke—thanks to the Yankees. The proof may still exist in the archives of the Albemarle or Appomattox County courthouses because Buckingham County was formed from those counties in 1761.

56. I have no evidence of this, only common sense.

57. See Appendix B for land references for Charles Rakes.

58. See Appendix C for Charles Rakes' will reference.

59. See Appendix C for Charles Rakes' will reference.

60. See Appendix B for land references for Samuel Rakes.

61. See Appendix C for Samuel Rakes' will reference.

62. See Appendix C for Samuel Rakes' will reference.

63. My editor suggests that perhaps she wasn't a beauty either.

64. See Appendix B for land references for Richard Randal Rakes.

65. See Appendix C for Richard Randal Rakes' will reference.

66. I have not yet found the deed or evidence of a purchase of 200 acres by C.M Rakes, but I have discovered the deed of sale by him and Ophelia to his brother, W.E. Rakes. Deed book 26, p. 312, Patrick County Courthouse, Stuart, VA.

67. See Appendix B for land references for Columbus McGruder Rakes.

68. There was an unexplained transfer of ownership of this farm from C.M. Rakes to Paul Simms to Ophelia Rakes back to C.M. Rakes over a 26-year period. I write more about that strange episode in our family's history in the "Sweetness" chapter.

2

James Robert Simms

Come on in, drinks are on the house.

James Robert Simms was my great grandfather. He died in 1928, long before I had a chance to know him. I have drawn my portrait of him and the "legend" surrounding him from interviews with his grandchildren, who did know him and who heard and retold the stories of his life—as well as the life of his second wife, Mary—which I now retell to you.

J.B. Simms Family Tree
(Abridged)

Caroline Cannaday (1820-1899) —— m 1841 —— Andrew Jackson Simms (1816-1855)

James Robert Simms (1844-1928) —— m 1872 —— [1] Lucinda "Betty" Cannaday (1851-1886)

Arthur	Mollie	Paul	Harry	Grace
(1873-1899)	(1875-1949)	(1878-1964)	(1881-1904)	(1883-1948)

m 1887 —— [2] Mary P. Shively (1866-1968)

Archer Gale	James	Bessie	Delma	Amy
(1888-1970)	(1889-1975)	(1896-1978)	(1903-1990)	(1906-2002)

James "Jim" Robert Simms c1924

James Robert Simms was the bad boy of the family (or one of them, anyway). He was a rebel, a redhead with a quick temper and an artistic bent, an expert craftsman with a wicked sense of humor, and a man who did love his "dram," especially in his later years. Jim married twice; he had ten legitimate children, five by each wife, and one illegitimate child from a youthful indiscretion. As if that weren't enough, he had a between-wives live-in "housekeeper" who refused to leave the premises even after the second Mrs. Simms arrived on the scene.

The bride (the second Mrs. Simms) was Mary P.—P for Pope, a name she hated and told people who were inconsiderate enough to ask that it stood for Patience, a quality she needed in great measure—Shively. She was 20 years old, compared to Jim (or Mr. Simms as she called him) who was 43 when they wed. Her step-daughter Mollie, a child from the first marriage, 11 at the time of the nuptials and not always on good terms with her Pa, wondered why a young woman like Mary would marry an old man like her father. She assumed that her new step-mother must have been desperate. It is hard to believe now, but in those days any woman not married by her 21st birthday was considered an old-maid—a dreaded state in life—the word itself a disparaging epithet. Without a good education, which was certainly unavailable to most women in the country, she would have had few choices. She could have lived with her parents or moved in with another relative—a married brother, perhaps, or she could have become a housekeeper, a washer woman, or taken some other menial job. Such was the pitiful state of women in the late 19th century.

Paul, Mollie's younger brother and another child from the first marriage, thought that there were reasons other than panic for Mary's decision to take on a man twice her age who had a ready-made family. He suggested that their father Jim had charm and a certain appeal to the ladies.

It must have been true. Even before he was 17, Jim and a young woman whose name we don't know were lovers. She became pregnant and, according to family legend, was snatched up by her mother and whisked off to western Virginia (later West Virginia), to avoid the shame of a bastard child and the whispering and tut-tutting of neighbors and friends.[1]

That unfortunate affair happened about 1861 when the country was on the brink of Civil War. Whether it was the scandal, the glamour of war, Southern pride, the desire for adventure, or just the opportunity to escape the demands of farm work and a domineering mother, Jim left home at a tender age to help the South to fight the Yankees. Like every veteran of combat, Jim had his share of stories of daring deeds, cold, hunger, suffering and death, but only a few of the stories he told (some of which may even have happened) have survived the more than 140 years since the end of the war.

We have always heard that Jim lied about his age, claiming to be 18, in order to enlist. The age requirement was set during the first years of the war, before things went bad for the South—when the once strict age limits were relaxed to include anyone male and still breathing. One of the ways young men got away with early enlistment was to write the number "eighteen" on slips of paper, put them in their shoes, then swear before God and the recruiting officer that they "were over 18." I never heard that Jim pulled such a stunt, but I would not be surprised if he not only did it, but invented the whole charade.

Jim was a private in Company A, 37th Battalion, Virginia Cavalry, a company recruited from Franklin County. The Battalion was organized by Col. Ambrose C. Dunn on August 2, 1862 (just before Jim's eighteenth birthday in September) and mustered in as "regular cavalry" in November 1862. James Claiborne recruited the boys from Franklin County. The unit established a boot camp in Salem, Virginia, in December 1862 and paid recruits $12 per month plus a bounty for their horses. Cavalrymen, even privates, had to supply their own horses. Jim not only took his horse, he also took a young black boy to be his body servant. (I suspect that this was his mother Caroline's idea). It was unusual for an enlisted man to take a slave to the war, but our grandfather was not a usual soldier or man. The young slave did not hang around long. At the first sign of combat, he skedaddled and left Master Jim to fight the Yankees without him. He sped back to the safety and comfort of home in Franklin County, and no doubt to an ear-thrashing from his mistress Caroline.

The account of Jim's experiences in the Civil War varied according to which relative was telling the tale. His grandchildren Earl Simms and Elva Simms Cannaday were sure that he joined the army when the war broke out, before his eighteenth birthday, and then later re-enlisted with his friends from Franklin County in the 37th Virginia Calvary in the fall of 1862 for the duration of the war. On the other hand, Harold Simms, the grandson who lived with Jim and his second wife Mary, thought his grandfather was in the 37th Cavalry only briefly, not much more than a year at the end of the war.[2] For most of the war the 37th Cavalry fought in the Shenandoah Valley and the western part of Virginia.[3] Jim told his children and grandchildren that his service as a scout in the cavalry repeatedly put him in real danger. Once he was out on a mission and happened upon enemy troops, so close that he had to hide quickly. To avoid discovery, he dropped down and stretched himself out beside a fallen tree trunk, holding his breath and plastering himself against that fortunate downed log until the Yankees rode away.

In late 1863 the 37th went west to the Cumberland Gap to support James Longstreet's failed campaign to capture Knoxville. In July 1864 the unit joined Jubal Early's effort to take Washington, DC. It was with Early when he burned Chambersburg, Pennsylvania in retaliation for David Hunter's raid through Western Virginia. They carried out this mission and returned to the Shenandoah Valley by way of the Cumberland Gap and Romney. The 37th covered Early's retreat and was almost wiped out at the battles of Fisher's Hill and Cedar Creek.

At some point during the war Jim Simms was wounded in his left shoulder, at New Market according to his grandson Earl, an injury which left him with a small but permanent disability for the rest of his life. He had trouble lifting his left arm even to shave and had to hold the basin close to his face to splash water on himself without lifting his arm. This romantic war wound looked less glamorous when Harold told me a different version of the story. According to him, the injury occurred long after the war had ended, after Jim had married Mary and was living at the home-place in Franklin County. Jim had finished setting the mill wheel at Nowlin's Mill several miles from home and rewarded himself with a little refreshment at the end of the work day, just enough whiskey to get intoxicated. On the ride home, he fell off or was thrown from his horse, but not completely. His foot got hung up in the stirrup, and the horse dragged him all the way home, bumping along on his pitiful shoulder. By the time he got home it was dark. He hollered for Mary to come rescue him from his misery. Grandma Mary didn't mince words when she told Harold the story; she said that Jim got drunk and fell off the horse and that's how he got that crippled-up shoulder.

Another version of the origin of Jim's crippled-up shoulder came from his granddaughter Mary Elizabeth Simms Whelby. She was sure that her Grandpa had been shoeing a horse when the animal kicked him and caused the grievous injury. So the wound was probably not the result of a heroic war effort at all. (We can only wonder how that war injury story got so corrupted and part of the Jim Simms' lore).

Late one summer during the war, probably in 1864, Jim was granted a leave to go home. No sooner had he arrived back at the home-place, than one of the slaves told him that a Confederate deserter had been raiding the family's cornfield that Caroline had managed to get planted the previous spring. Jim was furious that anyone would desert and then steal from his mother's garden. He grabbed a rifle, went in search of the thief, found the reprobate foraging in the corn patch and fired buckshot into the fellow's backsides. Caroline was aware of the thievery and must not have cared that the desperately hungry man was helping himself to a little of her corn. She sure didn't want anyone to tell Jim because she knew, considering his volatile temper, exactly what he would do. (This story has generally been told that Jim took on the deserter in the cornfield at the end of the war, soon after he came home, but that doesn't jibe with the growing season. Most crops, including corn, mature in late August; the war was over in April.)

If Jim took this leave in the fall of 1864 as I suspect, he returned to fight with his comrades at Cedar Creek in October. They spent the winter in Warm Springs. By that time not much was left of the 37th. By late 1864 15% of the men on the roster had gone AWOL or had deserted during the course of the war. According to the historian of the 37th, the battalion was in Buchanan at the time of the surrender. To get home Jim, Matt Spencer, and a Cannaday cousin from Floyd, took turns walking and riding the one horse they had, all the way back to Franklin County. Jim was 20 years old in April 1865.

Lucinda Elizabeth "Betty" Cannaday Simms, (1851-1886) J.R. Simms' first wife, Paul Simms' mother

For six years after the Civil War, Jim remained a bachelor. He probably spent those years with his widowed mother helping out on the farm. After the loss of her slaves, she would have needed him. He eventually became a fine carpenter and blacksmith and an accomplished millwright. He no doubt used that time at home to learn and perfect those skills.

In 1872 Simms married Lucinda Elizabeth (Betty) Cannaday (1851-1886); she was 21, he was 27. We know nothing about their romance and only the barest facts about their life together. Betty and Jim were distant kin, third cousins or first cousins with several removes, enough genetic distance not to cause problems. They shared a great grandfather, James Cannaday Sr. (1755-1817), a veteran of the American Revolutionary War and an early settler in Franklin County. Lucinda, or Betty as she was called, and Jim (wonder if she called him Mr. Simms?) were not only related, they were neighbors.

Jim Simms was born in 1844 and spent his first 11 years in Raleigh County, Virginia (WV), many miles from Franklin, but he moved there with his mother Caroline and his four siblings soon after his father, Andrew "Andy" Jackson Simms, died suddenly in 1855 at age 39.

In 1873 Betty and Jim began their family of five children, one born every other year or so. Arthur arrived first in 1873, then Mollie in 1875, Paul in 1878, Harry in 1881, and Grace in 1883. You would think that we would know where the Jim Simms' family lived during these years, but we don't. It probably was not Franklin County. Paul, we do know, was born in Floyd, a county adjacent to Franklin.

In 1886 the young family suffered a devastating loss, Betty only 35 years old, died of typhoid fever. We have only one photograph of her, one precious, visual reminder of our grandmother, Paul's mother. From the picture, we can see that she was a lovely, dark-eyed woman with long brown hair and full lips.

Both of Betty's parents, Isaac (1825-1875) and Polly Cannaday (1824-1870) had died by the time of their daughter's death. Jim's mother, Caroline, was the one who had to step in and help her son cope with the tragic loss of his wife. She knew what it meant to be a young single parent responsible for five small children. (Jim was 42, but he was a man, and no doubt helpless when it came to caring for a house and children). Soon after Betty's death, Julia Simms Griffith, Caroline's daughter and Jim's sister, came from Missouri to assist her mother in caring for her brother's family. She could only stay for a short while before she had to return home to her own children and husband, Turner Griffith. It was decided in some sort of family council, I guess, that it would ease Jim's burden if Julia would take two of the children home with her. They selected Paul, aged eight, and Mollie, aged 11, to go with their aunt, to take the long train trip to a strange new place. The other three youngsters, Arthur, the oldest at 13, Harry aged five, and Grace only three, would stay home with their father and a hired housekeeper.

The details of the trip to Missouri we can only imagine, but the story of the return to Franklin County was one Paul loved to tell. After a wretched year or two in Missouri, his grandmother Caroline Simms came to rescue him and Mollie from the frigidly cold Midwest where the wind blew all the time, from the frightening cyclone cellars they hid in when the threatening storms came, and from the harsh treatment of an aunt with a quick temper and a ready switch. Paul said that his Aunt Julia insisted that the youngsters work hard for her, churning butter until their little arms ached. When she wasn't around or paying attention, the children, including their cousins, climbed up on top of the churn and stood there plunging the clapper into the container. When she caught them, however, for that or for any other "crime," she whipped them for a fare-thee-well. It was with enormous relief that Paul and Mollie left that cheerless house, holding Caroline's hand as she helped her grandchildren board the train for Virginia. The first stop on the trip home required them to spend a night in a hotel in Chicago. The next morning, on the way to re-board the train for the ride home, Paul realized that he had forgotten his prized cap. Much to his dismay, his Grandma made him go back to the hotel by himself to retrieve the hat. It was probably only several blocks away, but to a 10-year old country boy unused to life in a busy metropolis, the walk was long and fearful and certainly one he never forgot.

Back in Virginia, probably in Carroll County, there was a new mother to get to know. Mary, Jim's second wife, was a stepmother unlike any other. As a new bride she faced several challenges right off the bat; the first was Jim's stubborn housekeeper. After Betty's death Jim had hired a woman to help with cleaning, cooking, washing, ironing, tending to the children and perhaps providing extra-curricular services. For some reason when Jim's new wife asked her to leave, she refused. Mary tried to persuade the housekeeper that she was now in charge and that the family no longer needed her. But there was no moving her, or else Mary at the tender age of 20 wasn't forceful enough to convince the woman, who probably had nowhere to go, to pack her things and take off, and apparently Jim was no help. So Mary called in the marines—her mother-in-law, Caroline. A few words from Mrs. Simms the elder, and the reluctant housekeeper was out the door. When someone in later years asked Mary what Caroline was like, Mary replied that her mother-in-law was a "tough old thing."

Mary's second challenge was coping with the post-war poverty and destitute living conditions on the Little Reed Island River in Carroll County, where she and Jim first settled. At least one baby, Archer Gale, was born there in 1888 before they moved back to Franklin County. Remembering those early years, Mary told her grandson Harold that "we liked to starve until we got back down here."

It may have been around 1890 that Jim and Mary returned to Endicott and Franklin County and moved into the residence we all remember as the Jim Simms "home-place." This farm had Runnett Bag Creek flowing in the back and a main road running in the front. I assume that it had been Caroline's home, the place she lived and raised her family—where she came after her husband died. At 70, considered old in 1890, she may have decided to leave and to live out her life with her daughter Virginia (Jennie) Simms Hancock in Rocky Mount. Caroline died there nine years later, in 1899.

At that time the house, like most of the first homes over in the country, was a modest three or four room log cabin. And like other homesteads, this one grew. With the help of his son Archer Gale (and probably some of his other children) Jim added rooms upstairs and down, installed a front porch, which they filled with rocking chairs, covered the logs with wood siding, and painted it white.

Jim and Mary settled easily into the family residence and the routines of their new life in Franklin County. For Jim it meant some farming, but he was primarily a carpenter, a "smith" and a millwright. In fact, he became a master millwright and traveled all over western Virginia and North Carolina setting water wheels and installing the complicated machinery inside the mills which he both designed and manufactured. His grandson Harold explained with pride how his Grandpa "would go to the woods and hunt him a suitable tree, usually a locust, for the spindle," the portion of the wheel which held the buckets. "He did all the work himself; he made the wooden gears, every one of them." Only the shaft which extended from the wheel to the interior workings of the mill was metal. "The rim on the wheel was solid wood, made from white oak if he could get it. He would cut the tree down and hew it out to have six sides, into a hexagon."

Grandpa Simms could do just about anything—certainly his children and grandchildren thought so. He often "allowed" them to help him in his carpentry and blacksmith workshop, which was behind the house down by the creek. In his business Jim was in constant need of sharp instruments, and it usually fell to his son Paul to keep his father's tools razor sharp by honing them on an old whetstone. It must have been an inefficient implement and mighty "dull" work for Paul, because he promised himself that once he had his own farm, the first thing he would buy would be an easy-to-operate pedal grinding wheel, and he did. In Jim's later years his grandson Earl, Paul's son, helped his grandfather by working the bellows in the blacksmith shop. Earl was just a little fellow, and he had to jump to grab the rope which controlled the "breathing" apparatus for the forge. Earl also worked for his Grandpa picking apples from his orchard, but it was Paul who paid his son for his labor, knowing that his father wouldn't. Those chores kept children busy in a useful way and especially so for Jim with that crippled-up left shoulder.

As a skilled carpenter Jim was called on to craft all sorts of things. He built the essential elements for stills—hogsheads, caps and worms. He constructed ground slides (wagon beds with runners made from sourwood that farmers used on the steep hillside slopes of their mountain communities), he made cradles, and he made coffins—something for the beginning of life and for the end.

The prized family cradle, which he designed and constructed for his little girl Bessie (born in 1896), and shared by his adult children for their own growing families, was rarely empty or at rest. With babies arriving regularly both in his own second family (Delma in 1903, Amy in 1906) and in Paul and Eula's family (Earl in 1905, Elva in 1907), at least five infants started their lives swaying to the comforts of soft singing and gentle foot-rocking in this well-used, well-made, well-loved cradle. Unfortunately that little baby bed did not end up in the family "museum." Many years after Jim and Mary's and Paul and Eula's children had outgrown the need for baby furniture, young Jim (Jim and Mary's son) and his wife Lera inherited the cradle and used it for their first born, Essie. Jim Jr., too, was a carpenter who had a shop of his own. He did not appreciate the aesthetic and historic value of his father's craftsmanship. While he was working on one of his projects he needed a particular piece of wood. He cast his eye around his shop and the house, and found exactly what he needed right there in the cradle. Being a practical, unsentimental man, Jim did not hesitate to break the baby cradle apart for that right strip of wood. When Eula heard about the destruction of this beloved little piece of furniture which she had used for two of her own babies, she was furious and never forgave her brother-in-law for this sacrilege, not that he was ever repentant or even knew of her anger. It would not have been like her to tell him what she thought of his ruinous action. The only irony or small justice in this sad episode was that after the cradle "unraveling," Jim and Lera continued to produce babies, at least five more. Those little ones probably had to begin life in a bottom dresser drawer; not that it inconvenienced or bothered the younger Jim one bit.

The loss of the baby cradle was but a disappointment in life. The need for a coffin was always a much sadder occasion. Grandpa Jim built caskets for people of all ages. All deaths were sad; the deaths of children were the saddest of all. One dark, rainy evening just after he and Mary had finished dinner, a knock came on the door. Jim went to admit the caller and found a man named Allen. The man held out a gun and asked Jim to take it. "I want you to have this," he said, "as payment for making a coffin for my little girl." It was the only thing of value he had to offer. Mr. Allen, overcome with despair and grief, said nothing more and left. Jim kept the weapon, an 1812 flint lock rifle made in Jamestown, North Carolina. Unlike the cradle, it remains in the family.[4]

For Mary P. Shively, marriage to Jim Simms brought the usual rigors of farm life—working 12 to 16-hour days, mothering Jim's five children and having five babies of her own. Archer Gale, the first born in 1888, James in 1889, Bessie in 1896, Delma in 1903 and Amy in 1906. This second installment of Simms children blended with the first. Paul, the middle child of the "original" batch, was 10 when Archer Gale arrived, 11 at Jim's birth, 18 at Bessie's, 25 at Delma's and 28 at Amy's, and by that time married and a father himself. In fact, his half-sisters, Delma and Amy, were not only aunts, they were also best friends of his and Eula's first two children, Earl born in 1905 and Elva in 1907.[5]

The tangle of generations, certainly not unique to our family, but a mess to explain, was great fun for the children who grew up with cousins and aunts and uncles and nieces and nephews who were around the same age—all of whom lived nearby and provided a ready pool of playmates.

The confusion created by relationships became downright hilarious at times. Amy, the youngest, the last born of the second lot of Jim and Mary's children, was only one year older than her half-niece, Elva. The two girls lived within a ten minute walk of one another and were best buddies for their entire growing-up years, until they went off to high school and got married. But, at times, in the universality of girlhood friendships, they sometimes "fell out." It was then that Amy would often pull genealogical rank on Elva, taunting her by declaring that she, Amy, was a daughter and by inference, somehow closer to God, or had a truer kinship with the past, or was in a more favorable state than Elva who was ONLY a granddaughter. But Amy had a scare, an ancestral nightmare that she was not, in fact, the natural child of Jim and Mary Simms. Her concern was prompted by knowledge that her brother Harold was not a brother at all; he was her nephew. He had been living with the family under false pretenses.

The sad truth was that Harold was the child of Archer Gale (Amy's older brother by 18 years) and Nola Dudley Simms. He was born in 1914, the same day, or a few days before his mother died.[6] When Nola realized that she was desperately ill and was probably going to die, she asked her mother-in-law to look after her new baby boy. Mary gathered up her son

James Robert and Mary Simms Homeplace

and daugher-in-law's newborn child and took him home, walking over the crossing log, the crude footbridge which spanned Runnett Bag Creek from one property to the other, and raised him as her and Jim's own. According to Harold and his wife Elvarine, when Grandma went for the baby, she asked the Lord to help her be good and kind to him and to love him (as if she could do anything else!) In all the years that she cared for Harold, Mary said she only slapped him once and that it had made her hand burn—then and whenever she thought about the one time she punished him. She felt enormous compassion for the little boy who had lost his mother.

For some reason Jim and Mary saw no need to tell Harold or their other children who his parents really were. He melted in with the others—belonging—an equal with them. There was no attempt to deceive anyone, it just didn't seem important to Jim and Mary to tell the children who Harold really was. They may have assumed that everyone knew he was their grandson. But everyone didn't know. When Amy found out about Harold's adoption, she began to wonder about her own paternity and maternity; maybe she was not a legitimate Simms either. When Amy put the question to her mother, Mary, calling on her rascally sense of humor, teased her little girl: "Yes, you are right, Amy, you are not a Simms at all, you are actually an Allen from Allentown." At that time Allentown was the poorest section of the county's community of log houses, located on a branch of Runnett Bag which flooded whenever the creek "got up." Even in Endicott, even in the country, the deep sticks, there was snobbery, a hierarchy of families, the ins and the outs. The Allens were the outs.

Harold didn't find out that his grandparents weren't his father and mother until he was six-years old and in school. (Ah, school, that great illusion buster—the place you discover the truth about Santa Claus, the Easter Bunny, the stork, and many other childhood fantasies.) He happened to mention something about his mother and father "to two little old gals sitting there," and they told me that you "ain't got no mama." He said, "Oh, yes, I do." They said, "No, she died." They told him that it was his grandmother that he lived with. He didn't believe them. "I studied about it all day long." Then when he went home, he asked Mary "Aren't you my ma?" She fumbled around a bit and said, "Yes." Harold told her "those little Hash girls said that you wasn't my mama, that my mama died." Then Mary sat down with her grandson and told him the whole story. That was the first he knew that his real mother was dead.

The blood-line bragging rights didn't end with Elva and Amy's generation, it continued on into the next. Around 1939 Amy's daughter, Jean, and Elva's much younger sister, Betty, were at Grandma Mary's house. The two little girls were both about ten-years old, playing with their paper dolls, or pumping music out of the organ, or involved in a game of croquet or tag, when something went wrong and play ended in an argument. Betty threatened to go tell Grandma "on Jean." But Jean fired back. She brought out the heavy artillery with the wounding shot to the heart, telling Betty that she, Betty, wasn't Grandma's REAL granddaughter, but that she, Jean, was. Betty argued that she was too Grandma's real granddaughter and the child's war was on—fought on that familiar battleground of "am too," "are not," "am too," "are not"—until Betty ran home to her mother for reassurance that she was, in fact, a true granddaughter, because she obviously had been treated like one. But Eula had to break the news to her little girl that she was only a step granddaughter; Mary was not her real grandmother. Betty, heart-broken, spent the rest of the day in her room dissolved in tears. She had lost something precious—the blood tie to Grandma and the war to Jean.

There were always children, grandchildren, great-grandchildren around the Simms homeplace. My own memories of visits to Great Grandma are limited to three big attractions: the organ in the parlor that had two large pedals to pump out awful, discordant whining sounds; the front porch with a swing and rocking chair; and a grape arbor with plump purple scuppernong grapes loaded with seeds and thick skins.

Mary and Jim Simms had a wonderful sense of fun, but Jim had a wicked—you might even say a twisted—sense of humor, caused I think by a mischievous bend in one of his chromosomes, a genetic trait bequeathed to many of his descendants. A favorite story that illustrates his devilment was a prank I call the "Chicken and the Eggs."

One of Jim Simms' pleasures was his daily newspaper which he picked up at the post office in the General Store in Endicott, a mile or so from his home on Runnett Bag Creek. Along the way he took a short cut across his friend Arthur Snead's property to follow the creek and save himself a few steps and a little time. Crossing the Snead farm, he passed his friend's barn and its one hen's nest.

After going by Arthur's house every day and seeing that one lone chicken's perch, Jim couldn't resist the temptation to play a joke on his wonderful but gullible neighbor. All farmers know that a hen lays only one egg a day, but Jim hoped to persuade Arthur that the laws of nature had changed in his favor. Every morning for several weeks, enough time to convince the man he had an extraordinary hen, Jim put an additional egg under his friend's layer. Before long Arthur began bragging about his double-laying hen to Jim and the local farming gentry who gathered at the general store to drink Cokes and swap tall tales. Jim slyly challenged this fantastic notion, saying, "Arthur, don't tell stories like that. Nobody would believe anything like that." Arthur, confident and proud of his chicken's prowess, rose to the dare: "I know good and well it is so, too. I been getting those eggs." So they got up a bet.

Arthur wagered Jim fifty cents (a substantial amount for those days) that the hen would, in fact, lay two eggs. The two men agreed to meet the next morning at the chicken coop to see the "miracle" of the double-laying hen. Bright and early, they convened at the hen's nest but, of course, there was only one egg. Arthur lost the bet.

We are not sure if Arthur Snead ever discovered the truth, but it is hard to imagine that Jim's misshapen chromosome would have allowed him to keep such a delicious secret for long. (He didn't because obviously, we all know about it.[7])

(Perhaps that is what is meant by the expression "egging him on".)

The story of the "Chicken and the Eggs" was a tale the family enjoyed telling and retelling for years after the event. There are others, less well known, some as harmless as this one, others more serious.

Jim's nemesis and sparring partner in pranksterhood was his friend and contemporary Matt Spencer (referred to as "Old Man Matt" by many members in the community, including the Simms' children). The two men were constantly playing jokes on each other. Matt lived a short distance from Jim, on the same road on land which had once belonged to James Cannaday II (Jim's grandfather.)[8]

One evening, just for the heck of it or maybe in retaliation for some nonsense, Jim piled a bunch of thorny blackberry vines outside the front door of Matt's house, grabbed one of Matt's chickens and made it squall. "Old Man" Matt had settled in front of the fire and gotten himself comfortable by taking off his brogans, when he heard the ruckus outside. (To make this trick work, Jim must have known that Matt would be shoeless; perhaps most farmers shed their heavy boots at the end of the day.) Matt jumped up, bare-footed, grabbed his rifle, ready to shoot anybody stealing his chickens and ran out the front door smack dab into the briar patch trap Jim had set for him. By then Jim was nowhere in sight.

Some pranks were just for fun, but some were quite rough, like the one on Matt's dog. The old hound had been making a nuisance of himself by constantly wandering over to the Simms property and invading the family's springhouse, their source of drinking water as well as the place they stored fresh milk and butter. Because the spring was some distance from the farm house, Jim and Mary didn't always hear or see the animal when he crawled under the springhouse door and got into the milk and butter. After discovering that Matt's dog was "tearing up his milk," Jim found a particularly vicious and effective way to stop the marauding canine. He ground a long cradle blade, an implement used to cut wheat, razor sharp; he "set up triggers to cause the blade which had a weight tied to it to cut the dog's head off" when the hungry, unsuspecting creature sneaked into the springhouse. And sure enough, the next time the dog crawled into the spring house, the blade dropped and hit its mark. Jim dragged the poor beheaded animal off into the woods and left him there. That was not the end of the story by any means. Several days later Matt went looking for his pet and found the dead and decaying dog in the woods. Furious, he got his revenge by tossing the corpse into the Simms' spring, fouling the family's drinking water and causing them to use another spring much farther up the hollow until they could cleanse the near water.

Matt not only had a pesky dog, he had ducks and geese that made the mistake of "visiting" Grandpa's garden. Disgusted by the "fowl" incursion, Jim snatched up the geese, poked their heads between the palings of the picket fence which adorned the yard, and left them hanging there, honking miserably until Matt came to their rescue.

The creative bent of Jim's slightly twisted mind didn't end with nasty and imaginative pranks; it continued on with an artistic flair. Jim was a gifted caricaturist. He could draw recognizable faces with only a few lines, often on a stump using a piece of charcoal. He did not paint or draw pictures of his children or wives, so now we have no oversized portraits of somber-faced family members, preserved for all eternity in elegant gold frames hanging over the wainscoting of our dining rooms like the aristocratic families who lived east of the Blue Ridge on James River plantations. No, Jim used his talent to draw insulting caricatures and cartoons of his neighbors and sent them out as Valentine "gifts." He got a good laugh at his "friends'" expense, irritating the heck out of them.

Jim's sense of humor relied heavily on insults and mockery. Another different illustration of this inclination was his reaction to the famous Allen shootout which took place in Carroll County in March 1912. Several members of the Allen family were certain they had been wronged by the judicial system and took the law into their own hands. The men, packing pistols and rifles, walked into the courthouse, murdered the judge, the Commonwealth's attorney, and the sheriff as well as wounding several others. This incident produced quite a bit of shocking gossip and conversation at courthouses all over western Virginia. When someone mentioned the Allen shoot-out to Jim, he said that he was only "sorry it didn't happen down here" in Rocky Mount. I don't know why he said or thought such a thing, probably to be funny. Maybe he, like many country folks, distrusted and resented local government and what they considered the over-reaching hand of law enforcement, especially when it came to moonshine.

You can't mention Franklin County without someone reminding you that it is known the world over as the "Moonshine Capital of the World." I have always been aware of its reputation, and until recently confident that my family had nothing to do with any of that business. Well, maybe they did make a little, on the side, for their own use.

As far as I know, Jim did not make illegal whiskey himself, but he did help those men who did, in other ways. In his backyard workshop, he crafted not only coffins, cradles, and mill wheels, he also made hogsheads, caps and worms for stills which he sold to his neighbors who were working in the booze business. His contribution to the success of the moonshiners didn't end with selling them the means to make white lightning, he was a consumer—a fine customer—and as the years rolled on, he was often drunk—a state his grandchildren most remembered him in, an unfortunate last memory of their grandfather.

Ignatius Andrew Jackson Simms, Uncle Jack, *J.R. Simms' younger brother*

As a younger man Jim just enjoyed his dram. He was an unsophisticated fellow, unfamiliar with the fast paced business world of the nearest "big city," Rocky Mount. There, his younger, financially successful brother, Ignatius Andrew Jackson Simms, lived in a modest house which he had ordered from Sears & Roebuck. Uncle Jack was a big man with a mustache and an ever present cigar hanging from his mouth. He owned an entire block of buildings in the heart of downtown with a saloon the most prominent and probably the most lucrative of the lot. But Jack made at least one bad business decision. He invited his older brother Jim to take care of the tavern for a few days while he was away. Once on the job, Jim grew big-hearted and generous at the sight of all that liquor, or maybe that misshapen chromosome of his pushed him into a little devilment. Much to the delight of the locals, he threw the doors of the bar open and invited everyone to "Come on in, the drinks are on the house." The good citizens of Rocky Mount took full advantage of the

Simms' brother's invitation and drank up every drop of alcohol in the place. No one seems to know how Uncle Jack reacted to such business incompetence, but Jim was never invited to tend bar again.

Perhaps Uncle Jack got even after all. Whether it was intentional or not, he managed to wrangle the family Bible away from Jim's family. The Bible had been left to Jim as the oldest and the one most in need of its message. At least that was the family tease. Some years after Jim died, Uncle Jack paid a call on his widow, Mary Simms, at her home on Runnett Bag Creek. While there, he noticed that the old family Bible and its wealth of the family's genealogical history, handwritten inside its cover, was falling apart and needed a new binding. He offered, out of the goodness of his heart, to have it rebound, promising that once it was repaired, he would return the Good Book to Mary. Uncle Jack died before he could do it, and no one from the Jim Simms' side of the family has seen the Bible since, not that they haven't tried repeatedly, even threatening law suits. Uncle Jack's children refused to honor their father's promise to return the Bible, and refused even to admit that they had it, or even knew where it was, which meant, of course, that they could not provide copies of valuable information on the history of our side of the family. It's enough to make your blood boil; no wonder there are religious wars.

J.R. Simms and his family at his 80th birthday party, September 9, 1923. Back row: Delma Simms Lumsden, Mary, Grace Simms Brogan, Jim Jr., Archer Gale Simms. Front row: J.R. Simms, Paul Simms, Bessie Simms Goode.

I never knew Grandpa Simms, my great grandfather, (Mary's "Mr. Simms") and can describe him only from the memories of others. As far as I know, there is only one series of photographs of him, made at his 80th birthday party on September 9, 1924. It was one of those elaborate family meals, served outside next to the house, under the shade of the trees, on a table covered with a clean, white cloth and laden with bowls and platters of food—truly a groaning board. From the photographs we can see that he was a rather short man, 5'5" or 5'6", dwarfed by his wife, who was self-

Frank and Mollie Simms Denison with son, Okema

consciously taller than he and hated to have her picture taken. Most of her images are blurs as she ran from the camera. Jim was a little stooped by age, fair complexioned with blue eyes, a hint of red hair amid the gray, and a bounteous mustache. Even at this age, in the old photograph, we can detect a mischievous look and smile on his face.

In spite of Jim's sense of fun and devil-making, he was often a harsh Pa to his children. Apparently Mollie had an argument with her father and left home as soon as she was old enough and could manage by herself; she fled to Missouri, probably to Aunt Julia's family. There she met Frank Denison whom she married in 1897. The newlyweds became "Sooners" and helped to settle Oklahoma, in the new town of Okema, the name they gave their first born son. Paul, too, had an unpleasant encounter with his father. Jim threatened to whip his almost-grown son, and the two of them came mighty close to a fist fight. That blow-up was the deciding factor. Paul too left home, but not to undertake anything as glamorous as pioneer life in the far West. For him it was the mines of West Virginia, where his brother Arthur had gone before him. But that's a story for another chapter. Not even Amy, the baby of the family, was spared her father's hurtful tongue. When he learned that she was planning to marry Grady Thomas at the tender age of 19, he said, "Well, I'll be damned, I wonder where they will live." And when she showed him her wedding dress he said, "I would rather see you in your shroud than wed to that Thomas boy." (Who, by the way, was a sweet, gentle man and a valued employee of Norfolk and Western Railroad.)

Jim's grandchildren were spared any such cruel treatment. In fact, they were greeted with open arms—"Here comes Shiney Eyes," Grandpa would say to Elva, his pet name for her. At his house there were children to play with and Grandma's "molassy" cookies which she made into recognizable shapes for them to eat. The very mention of such delicacies, even in modern times (more than 80 years later), brought smiles to the aged faces of Elva and Earl. When the two children returned home, they told their mother Eula about the delicious "molassy" cookies that Grandma had made for them. So Eula, who was one of the finest cooks anywhere, to please her children, made "molassy" cookies too. Earl and Elva, the little ingrates and cookie experts, told their mother that hers were pretty good, but not as good as Grandma's.

Grandma's talents did not end with cooking and desserts; she also had a fine sense of humor which was a nice counter to her husband's. One of the family's favorite stories about Mary and Jim involved a contest over a chair. The two of them were sitting in front of the fire one evening, Mary rocking Baby Delma, Jim reading his newspaper when the fire began to die down. Rather than walk out to gather wood to replenish the woodpile which was empty, Jim picked up the chair he was sitting on and threw it into the fire. Mary said nothing, just continued to rock the baby, but when the flames began to die down again, she picked up her chair and threw it into the fire. Jim reacted immediately; he rescued the chair and said, "Now Mary that's going too far." Apparently his was an old, worn out piece of furniture and hers was newer.

Obviously Jim Simms could be an exasperating husband. On one occasion during harvest season, he brought home the hired hands for a noontime meal. For some reason, Mary did not know she was having "guests" for dinner and was not properly prepared. She had to rush around and put the meal together, as best she could. When everyone sat down to eat, she apologized for what she considered a substandard effort. Her husband said, "Oh, hush up, Mary, it's better than they are used to." And even though he was probably right, she was embarrassed by his inconsiderate and thoughtless statement, made in front of those hardworking men.

Bessie Simms Goode and her mother Mary P. Shively Simms

There are several other "embarrassing" stories that involve Grandma, one that my mother didn't want me to tell, but one that other members of the family said I must. And it is funny, especially to those of us juvenile enough to enjoy bathroom humor. In the 1940s Amy and her family were visiting or living with Grandma, who was by this time a widow. Amy's daughter Jean had reached courting age and was sitting in the front parlor with her date, when the romance suffered a fatal blow. Grandma came in, wished the two young people good-night and climbed up the steps to her bedroom, but, poor woman, on every step she took, she broke wind. The noise was clear and unmistakable. Jean wanted to die and never see the equally embarrassed boy again.

In the early 1920s, I will guess, many years before the unfortunate dating scene, Mary and her daughter Delma were sitting in rocking chairs on the front porch when a man and wife who lived on Shively Creek passed by. They were in a horse-drawn wagon, on the way to Hurd's Branch to spend the weekend with their daughter and her family. Behind the wagon they had tied their cow and brought it with them, which, apparently violated the rules of country etiquette. Cows were supposed to be left behind when the family went visiting. Mary commented to Delma, "Look at that poor old cow, how she's hanging her head, ashamed and embarrassed to be tagging along with her owners."

Jim died in 1928. He left eight grown children, all married with families of their own. Two of his "boys," Arthur and Harry, children from his first marriage, had died in their twenties. And he left Mary, a widow aged 61. She lived 40 more years, most of that time in the home-place on Runnett Bag Creek. By the time of her death in 1968, Mary was the oldest, or one of the oldest, Civil War widows alive. As a widow of a Civil War veteran, she received a small pension.

Mary and Jim Simms were an interesting couple. He was a charming man with a devilish idea of fun, a talented craftsman, a father with a quick temper and an old man who drank too much. Mary was a perfect counterweight to her husband. She put a limit on Jim's nonsense. She was an unselfish woman who provided stability in what could have been an unstable home, and she provided love and laughter to all her children, step-children, grandchildren, step-grandchildren, and great grandchildren. It was easy to overlook her contributions to the lives of secure and happy children. She behaved the way all mothers, wives, grandmothers should.

Mary Simms at 20 married an "old" man of 43 with a ready made family of five, the oldest, Arthur, 14, the youngest, Grace, 4. She had to evict a reluctant housekeeper and in a year cope with her own first born child, Archer Gale. She managed to muster up equal portions of love and understanding for all her children and step children, grandchildren and great grandchildren. Everyone was welcome in her home, and everyone adored her—a feat that inspires wonder even now. When it came time to distribute family belongings, Grandma Mary made sure that the children from the first marriage, Jim and Betty's children, received the things that had been part of their lives. Paul was devoted to his step-mother and saw to her welfare after she became a widow, as did her other children—especially Amy, who unselfishly took care of her mother when she became sick and bedridden.

I wish I had known my great grandmother better, had paid more attention, had not taken her for granted. Of course I was just a little girl, and to me she was an old lady, with gray-white hair pulled slick back into a knot on back of her head. Her dresses were like sacks, always covered by an apron. I could not even begin to imagine a young person under the wrinkles and the bulky clothing, but she once was. She has left a legacy of love and affection that makes that modest woman one of my heroines. I never expected to admire her until I listened to the stories of those who did know and love her for much of their lives.

Notes for Chapter II, James Robert Simms

1. This child, a son, was not a complete stranger to the family. In the 1920s or so, when he was in his 60s, he sent a letter to Archer Gale Simms, his half brother, in an attempt to contact his "lost" family. He very modestly said that he did not want to cause the family any embarrassment but would like to meet them. As far as I know the meeting never took place.

2. Jim's war record on file at the National Archives, which the archivist was careful to point out was probably incomplete, shows that he was mustered into Company A of the 37th Virginia Calvary in December 1862, which puts a snag in the story that he enlisted early in the war, and that he was in service in 1864.

3. J.L. Scott, *36th and 37th Battalions Virginia Cavalry*, Lynchburg, VA, H. E. Howard, 1986, 49-76.

4. Mary Elizabeth Simms Whelby, J.R. and Mary's granddaughter, kept the rifle in her care until her death in 2004. Her son Joe Whelby inherited the weapon, which he has since given to his cousin James Simms.

5. I know this litany of children is confusing, so I am providing a brief genealogy of Paul and Eula Simms' children to help with understanding these family relationships.

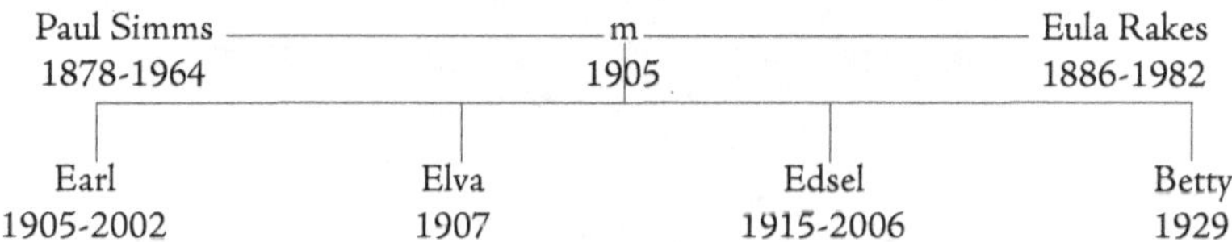

6. Brief genealogy for Harold Simms.

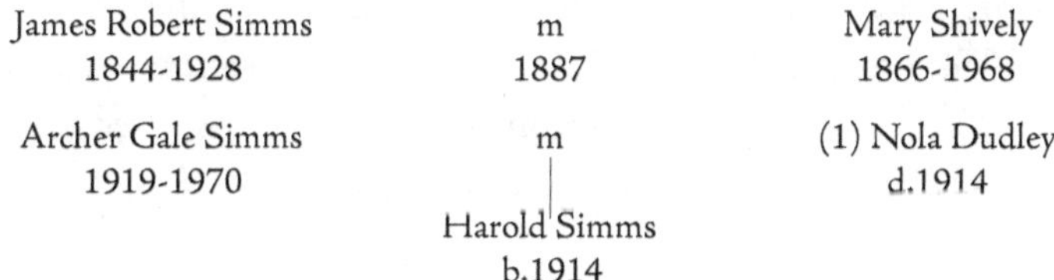

7. This story has several versions; this one is a composite.

8. According to Hughes Cannaday's history of the family. See Appendix E.

3
Columbus McGruder Rakes

Sweetness.

Columbus McGruder Rakes, Eula Rakes Simms' father, lived 57 of his 88 years, from 1893 to 1952, on a 150 acre farm at the convergence of Otter and Shively Creeks in Endicott, Virginia—no more than three miles from Paul and Eula Simms.

"Sweetness" is not a nickname anyone ever called Columbus McGruder Rakes, and I suppose it is odd to saddle any man with such a name. But from my own brief memory, and from the memories and stories of the people who knew him well, the adjectives kind, tender, caring, loving and every "sweet" word that comes to mind describe our Grandpa Rakes. So I choose "Sweetness" as his subtitle, and I am certain that he wouldn't even be mad at me for doing it.

Whenever I asked any direct-line grandchild of Columbus McGruder Rakes (affectionately called "Gooder" by his wives and his friends) about their grandfather, they would always smile just from the memory of this beloved, gentle, man. Then without fail, they would tell me that he had a special talent, a healing touch—an instinct with people and with animals. In fact, they liked to think of him as the non-diploma-ed veterinarian of Endicott.

The best-loved story of Grandpa's veterinary skill and quick thinking was his rescue of Tommy Snead's cow. Tommy was a friend and a near neighbor who lived in the first house over the hill, east of the Rakes' farm. His prize milk cow got into serious trouble when, while grazing under an apple tree, she tried to swallow an apple whole. The fruit got stuck in her throat. She was in distress, gagging and choking, when Tommy found her. He knew exactly who could help him with this emergency and ran across his pasture to get his friend Gooder Rakes, the local "vet." Grandpa rushed back with Tommy to the field. He examined the animal's throat, diagnosed her problem, and sent his neighbor home for two things: a flat iron (the implement once used to iron clothes) and a small wooden mallet. With these "medical tools" in hand, Gooder again felt the cow's throat to locate the exact spot where the apple had lodged, placed the flatiron on one side of her neck and struck the opposite side with the mallet applying just the right amount of force to smash the apple without damaging the windpipe. The "old" cow spit out the crushed fruit and began to breathe normally once more. Grandpa had saved her life and gained Tommy Snead's undying gratitude.

Grandpa had an extraordinary relationship with his own animals, especially his dogs—"Old Scott" in particular. (All beloved farm animals in our family were called "old," a title as respectful as "sir" or "lord" or "lady" might be for worthy humans.) Gooder gave commands to his adored canine by whispering in his ear, orders such as "go get the cows." The dog would "light out," brown fur flying, tongue drooping off to one side of his mouth, find the cows (three or so) in whichever pasture they were grazing, round them up by barking at their heels, and direct them to the milking gap.

The milking gap was a moveable spot, usually a break in the fence not too far from the house, where Gooder, his wife Ophelia, or one of their girls milked the cows. Why they (or the other farmers in the country, including the Simms family) did not perform this twice-daily task in the cover and protection of the barn, except during nasty weather, I do not understand, but my mother and her brothers insist that the country custom was to milk the cows at the "milking gap." (From my visits over in the country, I never remember a milking anywhere other than the barn at the Simms farm.)

"Old Scott" could not care less where the cows were milked; he just followed orders. Another command Grandpa gave this faithful and reliable dog was to guard an opening in the fence. Grandpa placed a jacket or a piece of his clothing on the ground and instructed his well-trained canine to stay there and keep intruders, whether they be animal or human, in or out. Old Scott sniffed the material, curled up on the garment and remained there, guarding the place until Gooder released him.

Grandpa was an expert shot with a rifle and enjoyed hunting small game, rabbits, squirrels, and opossums. On hunting days he took the rifle down from its keeping place over the doorway between the kitchen and dining room, called to this favored pet, and ventured off. One afternoon the two of them had a narrow escape when they were out in the woods. While nonchalantly searching for small animals, they were scared almost to death by the sudden appearance of a large mountain lion, an animal known to live in the hills, but rarely seen. The encounter could have been disastrous for both man and dog, or even for the mountain lion if Grandpa had gotten his rifle to his shoulder in time. The strangeness of the human and his canine companion was just as frightening to the wild animal as was the big cat to Grandpa and Old Scott. All three of them, startled at the sight of the other, jumped with shock and surprise and, like comedians on a vaudeville stage, ran away in opposite directions.

It was a sad day for Posey Queen (a man with a name that Dickens would have loved) when he discovered Gooder Rakes' ability with a shotgun. Posey was a young country upstart who thought he would take advantage of an old man by challenging him to a "shoot out." Posey bet Grandpa $5 that he could not hit a target 100 yards away. So sure was he of the outcome that he, Posey, offered his own black Stetson hat as the "bull's eye." Gooder not only had confidence in his marksmanship, he had a secret for keeping the shot from scattering. He soaked the shell in linseed oil so that it would act as a solid round. Once Posey had set the Stetson at the agreed on distance, Grandpa moved it even farther away—50 more feet, then aimed and blasted the Stetson squarely in the center, taking Posey's $5, ruining his new hat, and reducing his swagger somewhat.

Gooder Rakes' medical skills did not end with tending to animals. According to everybody who knew him, Grandpa would have been a wonderful country doctor; he had healing instincts and a compassionate nature, if only he had had the proper education. He did have a few medical implements: fleams (knives with three legs and rounded blades used for bleeding patients, gruesome medical tools he inherited from his father), and a pair of tooth pullers.

I never heard that he used the fleams, but he certainly used the tooth pullers. The preferred method of dentistry in the early years of the 20th century (in the country anyway) was to yank out any tooth that was causing great pain. One of Grandpa's patients showed up with a terrible toothache. To help the man get through the dental ordeal Gooder gave him some peach brandy and sent Lillian, his youngest daughter, into the house with instructions to play the organ, and to play it as loudly as she could while he extracted the offending tooth.

Friends and family relied on Gooder Rakes, dentist, veterinarian, and healer to help them with their ailments. One of his medical philosophies was: "You're all right as long as your miseries keep moving around; it's when they stay in one place that you are in trouble."

To illustrate this very point, his little granddaughter Elva Simms had a misery which had settled in one place. He noticed that she was constantly scratching around her torso. Her mother Eula tried to get Elva to stop picking at herself: "People will think you have the itch." Grandpa knew about the healing power of herbs, which he gathered and used in his "medical" practice. He brewed up a combination from wild plants and told Elva to bathe in the concoction. "Take this upstairs and wash yourself good with it; rub it all over," he told her. She did just as her grandfather instructed. Soon afterwards, large flat welts appeared around her waist, but almost immediately they faded and disappeared along with the dreadful discomfort and embarrassing itch. She was untroubled by this strange misery for another 30 years. It was obviously an allergy which, once it reappeared, was brought under control after visits to a "real" doctor, fancy

Ophelila Rakes holding Edsel Simms with Elva beside her, c1916

tests, shots, and salves to ease the irritation.

Elva adored her grandfather, who affectionately called her "chinquapin." It was much more than his bedside doctoring ways that she loved. Both Grandpa and Grandma Ophelia welcomed Elva and her brother Earl into their home with open arms. The children had no rules, no chores, no switches; there they were spoiled and allowed to be lazy.

Elva especially loved those visits because she was her Grandma's pet. Earl did not have quite the same relationship with his grandmother; he was the favorite child at home, or so Elva said. He was a picky eater and remembered that Ophelia was always trying to correct this shortcoming, encouraging him to have a little taste of this or that "repulsive" food. He also remembered her as a quarrelsome, unpleasant woman, fussing about one thing or another, constantly nagging her husband. Even Elva admitted that Grandma was something of a screamer; they could hear her yelling from the house to the barn.

"Dump," Gooder's pet name for his wife, "I think we ought to hoe the corn." And Dump would reply, "we are not going to hoe corn today, Gooder. Don't you have a grain of sense?" Or conversation to that effect. None of this yammering bothered Elva one bit because she was never the object of Grandma's temper.

Of the dozens of times she went to stay with her Rakes' grandparents, two visits stand out from the rest. By age nine or ten, Elva was considered old enough to walk the three miles from her house on Hurd's Branch, across the Griffith Hill to Otter Creek and to the Rakes' house all by herself and was even allowed to stay the night. One summer afternoon she left home in bright sunlight and walked a good part of the way, at least two miles, when an electrical storm suddenly blew up. The thunder and lightning and the great gushing downpour that followed, forced the little girl to seek shelter with one of Grandpa's neighbors—the Sammy Shivelys—a family Elva knew. The rain poured down with such ferocity that Shively Creek flooded the road and made it impossible to cross. Once the rain let-up, Sammy made a serious mistake. He gave Elva the choice of riding behind him on his mule to her grandfather's house, or having him fetch Gooder to take her to his house. Naturally, like any child in strange circumstances, she wanted her beloved Grandpa to come for her. That meant that Shively had to saddle up his mule, ride to the Rakes' farm in the still pouring rain, get Grandpa who had to saddle up one of his horses, (either Morgan or Daisy) ride back to the Shivelys' place and take Elva home with him. Gooder may not have been pleased by her decision, but he didn't tell her that, although she did catch a glimmer of his displeasure. The truth was that they were all relieved to have that precious child safe at the home-place on Otter Creek. Paul and Eula were also concerned about their little girl because they knew she could not possibly have gotten to the Rakes home before the storm struck. In fact, Paul had saddled up his horse and come to her rescue as well, but by the time he arrived at the Rakes home, Elva was there, drying off in front of the fire. He "sat for a spell" and relaxed with his in-laws.

Elva's other memorable visit with her Rakes' grandparents got her into big trouble with her parents. She had been invited to stay several days with the understanding that she would return home on the third day. At the end of the that day, Elva did not want to go back home, nor did Gooder or Dump remind or encourage her to leave, so she didn't; she stayed on. It was just so pleasant with them there on what Grandpa called his "plantation," that she hated to leave. Her parents, Paul and Eula, however, were not happy. They were torn between anger that she had not come home when expected and worry that something had happened to her. So they sent a "fetcher," Big Brother Earl, to collect her. Elva knew the minute she saw him coming up the road that her future looked dim. On the long trek home, Earl, with monstrous delight, told her over and over again what was waiting for her back at the Simms farm. "You are going to get it. You'll have to go down to the branch and pick your own switch from the willow tree and it is going to sting your legs and you are going to cry in pain." Aren't all brothers sadists? Elva and Earl actually had a very hardy sibling rivalry with inventive and creative "attacks" and "counterattacks," enough for an entire chapter in a book.

At the Rakes "plantation," Earl and Elva reveled in freedom, grandparental love, and enjoyed young playmates. Like Jim and Mary Simms, their other grandparents, Gooder and Ophelia Rakes had a later generation of children—two more girls—Effie, born in 1898 and Lillian, born in 1903. These girls were less than ten years older than Earl and Elva, so they were more like cousins than aunts.[1]

As the oldest Effie took full advantage of her seniority. Anyone who ever knew Effie Rakes (Snead) would not be surprised to learn that she was a bossy and manipulative teenager. She began at an early age to demonstrate potential for the shrewd businesswoman she grew to become. She managed to get the other children, including her younger sister Lillian, to do her chores, promising them such treasures as colored picture postcards (used) in exchange for ironing a certain number of linens or pieces of clothing.

Perhaps an event from Effie's deep past had an important psychological effect on the development of her personality. When she was an infant, her older sisters Eula and Iva almost killed Effie by trying to baptize her. One Sunday morning after the girls had been to a baptism conducted by the preacher of Long Branch Primitive Baptist Church, they had an inspiration. Impressed, as well as amused, by the custom of baptism by complete immersion, they decided to hold a service of their own. What better subject than their baby sister Effie?

Eula and Iva knew Effie would need a proper outfit, and a source of water for the "religious" ceremony. So they made a tiny dress for the new little Christian. Otter Creek, which flowed behind the house, was a ready body of water for the occasion. As they were putting a cap and "christening gown" on Effie and making preparations for the dunking, their mother Ophelia "got on to it" and put an immediate halt to the unofficial baptism, perhaps saving her baby from premature death by drowning.

Whether it was this earliest attempt to save her soul, or some other trauma, Effie remained unbaptized until she was a grown woman living in Roanoke and joined the Grandin Road Baptist Church. This was a church she helped to found, and she remained a sustaining member until her death in 1999 at the age of 101.

The other sister, Lillian, the youngest of the Rakes' girls, was often out-smarted and out-maneuvered by her older sister. But sometimes, at least once, Lillian, with help from her nephew Earl, out-manipulated Effie.

The two girls were playing outside and one of the family's horses (either Morgan or Daisy) was grazing in the front yard. Both sisters decided, simultaneously, that they wanted to ride the horse and made a dash for him. As usual Effie won. Not to be outdone this time, Lillian planned revenge; she enlisted Earl to assist in her scheme. To frighten Effie the conspirators decided on a surprise attack with an umbrella as their weapon. They crept out the back door and around to the front of the house, snuck up behind the horse with big sister sitting smugly astride, and jerked open the umbrella. Instead of frightening Effie, they startled the horse. The usually gentle animal reared up and Effie slide off his backside, surprising everyone. Fortunately for Lillian and Earl, Effie escaped unharmed with only her dignity in shambles.

Effie may have been the dominant sister, but Lillian had her own claims to fame. For one, she was a lover and collector of cats. At least six felines followed her everywhere she went, especially to the milking gap. There she fed her pets "directly" from the cow's teats by squirting a stream of milk into their open, waiting mouths. For another, she was an amateur fortune teller. During World War I, when Lillian was a young teenager, she sent off for a booklet on how to tell fortunes—a seemingly harmless hobby. She studied the handbook to learn the mysteries of reading the future in palms, teas leaves and coffee grounds. After practicing her craft on various kinfolk, including nieces, nephews, and young friends, she acquired a reputation as something of a soothsayer. While one of her friends, Lelia Gillespie, was visiting at the Rakes Farm, Lillian made a dire prediction. Lelia was concerned about her fiancé Virgil Shively, who was in basic training at the Norfolk Naval Station, and asked Lillian for a "reading." "When will I see him again? What will become of him?" Lillian had Lelia pour coffee out of her cup, then turn it right side up. After careful scrutiny of the fateful coffee grounds, Lillian predicted that Virgil would come home by the end of the month to be with Lelia and would not return to the service. If he went off to war, he would die. Amazingly, Lillian's prediction came true. Virgil came home, and he came home to stay, except for the couple of years he spent in prison for going AWOL. He must have decided that Franklin County was a lot safer than going to war on foreign seas. We don't know if Lillian's prophecy was the source of his troubles or if it was his own timidity.

Children from all eras get into mischief, delight in sibling rivalry, and love to play dress-up. One Sunday morning, with the adults safely off at church, Elva, Earl, and Lillian decided to explore the attic of the Rakes' granary (a barn-like building used for storage) where they found a trunk filled with old clothes. They had a wonderful time dressing up and admiring themselves in the old-fashioned grown-up outfits. Then Elva discovered a corset tucked away among the garments and put on the body-girdle with help from Lillian, who cinched it up nice and tight. Elva prissed around in the "naughty" underwear, enjoying the risqué experience until she got into trouble. Try as she might she couldn't unlace the corset; she was stuck and her grandparents and parents were due back any minute. Neither Lillian nor Earl would help her out of her dilemma. In fact I imagine that they, especially Earl, were rolling with laughter at her distress. Eventually Lillian gave in and helped Elva escape from the clothing trap.[2]

The fun of playing with their young Rakes' aunts and the loving reception the grandchildren received when they visited were the main attractions at their grandparents' home, but they weren't the only ones.

Gooder and Ophelia Rakes' homeplace was one of the most agreeable settings in all of Endicott. Finding a stretch of land appropriate for farming among the valleys and hollows in the foothills of the Blue Ridge Mountains was a challenge all settlers on this edge of Franklin County faced. The Cannadays and the Simmses claimed and clung to fertile, generally level land along Runnett Bag Creek. The Columbus McGruder Rakes' family, however, bested them by acquiring 150 acres of prime farm land between two streams, Shively Branch and Otter Creek, and creating a bottomland by re-routing one of the creeks, making it ideal for planting. Their home was on a gentle rise, surrounded by pasture and woods. They purchased this prize property in 1893 for $1,500

Before they came to Franklin County, Ophelia, who was originally from Floyd County, and Gooder lived on a 200 acre farm in the Poplar Camp Creek area of Patrick County, near land the Rakes ancestors had settled in the late 18th century. It had been "home" for over 100 years. We think the couple met at a Republican Baptist Church social. They married in 1885 and had their first two little girls—Eula Mae born in 1886 and Iva Nora born in 1888—in Patrick County. Eula was a premature baby who survived, they were sure, because she was born in the warm month of August. In March 1893, they decided to sell their Patrick County home to Gooder's brother W.E. Rakes, leaving behind all that was familiar, and moved to a new home in Franklin County. Perhaps the uprooting was to appease Ophelia, a bossy and difficult woman who never seemed happy or content.

Certain years stand out in a family's history. For Columbus McGruder and Ophelia Rakes one of those years was 1893, the year of the move and the year of the birth of another baby, Pearl. Before the early 20th century very few families escaped tragedy. The Rakes family was no exception. In 1896, three years after settling into their new home, Little Pearl died. Her death caused sadness I can only imagine, but Eula, my grandmother, even in her oldest years, could not speak of her little sister without getting a faraway look in her eyes and drawing in her breath. The Rakes family never recovered from the loss of their child, but they did get on with their lives. Several years later they had two more girls, the previously mentioned, Effie and Lillian. Grandpa always called the children "his boys" because all of them, especially Eula and Iva, had to work as hard as field hands or farm boys.

The Rakes' 150 acre farm came with a modest four-room house which has remained relatively unchanged since the time they bought it in 1893. It was a casual, unpainted frame house with, what I would describe, as flexible rooms. Except for the kitchen, any room in the house could have beds or pallets or sitting places, depending on need. If it was cold or someone was sick, they slept in the room with the best fire. If there was company, they might visit in the front rooms, or the kitchen, or the porch, and if the company stayed the night, (depending on the number of guests), they might sleep in every room in the house. The covered front porch overlooked fields and gardens, as well as any traffic passing along on the hard-surfaced road a hundred yards or so from the house. The outbuildings included an unusual barn that stood between the front porch and the road. This now ramshackle building, covered with a tin roof, was divided into three sections. The center portion was an open area into which Gooder could drive the wagon and unload hay into one of the rooms on either side, which he used for horse stalls and storage. At one time a swagging roof attached to the barn almost touched the ground. On that handy roof extension Grandpa spread out his apples to dry on feed sacks. The apples, peeled and thinly sliced, needed three or four rainless days to dry out properly. If the weather did not cooperate, the children had to dash down to the barn and rescue the fruit. Some of the dried apples they sold, and some they hung on a string in the kitchen to be used as the main ingredient for fried apple pies. To make that delicious dessert Ophelia started with a circle of pastry which she filled with the dried fruit, sugar and spices, then she folded it over into a half-moon shape, crinkled the edges with a fork, and fried it up crispy brown in a black iron skillet of hot lard.[3]

Our great good luck is that this farm, and the land that goes with it, has never left the family. It remains in the hands of the Rakes' descendants, Paul Keith Simms and Mark Simms, (Gooder Rakes' great-great grandsons, and Earl Simms' grandsons.) There is, however, a mystery about Gooder and Ophelia's "plantation," one that was only recently uncovered by folks nosing into the history of the property. As far as we know, no one involved ever discussed the odd purchases and repurchases that took place over 15 years early in the 20th century. Those who could answer our questions are no longer with us.

Here are the facts of the story:

(1) On March 21, 1893 "C.M. Rakes of the County of Patrick" purchased 150 acres more or less "on the waters of Otter Creek" in the County of Franklin from Ruth A. Shively and John E. Shively "in consideration of fifteen hundred dollars in hand paid." The layout of that land was described in ways that we could never verify—from white oak trees to red oak bushes to dogwoods; the trees died and the boundaries disappeared.

(2) On August 3, 1906, Paul Simms, the new son-in-law of C.M. and Ophelia Rakes, purchased from them 165 acres for $1,500—$100 in hand, $700 due one year later, the balance due in two years, August 3, 1908. We assume that C.M. Rakes sold his farm (the property he bought in 1893) to Paul, even though according to the deed, the number of acres varied by 15. The description of the land began at the same point, "the white

oak corner in John C. Sigmon deed" but the property owners named in the deed were different from those named in the first deed. That was not surprising because 13 years had gone by. A side note on the deed read, "The vendors lien (Paul's debt to Rakes) retained in this deed has been satisfied in full this 27th day of September 1907. O. H. Price, attorney in fact."

(3) On September 21, 1907, a little over one year after Paul's purchase of the Rakes property, Paul and Eula Simms resold the property whose description was exactly the same as the description of the land he bought on August 3, 1906, but this time it was recorded as only 110 acres. The sale price was $1500 cash in hand. The purchaser, however, was Ophelia Rakes, not Columbus McGruder Rakes.

(4) The final intra-family transaction took place on January 28, 1920, when Ophelia sold the same property, 110 acres, to her husband C.M. Rakes for $1500 cash in hand.[4]

In those days transacting legal business required a long, arduous 20-mile buggy ride to Rocky Mount, as well as paying a lawyer and court costs. It is hard to imagine they would have gone to all that trouble without good reason. It seems probable that Paul and Eula were shielding C.M. Rakes and his beloved "plantation" from some legal or financial threat. If it was financial, why didn't they just lend him money? Why did they resell the farm to Ophelia alone and not to Gooder? Could our grandfather, who was not greedy or particularly ambitious, have been in trouble with "the law?" In that part of the world, being in trouble with the law almost always meant making illegal whiskey. Grandpa did have a license to make a small amount of liquor, and as far as anyone knows his manufacture of alcohol was limited to peach brandy. (Any profit from moonshine business would have come from the sale of alcohol larger than the amounts permitted by the license.)

The discrepancy of the 55 acres is fascinating. Paul appeared to have come out ahead in this property swap, but even though he was ambitious and a cunning money manager, he was a fair man and would not have taken advantage of his father-in-law. The description of the 165 acres in one deed (1906 deed transfer from C.M. Rakes to Paul) and the 110 acres in another (1907 deed transfer from Paul to Ophelia) was exactly the same.

The Rakes sisters-Eula, Iva standing, Effie and Lillian seated

So I suppose the real cause of the discrepancy was an error made by the clerk and overlooked by Simms and Rakes. Paul resold the property to his mother-in-law Ophelia, who remained the legal owner of the land for 13 years. In 1920, the year she fell ill with tuberculosis and died, she sold "the plantation" back to her husband.

Thus we still have an unsolved mystery.

There was no mystery with the farm after 1920. Gooder retained ownership until his death in 1952 when his widow Sally Willy, inherited it. She remained on the farm for a few years before she decided to move and put the property up for sale at auction. Earl Simms, Gooder and Ophelia's grandson, learned from his friend and lawyer Virgil Goode Sr., that his grandfather's land was on the market. Without hesitation he, together with his mother Eula, bought the Rakes farm for $9,500. It has remained in the family ever since then.

But I am getting ahead of my story. As a farmer, Columber McGruder Rakes had his own way of doing things, a reasonable, sensible approach to growing and tending crops without "killing" himself—although that almost happened. During the blistering heat of mid-day, Grandpa stayed out of the garden. He worked the edges of the day—in the cooler early mornings and late afternoons. However, that practical routine did not spare him, however, from the whimsy of spring electrical storms. One year while taking a break from plowing his rich bottomland in preparation for April planting, a sudden storm came up and lightning struck Grandpa right in his tracks. The horse, either Morgan or Daisy, spooked and left him there in the field. The animal, dragging the plow behind him, walked alone across the road, up to the house. When Ophelia saw the master-less horse, she became alarmed, ran to the field, and found her husband just regaining consciousness. It happened so fast, he literally never knew what hit him. There was no long-lasting effect from that smack of electricity, but there was probably a blast from "Dump" lambasting her husband: "Gooder, why in the world are you out working in the field now. Don't you know any better?" (As though he was supposed to have been aware that his life was at risk.) I don't know that Ophelia said anything like that, although none of us would be surprised if she did. It was her way of saying that she was worried to death about him and relieved that he was safe.

It does seem as though dangers lurked all around my great grandparent—mountain lions, unpredictable storms, death of little children, and potential legal problems. In fact it was trouble with the law that became a great threat to the Rakes' daughter, Iva, her husband Will Bowling, and their eight children who lived on a nearby farm.

Will had violated one of the moonshine laws, gotten caught by the revenue agents, been convicted, and sentenced to prison. He was out on bail and had decided that he wouldn't stay around to serve his time. He gathered up his family and was preparing to make a run for it. To give him credit, Will was an honorable law-breaker; he returned the $200 to the bondsman so the man wouldn't lose money when Bowling jumped bail.

It was around 1918 and Iva was in her late 20s when she, Will, and their brood left their home to spend their last night in Franklin County with her mother and father. Iva's big sister Eula, her husband Paul, and their three children, Elva, Earl and baby Edsel were there, too.[5]

The family wanted to be together, to help, and support one another through the ordeal. On that last night, Ophelia, with Eula and Iva's help, fed and provided beds for the six grown-ups and 12 children who slept on pallets on the floor in that four-room house. The children knew from the whispering that something was seriously wrong. The next morning, before sun-up, the Bowlings crowded into their Ford four-seater touring car—baby Larry in his mother's arms, Reuben and Leonard, the older boys, clinging to the side of the car riding on the running boards, and the other children sitting on one another's laps. They had as many of their essential belongings as they could find room for, jammed into and tied onto the back of the automobile. (They must have looked like the Jode family in *The Grapes of Wrath*, leaving Oklahoma for California.) Grandma and Grandpa Rakes, Effie and Lillian, Paul, Eula, and their children waved a sorrow-

Iva and Will Bowling, standing, with Eula, baby Earl, and Paul Simms

ful goodbye to their loved ones as they fled Endicott, Rocky Mount, Franklin County, and Virginia. The Bowlings didn't know where they were going; they were just getting away from the Feds. They headed west, ended up on the Little Miami River in Morrow, Ohio, settled on a farm in a bend of the river where they began a new life. In time they added two more children to their flock, for a nice count of ten. The local papers turned Bowling into something of a celebrity by publishing a story about his escape titled "The Flight of the Red Fox."

But the story wasn't quite over. Some years later, the long arm of the law reached into Ohio, seized the "Red Fox," and brought him back to justice in Virginia. After only six months in prison, Will was released for good behavior. Back home in Ohio, he proved to be a troublesome husband who was not good to Iva. They divorced, and he returned once again to Franklin County, where he remarried and had another ten children. Iva never remarried. She struggled mightily to eke out a life for herself and her children on the farm in Ohio; she remained there for the rest of her life. She did return to Endicott for visits, but of course it was never the same.

With Iva and her family in Ohio, life changed for Gooder and Ophelia. And in just four years, another tragedy struck the Rakes family hard. This time it was Ophelia.

Ophelia "Dump" Thomas, our Grandma Rakes, appeared to be dissatisfied with her lot in life. We wondered if she had had high expectations as a young woman which she never realized, making her cantankerous and irritable. She took her frustrations out on her gentle, forgiving husband—not that he was the only one to suffer the fury of her tongue lashings.

Once, Gooder and his neighbor Peyton Rakes (distant kin, but no one wanted to check too closely) took a day off to go to Rocky Mount on business, intending to return home by supper time. The men were several hours late, and Dump was furious. When they finally appeared, she let them have it, saying something like, "Where have you two been? Why are you so late? I've been worried sick, and dinner's right here on the table getting cold. You inconsiderate 'so and so's.'" Peyton did not just shut up and "take it" the way Gooder did. "By God, Ophelia, we are late because we started late." His snappy reply to her outrage relaxed the tension, and they all broke out laughing.

Ophelia may have been a shrew, but, by way of compensation, she was a talented seamstress. In those days all women in the country made clothes for their families, but Ophelia's hand work was exquisite. She could see a dress or an outfit once and copy the design without a pattern. She crocheted bedspreads, some for wedding presents which she sold for $9. She knitted caps and gloves for the family's babies and made a "famous" little red fur coat for Elva when Elva was in first grade.[6]

In spite of her crusty disposition, Ophelia was close to her children and grandchildren. They were alarmed when she fell ill with tuberculosis in 1920, when she was only 50 years old. Eula, who had inherited her father's instincts for nursing, spent most of her time during that winter at the Rakes' home-place caring for her mother. Elva, who was12, remembered those days as cold and lonely. When she came home from school there was no one to greet her, no fires in the fireplace to warm her, and only her father to prepare dinner. Worst of all, her beloved grandmother was desperately ill. Even with their tender care, Eula and Gooder could not save Ophelia. She died in March of 1920.

The two years after his wife's death—the between years (between wives, that is)—were ones of upheaval for Gooder. Not very long after Ophelia died he moved all the furniture into the back bedroom, rented out his house and farm, and took turns staying with family members.[7] Eventually he grew weary of this vagabond state and imposing on his loved ones, and he decided to reclaim his home.

During the months he spent with Eula and Paul Simms, he helped in any way he could with work around the farm. In the fall everyone pitched in to harvest fodder, stripping by hand the last of the useful portion of the corn, which was later fed to the animals. This particular chore Elva hated because of the stinger worms, nasty little wooly creatures, that were several inches long and "hid" among the leaves and stung with a mighty hurt anyone who disturbed them from their "meal." She had been their victim on several occasions and was very careful pulling off the fodder. This made her slow about her work, falling far behind on her row. Grandpa, that sweet guy, knew why she was so cautious and came to her rescue, helping her until the awful job was done.

He came to her aid another time. In fact, he almost did the unthinkable—he almost whipped one of his grandchildren. It was probably during the summer of 1922 when Edsel was six, and Elva was 14 (old enough to know better, she said later). Grandpa and the two children were sitting outside under the locust trees in the Simms' front yard, when Elva, for some reason—either from boredom, a visit from the devil, or the irritation of having to constantly tend to her younger brother—started teasing Edsel about a girl, little Macey Midkiff. Too bad for Edsel—Macey was "in love" with him, but he of course, hated her guts, couldn't stand the sight of the little brat, who, he said, was always wiping her snotty nose across the sleeve of her dress. Edsel's disgust made the pleasure of taunting him just that much more delicious for Elva. "Edsel and Macey sittin' in a tree, k-i-s-s-i-n-g" or "Edsel loves Macey" said in a sing-song whiney voice. It was enough to cause a six-year old boy with any self respect to strike back, to pick up his grandfather's walking stick and whack his hateful, older sister across the head and knock her to the ground. Grandpa hadn't heard all the teasing, and didn't know about the torment that Edsel had endured, but he did see his grandson hit Elva and decided it was time that Edsel "learned a lesson." Even so, he just couldn't bring himself to spank a child. Eula took care of the naughty boy with a good switching.

During the "between times," when Gooder was back home on his farm, Edsel occasionally stayed with him to keep him company over those lonely days. Edsel remembered that when his grandfather heard a new story or learned something unusual, he would say, "That's a new wrinkle on my persimmon." Edsel also remembered Grandpa's extremely effective method for keeping his little grandson out of the woods and creeks, while he, Grandpa, was working in the garden or milking or away in the pasture and couldn't take the boy with him.

To protect Edsel and to make sure he stayed close to the house, Grandpa, who had not studied child psychology or read Dr. Spock, told his grandson that there were fierce, old shepherd dogs that roamed the local forests and that they would eat little boys and girls if the children wandered into their territory, and they would never be heard from again. This "protection" strategy was so effective that Edsel carried his fear of the woods and the old shepherd dogs back to his own family home over on Hurd's Branch. He became afraid even to walk the quarter-mile from his house to the mailbox on the main road. In Edsel's mind, dark, treacherous woods loomed on either side of the road with old shepherd dogs lurking, just waiting for a nice juicy little fellow to pass by so they could eat him. Taking out letters and picking up the mail were often one of Edsel's chores but, thanks to Grandpa Rakes, the boy tried to stay out of danger by "mailing" letters under a rock near the house. When he could not delay the trip through the "forest primeval" any longer, he ran like the wind, taking the "mailed" letters, picking up the incoming mail and the newspaper, then speeding home as fast as his little legs would carry him. Grandpa meant no harm, just the opposite; he wanted to keep his loved ones safe.

Elva's fondest memories of her visits with her "bachelor" grandfather were of his culinary skills. He made mud turtle soup, potatoes—the best in the world—roasted for an hour in hot coals, birds—probably quail or grouse—hung from a string over the open fire, heat rising to create an automatic rotisserie, and eels. These snakey fish he caught with a gig in Otter Creek after a rainstorm had stirred up the water and made it nice and muddy.[8] In the summer eels migrated up from the Smith River to lay eggs. After he caught them, Grandpa nailed their heads to a board and cut a ring around their necks to skin them.[9]

The easy days of Grandpa's stays with the Simms family and of their overnights with him came to an abrupt end in 1922 when he married a most unlikely and unsuitable woman—Sally Willy Sigmon. She was 25 years younger than Grandpa; he was 58, she 33. She was a big woman, big as a house. Okay, she was obese. She made three of Grandpa. She intimidated him. And why not? She was a fearsome woman—rumored to have

Grandpa Rakes with Sally Willy and her adopted daughter, Ossie, c1922

shot her first husband, and she for sure broke up a still she found on the Rakes' property on a ridge near their house. The owners of the still had been pumping water from Rakes' branch without their permission or rights to be there. Grandpa probably knew about the trespassers, but he did not want to incur their wrath, so he ignored them. But not Sally Willy. When she found the still, which she probably just stumbled across, she went home, grabbed an ax, and chopped the thing to pieces.

She was a much younger woman than Gooder, but she had not one ounce of sex appeal that anyone on the planet Earth could detect. If ever there was a marriage of convenience, this was it. He needed a housekeeper and she needed a home for herself and her adopted daughter, Ossie, who was eight or nine at the time of the wedding.

Naturally Gooder's daughters were distressed by their father's inexplicable choice of a mate. At first they had hard feelings and treated him with a cold chill of silence, but they loved their father and did not want to hurt him. Eula found a clever solution to the problem, a fine way to heal the wound, to end the conflict and make things right with her wonderful father. She sent Elva, her 14-year old over to the homeplace to be a "dove of peace." She saddled up Old Stormer, helped the girl mount the horse, smacked his backsides and Elva rode off to "welcome" the new bride into the family. This gesture made things tolerable and righted the relationship as best they could. Few, if any, of the children or grandchildren ever again spent the night with Gooder and the new Mrs. Rakes on his "plantation."

They did pay day visits, Sunday afternoons, mostly. Grandpa continued his gracious welcome, greeting everyone with a whistle and a

Betty (on left) with Grandpa Rakes, Elva (on his right) and two cousins

"Whoowee, what have we got here?" Eula almost always brought her father a gift from the store—groceries, like coffee and sugar—things he couldn't grow in his garden. At one time they took him a little money, but stopped that when they saw Sallie Willie snatch it from her husband and deposit it in her bosom.[10]

To Betty, the last of the Simms' children and the baby of the family, for all intents and purposes an only child, those Sunday afternoons with Grandpa and Sally Willy (whom her mother DID take the trouble to point out was not her REAL grandmother; none of that woman's blood coursed through Betty's veins) were interminable, especially during cold rainy weather, when there was no escape to the outdoors. With no other children to play with—all of her own siblings were much older and married by the time she was 11 and Ossie, Sally Willy's adopted child, grown up and gone—Betty spent much of her time listening to the clock tick and shooing away flies while her parents and her Grandpa talked about the boring old days, or the boring neighbors, or the boring farm.

Sometimes she would play "chopsticks" on the pump organ, which the Rakes kept in the back room, and sometimes Grandpa would offer her a sip of his coffee lace. This treat he shared with all of his grandchildren at one time or another when they visited him, an experience they all remembered well. In the morning Grandpa would brew up a pot of coffee, pour out a cupful, and add a dash of brandy. When a grandchild would climb up into his lap, he would offer her a spoonful of this delicacy. Betty didn't much like the taste, turned her mouth down and said something on the order of "yuck." Gooder drank the rest himself. (Elva, on the other hand, enjoyed Grandpa's coffee lace.)

Betty also remembered the constant annoyance of ever-present flies. For reasons no one could ever understand, Grandpa considered screens for windows and doors a modern "contraption" he wanted no part of. He preferred the conventional, old-fashioned fly minders to keep the insects from irritating him to death. These were fans made of newspapers rolled across a stick and cut into strips, then waved in front of the face or over the food to keep the dirty buzzing pests from landing.

Grandpa was not always unconventional. In his last years he joined the Primitive Baptist Church. The congregants dammed up a section of Otter Creek between Thomas Snead's store and Grandpa's farm, and created a deep pool to baptize him in. In consideration of his age, the preacher allowed Gooder to be seated in a chair for his ritual dunking.

We must allow Grandpa a few peculiarities, even a mistaken marriage, because for the full measure of a man, Columbus McGruder Rakes was a treasure. To the day he died he never lost his special way with children, his gentleness with animals, nor his wonderful sweetness.

Notes for Chapter III, Columbus McGruder Rakes

1. Brief genealogy of C.M Rakes family:

C. M Rakes	m	Ophelia Thomas
1864-1952	1885	1867-1920

Eula	Iva	Pearl	Effie	Lillian
1886-1982	1888-1977	1893-1896	1898-1999	1903-1995

2. Or that is what I suspect happened. Elva couldn't remember her release, only her predicament.

3. This delicacy is available at Blue Ridge Festival held at Ferrum College in the fall.

4. Franklin County Courthouse, Deed Book 43, p. 598; Franklin County Courthouse, Deed book 55, p. 15; Franklin County Courthouse, Deed book 56, p. 35; Franklin County Courthouse, Deed book 69, p. 575.

5. Iva and Will's eight Virginia children were: Reuben, Leonard, Lena, Noel Ned (Dick), Vivian, Thelma, Muriel, Lawrence.

6. Judy Simms Strawn, Ophelia's great granddaughter, has a crocheted bedspread made by Ophelia. Rubye Snead Nixon, a granddaugher, has a pair of hand-knit baby gloves.

7. Effie was married to Charles Snead by this time and living in Roanoke; Lillian at 17 left her father and took turns visiting her sisters in Ohio and Roanoke.

8. A gig is a spear used to catch fish by jabbing it into their bodies.

9. Once Philpot Dam was begun in late 1940s, the eels could no longer make it up Otter Creek and the gigging came to an end.

10. The tradition of hospitality in the country not only meant a congenial greeting, it also meant food. The guests brought food when they arrived and were given food when they left. I don't know that Sallie Willy was a traditional kind of gal.

4

Paul and Eula, Marriage and Before

Wedding photo, 1905

There are long, silent gaps in the early histories of Paul Simms and Eula Rakes, but there are also fascinating stories to tell.

"I thought she was the prettiest thing I ever saw," Paul told me some 50 years after he first caught sight of his future wife. They met when he began working for her father, Columbus McGruder Rakes, on the family's farm in 1904. Paul and Eula had grown up, not more than three miles from one another, but they had not met until then—or maybe they had and just not paid attention—for some very good reasons. There was a significant age difference—Paul was eight years older than Eula; and, there was a church-going difference—her family attended the Long Branch Primitive Baptist Church and his the Trinity Methodist Church, when they went. Paul had been away from Endicott for years, working in West Virginia.

Paul and Eula's children only knew the sketchiest details about their parents' meeting and romance, other than the wedding date, January 19, 1905.[1] Their love story they kept for themselves. Perhaps those memories grew dim over the years from the lack of telling, and from the soon-as-possible arrival of children, and the crushing work and struggle that was essential to the life of a farm family in early 20th century Virginia.

Eula was 17 when she met Paul. She was a very young woman, but she had already experienced some of the hardships of life. She had been uprooted and moved to a new home, lost a baby sister, and learned all too much about the rigors of farm life. The Rakes family left the Poplar Camp area of Patrick County in 1893 when Eula was seven years old, her younger sister Iva was five, and baby sister Pearl an infant. They moved to their modest house on 150 acres, at the convergence of Otter and Shively Creeks, on one of the most agreeable farm sites in that part of Franklin County. Only three years later, in 1896, little Pearl Rakes died, a tragedy from which they never completely recovered. Gooder and Ophelia Rakes continued to have babies—hoping for boys, of course, but with no luck. Two more girls were born—Effie in 1898 and Lillian in 1903.

Education for their daughters was rudimentary. They attended the Dry Hill School, a one-room school house, that was a mile walk up the rise above their home. Eula talked about one of her teachers whom she considered incompetent. Instead of concentrating on the basics, the three R's—reading, writing and arithmetic, he spent the whole day "inflicting" Shakespeare on little mountain children who could not understand or appreciate the Bard's beautiful but "foreign" words. The youngsters rolled their eyes in boredom. But he, or perhaps his successor or his predecessor, must not have been completely inept because someone did teach Eula to write, do sums and, best of all, read. In fact, reading became one of her greatest pleasures in life, a passion she never had enough time to satisfy while living on the farm, but one she shared with her children whenever she could steal time for such "whimsy." Whether it was from her teachers' example, or from natural insight, Eula realized the value of education and knew that if she had children, their future success would depend upon it.

For the Rakes children, school was an escape from the chores at home, especially for Eula and Iva, who had to work as hard as any field hand. Their father even called them "his boys." With no other male on the place, and with a never-ending need for labor, he had no choice but to use the only help he had available—his daughters. Maybe when Paul showed up with his good looks and his work ethic, that proved to be among his greatest attractions. He was like a son to Gooder and worked his heart out for this family, which relieved "the boys" from some of their onerous chores.

By the time Paul met Eula he had already had quite a few life experiences of his own—several miserable years as a boy living in Missouri after his mother died, a basic education from the local schoolmaster, and adventurous days in the coal fields of West Virginia.

Paul's boyhood years were tough and sad. He lost his mother when he was nine years old, and was then sent to live in cold, cyclone-infested Missouri with his father's sister, hard-hearted Aunt Julia, for several grim years. Fortunately he was brought back home to Virginia by his grandmother Caroline Simms to the Simms homeplace on Runnett Bag Creek. There he lived with his demanding and often difficult "Pa" and a new mother, Mary Simms, a stepmother unlike those of legend. She was as sweet and good to Paul as if he were her own natural child. It was a soft landing for our little boy.[2]

Back home, when he wasn't helping his father on the farm or in his blacksmith shop, Paul attended the one-room schoolhouse at Long Branch, a mile or two walk from home. The school-master was Hughes Cannaday (a first cousin of Paul's father), always called Cousin Hughes by the family. This notwithstanding his student Paul called him Mr. Cannaday, to show proper respect for his teacher. Hughes was only about 20 years old, but he had a certificate of achievement from an Academy in Floyd and enough education to stay several steps ahead of his pupils.

Cousin Hughes taught Paul through the 6th grade or, at any rate, the family always said Paul had the equivalent of a 6th grade education. He was very smart and learned educational fundamentals from Mr. Cannaday well enough to be a successful farmer and businessman. Cousin Hughes was not the best teacher in the world and used methods that were considered old-fashioned in 1888, some of which amused his pupils. For example he taught reading by first reading a sentence from a primer and then having the pupil read the same sentence after him, following each word with his finger. During one of these sessions, something diverted "the professor" from his instruction and forced him to tend to whatever emergency had arisen. When he returned to the lesson, he asked his student, "Now where were you?" The little fellow replied: "I was right where you were, Mr. Cannaday." Writing he taught by putting quotations up on the blackboard and having the students copy the words down on their slates. One of those "sayings" was "Think twice before speaking." Soon after that exercise assignment Cousin Hughes backed up a little too closely to the pot-bellied stove which stood in the middle of the classroom floor. One conscientious student with the adage still fresh in his brain said, "Mr. Cannaday, I think, I think, your coattails are on fire." We can only imagine the hilarity that followed; Paul certainly remembered that story from his school days and told it with relish over and over again.[3]

It was a long way from Long Branch School in Endicott, Virginia to the coal fields of West Virginia. Around 1896 or 1897, when Paul was 17 or 18, he left home, following his older brother Arthur who was already there, and headed west to the mines. It wasn't just his brother's example which determined Paul to leave Franklin County; it was a final blow-up with his father. Jim Simms could be a cruel and unreasonable man, and when he threatened to whip his almost grown son—for what, we don't know—Paul rebelled against the injustice, against treatment he considered unfair. That unpleasant confrontation convinced him it was time to leave home.

The flight to West Virginia was not unusual for young men in Franklin County; it was almost a rite of passage. In courthouse and genealogical records I noticed that many young Cannadays and Simms men had been lured to that part of the state by jobs or adventures that they couldn't find at home. The destination of many of the earlier pioneers, including Paul's grandparents Caroline and Andrew Simms who "went West" in the 1840s, was Raleigh County. There our great grandparents bought land and settled down. But their lives did not go as planned. Andrew "Andy" Simms died in 1855 when he was only 35 years old. Caroline sold their property and returned with her five children to Endicott and the family farm on Runnett Bag Creek.

Most families, including ours, are touched with irony and at least one lost fortune story. The land Caroline and Andrew Simms owned in Raleigh County, VA, (later WV) was rich in coal, a fact unknown to them. If Caroline had not sold the West Virginia land, her grandsons might have been mine owners instead of mine workers. But she did and they weren't. And if that particular "what if" had come true, it would have deprived Paul of an adventurous, character-building journey and all the tales that went along with it.

He and another young man, perhaps his cousin Jim Cannaday, walked more than 100 miles from home to their destination in West Virginia. We aren't sure of the exact route the two young men followed. They, no doubt, began their adventure by climbing the three steep miles up Cannaday's Gap, the closest Blue Ridge Mountain peak to the west. At the summit they were in Floyd County. From there they journeyed on to Christiansburg and the New River, which they swam across. Paul and Jim eventually "landed" in either Mercer or McDowell County, two of the counties in the southernmost tip of West Virginia, ten miles from where Paul's brother Arthur worked.

On their way Paul and Jim ran out of food and money—if they had even taken any in the first place—and got so hungry that they resorted to stealing corn from a farmer's corn crib. Paul said that that was the only time he ever stole anything in his life.

Starvation was just one of Paul's potentially tragic experiences in West Virginia. One night he was walking along a railroad track (why he was in such a peculiar place late at night will have to be left to our imaginations) when he heard, or saw, or was aware that a panther was stalking him. Whether from an old wives tale or an earlier experience, Paul knew that the way to frighten such a beast was with light, so he struck a match, lit his lantern, and frightened the panther away.[4]

Once there (wherever there exactly was) at the "promised land," the place with ready jobs for desperate young men willing to spend their days in a black, filthy hole, hacking out coal for $1 a day, Paul soon changed his mind. It only took a few days under the earth, in the pitch-dark and in grime so persistent it would not wash off, for Paul, who was a fastidiously clean man, to decide that mining was not for him.

He did not leave West Virginia, however. He stayed and found employment in the bright light of day, working for a prosperous landowner. Whether from ambition to succeed, a desire to stay out of the black and cold of the mines, or a resolve to do what was right (perhaps following one of Cousin Hughes' maxims) or a combination of those reasons, Paul was determined to excel—to be the best "hand" this man had ever hired, better than anyone else. He would plow more fields, hoe more corn, cut more hay, do whatever job needed doing and do it to the best of his ability. As you might imagine, this farmer loved Paul Simms and kept him on for as long as he stayed in West Virginia.[5]

Paul and his cousin Jim either lived in the farmer's bunkhouse or in a boarding house—somewhere that had a cookstove. The two country boys were used to having eggs, gathered fresh from the hen house every day. They made a slight miscalculation in their new circumstances. In an effort to save money, they bought an entire crate of eggs, not realizing that buying perishable goods in bulk without a way to store them was a serious mistake. Paul and Jim had fried, scrambled, or boiled eggs every morning for a quite few days, until bacteria took over and spoiled the remainder of the eggs. Paul hated that kind of waste of food and money all of his life. Even after they were married and Eula wanted to throw out old, but still edible canned goods, he would give them away rather than toss them in the trash, and let them go to waste. Her philosophy was that if the food was not good enough for her own family, it was not good enough for anyone else. He disagreed.

In West Virginia Paul probably earned $1 a day, which was the general daily wage in those days for working on a farm, and paid $1 per week for room and board. This meant he had to be extremely frugal, a trait which came naturally to him.[6] With careful management he was able to save money to purchase a place of his own.

In early October 1899, everything changed. That was the day Paul saw his father crossing the bridge that led to the farm where he was working. He knew the minute he saw his "Pa" so far from home and the expression on his face, that something was dreadfully wrong. Paul's brother Arthur, who had been working eight miles away, had died, either from consumption or in a mining accident. The mining company authorities had notified Jim Simms that his son was on his death bed, or maybe that his son was dead. Jim had traveled the 150 miles by train, we assume, to take

Arthur Simms, Paul's older brother

care of Arthur's funeral and to tell his other son, Paul, who didn't know that his brother was sick or injured. They buried Arthur on October 8 in Sand Lick, West Virginia.

Arthur Simms had not been an ordinary miner, although he started out that way. Somehow the owners of the mine discovered that they had a young man of superior intelligence in their employ and sent him to school to study mine surveying. There he learned how to "attack" a seam of coal—how to locate the mine entrance. He earned a certificate of achievement and became the "point" man for the mining company.

The one precious picture of Arthur that we have was made in Hunt's Studio in Welch, WV, in McDowell County. Even though the sepia-toned photograph has faded in the hundred plus years since it was made, there is no doubt that Arthur was a pleasure to look at. He had regular even features, brown hair and light brown eyes and was dressed "fit to kill" in a three-piece suit and a bow tie. Arthur's death at 26 was a terrible loss to his family, especially to his younger brother Paul who adored him.

We think that it was not long after Arthur's death that Paul, who had just turned 21, came back home to Endicott. This was not the last of the tragedies experienced by Paul's family. Five years later in 1904, another brother, Harry, three years younger than Paul, died of typhoid fever. Paul remembered that the men preparing Harry's grave hit rock and had to dynamite the hole. He never forgot the terrible, heart-breaking sound of the blasting.

On December 15, 1903, not long before he lost this second brother,

Paul purchased 100 acres of Cannaday land from his father on December 15, 1903 for $200 ($2 an acre), a bargain even in those days. This was the tract that J.R. Simms had inherited from his mother Caroline, the same land she had purchased for $200 in 1864 from her brother Peter, three years after their father James Cannaday II had died. Without much doubt, it was land Peter had inherited and wanted to sell because he was moving away.

In January 1905, a little over a year later, Paul married Eula Rakes and moved into one of the log cabins already standing on their new farm. Following the custom in the country their wedding ceremony was a simple affair. The preacher married the couple at the Rakes home with only the family attending. Eula's mother Ophelia, a gifted seamstress, made her daughter a beautiful, stylish new white dress with a high neck, leg of mutton sleeves, and a full bodice that accentuated her slender waist, with ruffles galore. The couple recorded the occasion by having their portrait taken by a photographer in Roanoke. On the walk to the studio, Paul managed to step on Eula's dress and rip it slightly. She was a little irritated and fussed at him for ruining her wedding gown, but she was not so bothered that it affected her smile for the picture, which is now a family treasure. We can see that she was, as Paul told us, a beauty with a full, lush mouth, a feature Paul teased her was too large (so unlike his own mouth which was a mere slit), bounteous dark hair piled atop her head, and high, distinctive cheekbones in her open face. Paul was handsome, of course, in a serious sort of way, with a generous nose (the feature Eula teased him was too prominent), thick dark brown hair parted in the middle, and a determined set of the jaw.

Determined. There are a multitude of descriptive words to describe Paul and Eula but the one, undeniable adjective for them both—expressed in their own way—was "determined." You will see this over and over as I tell you their story.

Notes for Chapter IV, Paul and Eula, Marriage and Before:

1. In 1998 while looking through photographs and other memorabilia in my Grandmother's house, 16 years after her death, I came across a note on a 1970's calendar (she wasn't good at throwing things away). On the January 19 day square, she had penciled "Paul and I were married on this day." For me that simple notation was a heart-wrenching entry. By the time she wrote that, she had been a widow for at least ten years; I knew that she was lonely, that she missed Paul and their full and robust life together, which had come and gone too fast.

2. See J.R. Simms chapter.

3. Later on Cousin Hughes taught at Laurel Bluff School, which was located a mile or so in the other (west) direction from the Simms' home-place. The family couldn't help noticing the school teacher as he walked or rode by their house on his way to his post carrying an axe, which he probably used to cut wood for that school's pot-bellied stove.

4. The current map of WV shows a park in Mercer County called Panther State Forest with train tracks located nearby. Maybe that was the site of Paul's "big cat" encounter.

5. This same man, whose name was possibly Poff or Tinsley, eventually moved to an elegant home in the Glenvar section west of Salem, Virginia, a few miles from Paul's retirement home. In fact, Paul visited his old boss at least once after he and Eula had retired to Salem.

6. He may have earned only 25 cents a day; people's memories vary.

5

Over in the Country

By the late 1940s, about the beginning of my conscious memory, my grandparents' farm was fully established. I remember it well—a comfortable white frame house shaded by locust and maple trees nestled in a low, level valley with ridges on either side and a spring house within easy walking distance. A squeaky screen door on the side of the house slammed shut to announce arrivals. There was a sleeping porch (everyone's favorite bedroom), my young Aunt Betty's room filled with love letters and make-up "to get into," a mahogany brown banister—polished slick enough for a good slide, the ever-active kitchen, and the fireplace, the main source of warmth and the ideal place for conversation and story-telling.

There was another house, the one we called the upper house, located on a rise directly behind the main house. Built in the 1930s and considered quite modern, this large rectangular building, constructed of concrete block and wood siding, had a dual purpose. The front portion was my grandfather's store; the back was for overflow company. One of the blessed amenities of the upper house was a bathroom with a flush toilet, a feature which beat the heck out of the still functioning outhouse, available for emergencies only, as far as I was concerned. Simms' cousin Rubye Snead (Nixon) who grew up in Roanoke and, like me, was spoiled by the convenience of indoor plumbing, claimed that she stayed constipated when she visited the Simms family because she was afraid of the outhouse.

Scattered around the farm were outbuildings. Just back from the house sat the granary, a barn-like structure with a storage area and a shed roof to keep, among other things, my Grandpa's school bus. On beyond the granary, out of sight of the house, was the barn for cows and horses. Several ridges over was the "far barn" used to store hay and alfalfa grown in nearby fields. A tenant house was tucked away at the end of a lane, an eighth of a mile or so from the upper house. The tenants had a certain amount of privacy, but on the way home they had to pass the pig pens, full of oinking, muddy, and stinky porkers. Over the long years of its life, this little house was home to family members and workers, many of whom became friends, dedicated to Mr. Paul and Miss Eula. It burned down, was rebuilt, remodeled and still stands today, a small well-tended house and farm.

My grandparents had planned their farm and outbuildings carefully and well, except for one feature I considered out of kilter with the rest. It was the hard surface road over to Hurd's Branch, which sliced directly through their property. Automobiles zipped by whipping up dust in a rolling boil. The location of that particular "highway" was no accident, however. It was a "devious" plot concocted by my grandfather to route potential customers by his store.

Across this road from the main house was a half acre or so of bottom land, kept fertile, plowed and planted with enough vegetables to feed the family and their scores of guests for a year, with plenty leftover to give to anyone in need. Along the back of the vegetable garden a slow-moving stream of water, we all called "the branch," meandered to a meeting with the cold, fresh water flowing out of the mountainside that we called "the spring." The branch provided endless amusement for children, from my mother and her brothers and sister, to my cousins and me.

The Ivy Hill rose above the spring house. The ivy, actually mountain laurel and rhododendron, formed a tangle of woods with lush beds of soft green moss growing under this thicket—another haven for children. The star of the hillside, however, was a swing or THE SWING, as anyone who ever thrilled to its ride over laurel shrubs and treetops knew it, an amusement beyond any Disney ever invented.

There were other magical and secret hideaways in this best of all places. But almost 50 years before it was a complete and fully realized farm and before my child's memory of my grandparents' home-place, it was 100, mostly wild, uncultivated acres, a mountain hollow with a flowing spring and several log cabins.

My grandfather Paul purchased the farm from his father, Jim Simms, for $200 in December 1903—13 months before he married my grandmother Eula. It was located just up the road from his father's farm. The two parcels joined and fit together like a jigsaw puzzle. One leg of Paul's land touched Runnett Bag Creek, the stream claimed by the Cannaday clan—part of the land purchased by settlers in Franklin County in the late 18th century. Even though this plot of land had belonged to Cannadays and Simms for over 50 years, it was identified in the courthouse deed as "the Martin land."[1] No doubt Martins had lived there in the past. In fact, the mountain which dominated one portion of the Simms' farm was called Stan Martin Mountain.

My grandparents were not the first occupants. By the time Paul purchased his property, it had been partially cleared, and a few old log cabins constructed on it. One of those cabins, the one Paul and Eula settled in, was the scene of adventures both good and evil. If walls could talk, that little house had stories to tell.

The most infamous story involved a man named Moore who came to a very bad end. Some years before Paul and Eula set up housekeeping, Moore had lived in the cabin. He was despised by his neighbors, as any human rat would be. He was an informer, a snitch, who told revenue agents the location of stills operating without the required licenses. After the local folks had had their fill of "businesses" destroyed and friends and neighbors locked up in jail thanks to Moore's treachery, they formed a posse, went to his cabin, and shot him dead. According to legend they ringed the man's head with bullet holes. There was an investigation, of course, but no one cooperated with the officials, including Jim Simms. Paul's father did not participate in the murder. After all, he did not have any reason to; he restricted his interest in moonshine to consumption alone. He knew the plot was brewing and when the posse was going to visit Moore. On the day of the murder, he went to his door repeatedly to listen for the shots, which he finally did hear. When an investigator asked Jim if it didn't make him feel strange that a murder had happened so close to his home, he replied with his own kind of defiance, "It's better that it happened there than not at all." Not surprisingly, that crime was never solved.

Paul and Eula, undeterred by the gruesome incident, moved in and lived in the cabin for four happy years. The cabin had only one room downstairs for living and a loft upstairs for sleeping—okay for a "starter" house but too small for the ambitious young couple. When Earl, the first baby arrived—just over the nine month wire in October 1905—and another, Elva, two years later, in December 1907, they needed a larger house as soon as they could manage it. In 1908, Paul and two of his cousins, Hanford and Virgil Cannaday, had the new house under construction. The men harvested trees from forested land up the hollow, and used the Cannadays' sawmill to cut the lumber for the house. Eula kept the men well fed. One morning while she was preparing one of her sumptuous breakfasts, the leg of the cookstove fell off. Virgil did not want anything to impede her progress, so he held up one end of the stove while she continued to cook their morning feast.

Little Earl noticed that the crew working on the new farm house made fires from wood chips to warm themselves and to dispose of trash. So he decided to help out. The stairs to the loft climbed up beside the fireplace mantle, the natural place to keep a big red box of matches. Unfortunately this put them within easy reach of little fingers. Earl gathered up a few wood shavings, took down the matches, and started his own fire just outside the cabin door. "Oh, Lord a mercy!" Eula said, her usual exclamation in emergencies. She put out the fire, then spanked the bad child, or was it the other way round? In spite of helpful little boys, the cabin remained standing for several years after the Simms family moved into their new house. For a while it served as the kitchen, and later as a school house.

All their lives my grandparents, especially Eula, did everything they could to see that their children, as well as other neighborhood youngsters, received as much education as they could manage. They gave land and materials to build a new school. They boarded and fed the teachers, and sent their own children off to a residential high school and on to college. They got an early start on this educational campaign when they turned the log cabin over to a teacher, Miss Lucinda Gussler, and her pupils, one of whom was Earl, just old enough to attend first grade. Elva at four was too young. When she saw the other children congregating in her front yard, laughing and playing, then going into the schoolhouse, she wanted desperately to go too. Determined to join them, she banged on the door and cried, "Let me in." But the teacher would not allow her inside. In an angry protest Elva hurled rocks against the school house, smashing them against the side of the building.

A year or two later both Elva and Earl and the other children were attending the Bitty Hill School, a new one-room schoolhouse built on a nearby hillside, on land donated by Paul and Eula, and constructed by Paul's brother Gale. The county of Franklin agreed to pay the teacher's salary if local residents, like Grandma and Grandpa, would provide the building and house the teacher. With a new school in operation and the Simms' farm house well under way, there was no longer a need for the log cabin, so they tore it down. It had served the young family well.

In those days, the evolution of many farm houses began with a log cabin and grew from there by adding rooms and floors and porches. That was the case with the J. R. Simms home-place, though not with Paul and Eula's. They started fresh by building a brand new four room, story and a half building, two rooms downstairs and two up. For a reason I never understood, my grandparents oriented their house to the southwest, with the front facing the Ivy Hill and the branch—and eventually the road to Hurd's Branch. The lane leading to the farm ended in back of the house. Naturally everyone, whether riding in a horse and buggy or driving a Model T Ford, parked at the rear and walked to the screened door on the side of the house. Few if any visitors, certainly not family or friends, ever entered through the front door.

The next improvement Paul made was the addition of two rooms on the rear of the house, a "formal dining room" furnished with a tall cupboard filled with my grandmother's beloved dishes and an expandable solid oak table, and an extensive kitchen. The front hallway led to and through the new dining room into the largest room in the house—today we might call it a great room. Great it was; fancy it wasn't. It was the kitchen and the family's room. It had a long, narrow table, which was the site of thousands of meals and hundreds of games of checkers and dominoes. The fireplace, a major source of heat for that part of the house, sat squarely in the middle of the back wall. It measured approximately four feet by three feet wide and two and a half feet deep and was built to hold back logs and to provide a good draw to waft smoke up the chimney.

For the next major change to their house, Paul and Eula decided to turn the half story into a full second story by raising the roof. That improvement did not happen without a major problem to make the construction memorable. With the old roof stripped away, and the house fully exposed

The Simms' Farmhouse *by Elva Simms Cannaday*

and vulnerable to the weather gods, the skies opened and rain poured into the house, ran down the stairs and formed a deep pool in the middle of the first floor hallway. Paul refused to be stymied by a little water. He found a clever way to rid the house of the unwanted flood before it caused significant damage. He bored a hole about the size of a silver dollar in the middle of the hall floor. Eula was glad to have the water out, but she was sure her husband could have found a less conspicuous location for his drain: "Paul, I can't believe you drilled a hole in the middle of my floor. You've got to fix that awful thing." He covered up the eyesore with a wooden peg and a well-placed rug. By "my day" in the late 40s, this same hall sported a wavy, polished linoleum floor, ideal for running and sliding on in my socks.

The final additions were the double porches which spanned the entire front of the house. They were about ten feet wide, had a two inch slant for draining water away from the house, support posts turned with decorative cuts, and three-feet high pickets along the base of the porch. On one end of the downstairs porch was a two-seater swing, hung from the ceiling by chains which made a comforting creaking sound when "customers" were aboard.

The best place in the house, once you had left the kitchen full of my Grandmother's fried chicken, was the sleeping porch—the upstairs half of the double porch. The sleeping porch, as its name would suggest, was an overflow bedroom, the ideal place to spend a summer's night, to fall asleep to the familiar sounds of hoot owls, frogs, crickets and cicadas and the sweet perfume of roses and honeysuckle. It was screened in, furnished with an iron double bed and several army cots, all with strawtick mattresses. It had green striped, interior awnings to roll down in case of bad weather, and the added advantage of access to the two bedrooms through windows which opened out onto the porch. All children loved the sleeping porch, especially if they could persuade their father/uncle/grandfather Paul "to tell them a tale" before they fell asleep. Paul was an imaginative storyteller who took delight, not only in entertaining, but also in scaring the bee-jesus out of his young listeners. The most famous of Paul's sleeping porch tales was the story of the Whippenpoo.

Earl, Eula, Paul, and Elva Simms by the side of the house, c1913

One summer evening cousin Warren Snead was over in the country staying with the Simms family. The ten year old was in bed on the sleeping porch when Paul decided that it was such a pleasant night that he would join him. No sooner had he arrived than Warren began to beg, "Uncle Paul, please tell me a tale."

Paul asked Warren, "Have you heard about the Whippenpoo?" "No I haven't," he responded. "Well, I'm surprised," he said, "because the Whippenpoo is an enormous black beast with a six-foot wingspan and a 20-foot long forked tail. He hangs out over there on the Ivy Hill, and when he gets hungry, he flies over houses where little boys are visiting. He lands on the roof and drops that forked tail of his down into the boys' bedroom. He spears them with it while they are asleep and takes them back to his lair for his 'next meal.' The children are never heard from again."

At this point Warren, frightened to death said, "Uncle Paul can I come get in the bed with you?" Paul said, "Yes, come on." Once Warren felt safe and brave enough to hear more, he said, "Okay, now Uncle Paul tell on." As far as anyone can remember, the story ended there. When Paul grew sleepy, he would yawn and say to children pleading for more, "to be continued," and that was that. No amount of begging helped, and you didn't want to rile "Uncle Paul." There were variations to this oft-told tale. When Grandpa was entertaining a girl child or both girl and boy children, he indicated that the Whippinpoo did not discriminate; he was an equal opportunity monster. He took children of both sexes from their beds at night, and when he was finished with them, left the girl bones in one corner and the boy bones in the other.

With the addition of the double porches my grandparents had completed work on the main farmhouse, and Grandma then turned her attention to her yard and her flower garden. She once told me, "One of the best things I ever bought for the house were the locust trees which are growing in the side yard. I got them from a traveling salesman and paid a lot of money for them. But they were pretty good size, and grew fast, and began to shade that old kitchen which got unbearably hot in August, especially during canning season." She planted pink climbing roses, dahlias and pansies in her flower beds and a large, white snowball bush in one corner of the yard—what farmhouse would be without one of those familiar shrubs? Not far from the snowball bush she grew a small round shrub with fleshy, oval leaves—a succulent plant much like a tiny cactus, but without spikes. My cousin Judy and I loved to play with the leaves of that plant. We discovered that we could turn the plump leaves into small balloons if we handled them just right. We would squeeze and gently rub the leaves to separate the "skins" without tearing them; then we would blow a short puff of air to inflate them into little bladders. Under Grandma's locusts trees we grandchildren played on metal, latticed chairs which had runners and were painted light green. They were heavy, but flexible enough to rock back and forth and light enough to turn upside down to make imaginary play forts.

In the shaded yard in the late afternoons, everyone—children, visitors, men—all pitched in to help with food preparation, whether it was stringing beans, peeling potatoes, shucking corn, slicing tomatoes and cucumbers, or peeling apples. There were always apples, apples, apples, and more apples, and no such thing as a meal without them, or so it seemed. There were informal apple-peeling contests—not for quantity but for efficiency, the cleanest peel, an unbroken circle of skin with the least amount of fruit attached, the winner—the dangling spiral held high to ohhs and ahhs of appreciation. Grandma Mary Simms was the queen of apple peelers.

Pitching in to do the shucking, the stringing, and the peeling was part of the fun of farm life for children, but nothing beat playing in the branch and riding the wind on the Ivy Hill swing. The branch, "born" on the Simms farm, joined water from the spring to form a larger stream which emptied into Runnett Bag Creek farther "down the road." In summer young folks—Simms children, visiting friends and cousins, then grandchildren—spent hours playing in the branch, wading, catching crawdads in glass jars, "swimming" in a three-foot hole, and constructing flutter mills. These inventive little toys Earl and Elva created by making a wheel from the small, lightweight wooden partitions that surrounded squares of honey. They erected a tiny dam out of rocks and brambles and allowed the water from the dam to run over the wheel, turning it like a miniature mill wheel.

The abundant and reliable spring never went dry in the 50 years the Simms family lived on the farm. Like the well-constructed fireplace, it was a source of pride; two essential elements—water and fire—necessary for the success of any farm. The water from the spring was cold enough to keep milk and other dairy products fresh even during the sweltering days of summer. The Simms kept a dipper there for any thirsty passerby to use.

The spring house, built on a concrete foundation, was surrounded by touch-me-not wildflowers, and frequented by ruby throated hummingbirds. Inside the spring house Grandpa constructed a trough for water to flow through, and placed crocks of freshly "squeezed" milk and newly ripened watermelons in it to chill. One side of the little house had three inch wooden slats with air spaces between them, and the other side snugged up against the hillside. It had a retaining wall of rocks with tops flat enough to set jars on. Just above the branch and the spring house was the Ivy Hill, another haven for children. Under the rhododendron thickets, on luxurious green moss carpets, youngsters gathered white rocks, built imaginary rooms using pebbles for furniture and played with their dolls in the outdoor playhouse.

In the clearing above the mountain laurel stood a cucumber magnolia tree, at least 70 feet high. From a branch of this fantastic tree hung a swing with a wooden seat, with triangular notches on each end to fit snugly into the looped chain and just the right size for a child's bottom. Little ones like my brother Ken had to be lifted into the swing seat, bigger ones, like my cousin Judy and me, backed into the swing, jumped on and held on for dear life while someone, often Grandpa, pushed us with all his might. We glided over treetops like soaring birds riding warm thermal currents. I guess if any one of us had fallen out, it would have been instant death—a fact that did not escape my Grandma who hated the dangerous swing. Grandpa loved it.

Because he took such delight in The Swing and in pushing the children to its limit, I always assumed it was my Grandpa's invention, but I was wrong. The credit for the construction of this greatest of joy rides goes to my Uncle Edsel.

When he was only 16 or 17, he designed, engineered, and installed the swing, all by himself with only Old Buddy, the family's beloved shepherd dog, stretched out in the ivy patch, watching. Edsel cleared brush from the ground under the swing, sighted the distance from the ground to the limb, and calculated that he would need 100 feet of chain. Papa Paul, who fully supported this venture, took his son to Nelson's Hardware in Roanoke to buy materials. The store only had 97 feet of chain, 3 feet short of Edsel's estimation, but he figured he could manage. As it turned out, he only needed 87 feet, so he used the extra 10 feet for additional support. To protect the tree from the friction of chains rubbing the wood, Edsel cut up an old tire to use between the chain and the tree limb. He tied kite twine onto one end of the chain, put the nuts, bolts, and washers he would need to anchor the chain in a bag inside the tire cuts. As he climbed the tree, he pulled the chain up by the tough kite string which he held in his mouth; at the same time he lugged the pieces of tire with the hardware inside. When he reached the branch with his burden, he dropped the chain over the limb. Edsel accomplished the installation with only one climb. He had thought everything through before he took his first step up the tree. The swing stayed securely in place for 20 years. No one ever again had to undertake that treacherous 30 foot ascent to make any repairs or adjustments, as far as Edsel knew.

Soaring on my Uncle Edsel's swing was about as much fun as any child could ever have, but there were many other places to play around my grandparents' farm—the granary, for instance. That outbuilding, about 50 yards from the house, was a barn-like structure with a shed roof. It had multiple uses over the years—grain storage, automobile and school bus garage, and home of Grandpa's first store which he opened around 1920.

For some reason, the granary was a place children got into trouble; it was an attractive nuisance, you might say. When Earl was a little boy, he cut a ragged hole along the edge of a storage bin inside the granary. His intention was noble; he wanted to allow the cat to go inside the granary to catch the mice he had seen scurrying around in there. The same "way" in for the mouser was the "way" out for the wheat which seeped through the crude opening and spoiled. Losing the grain upset Earl's Papa who was not impressed with the hole Earl had cut in his bin and whipped the well-meaning "culprit."

The "attack" on the granary continued. More than 25 years later, Betty, Earl's baby sister, and Earl's son, Keith (Betty's nephew)—those mixed up, tangled up generations again—amused themselves by taking turns boring holes in the storage bins using a brace and bit—a tool they found fascinating to operate. When Paul discovered this particular mischief, he was not fascinated—he was furious. He demanded, "I want to know who did this." Keith bravely spoke up and said, "Grandpa, I did it." Chivalrously, he did not implicate Betty. After all, he said, "I knew I was in for it, so why should she be punished too?" Consequently he was the only one who "got it."

That did not conclude the end of Betty and Keith's tomfoolery in the granary. In the loft, far enough away from the house to avoid detection, the two little rebels took up smoking corn silks. Even so, Betty would have been in big trouble if her father had caught her. He did not believe that females should smoke anything.

Besides the granary, the farm had several barns—one, on up the hollow out of sight of the house was the main residence for horses and cows. The other, several ridges beyond the tenant house—the far barn—was a newer building used to store freshly cut hay and alfalfa. Paul kept cats and black snakes in all these out-buildings to keep down the mice and rat populations. Once when he was driving his pickup truck with Betty sitting next to him in the passenger seat, he jammed on the breaks and stopped dead in the road to collect one of those treasures, a black snake that lay stretched out, sunning himself on the warm pavement. Betty reacted the way most girls do at the sight of a snake, screaming, "Oh, ooh, yuk, it's a snake!" Paul jumped out and snatched up the reptile. Before he put it in the burlap bag which he kept stashed in his truck for just such good fortune, he tormented his squealing daughter, holding out the black snake, saying, "Here, Betty, take it, take it." Then, pleased with himself, he tossed the slithering creature over into the back of the truck, much to Betty's disgust. Later Paul deposited the snake in the far barn to patrol the area and keep out rodent threats to his stored crops.

One of the outbuildings that especially pleased Paul was the chicken coop. He hated the fowl creatures and often said, "The only good place for a chicken is on the table." Eula, however, was determined to have them. After all, they both loved fried chicken for Sunday dinner and fresh eggs every morning for breakfast. At one time they had "free range" roosters and chickens running all over the place, getting in the way, creating ugly little messes. Paul would turn up his nose and say, "Shoo chickens, shoo chickens." He solved this problem by building a chicken coop and putting it as far away from the house as was practical, high up on a rise near the road to the tenant house. He enclosed the lot with chicken wire, to confine the nasty cluckers and keep them out from under foot. Of course, having chickens so far from the house meant that someone had to haul feed and water to their new residence. Eula planted a row of hollyhocks beside the chicken house to pretty it up a bit.[2]

One of my most vivid childhood memories was my grandfather killing a chicken for Sunday dinner. He, or my Grandmother, usually whacked the chicken's head off with a sharp axe on the chopping block. This time, however, Grandpa decided on a different means of execution. He took his .22 rifle, steadied the barrel on one corner of the granary and, with me safely behind him and the hen at least 20 feet away, neatly shot her head off. Fire exploded out of the gun barrel and the headless and pathetic chicken ran hither and yon around the yard, flapping her wings, before finally toppling over dead. I suspect he did this to shock me, as well as to get a little practice shooting and have some fun for himself.

The most ambitious addition to the farm complex was the upper house my grandparents built in the 1930s. Completely apart from the main residence and separated by a spur road—a driveway really—this long, rectangular building, cinderblock below and wooden siding above, was tucked into the hillside directly behind the farmhouse. Unlike the main house, which had a certain grace and architectural refinement, the upper house was squared up, sturdy, practical, and ugly. Somehow I think it was my grandfather's design because the important front half housed his "new" store, which he moved from the less-than-ideal location in the granary. Eula was always lukewarm on the store. It was one more thing for her to tend to while Paul was off mowing the back fields or at market in Rocky Mount or Roanoke. To "help her out," he rigged up a bell for customers to ring when they needed assistance with merchandise in the store. When the bell sounded in the house, she had to drop everything, rush up to the store, and wait on customers. Before Paul installed the "helpful" ringer, folks came to the gate and yelled out—"Anybody home?" when they wanted something. To compensate for the inconvenience of having to tend to the store, Eula probably insisted that Paul give her one part of the new building. There, in the back half of the building, she installed a modern kitchen, which she rarely used, and a lovely bathroom with a flush toilet and a shower, the jewel of the place as far as I was concerned. Upstairs there were three rooms. I remember that the first had an old-fashioned Victrola record player, the second—which was the largest—had a bed with a quilting frame ominously strung up over it, a sofa, a fancy Eisenglas stove, and a black upright Baldwin piano, with yellowing keys and always out of tune. Beyond this large main room was a smaller one with an iron cot and the entrance to the storage area over Paul's store.

The store may have been a nuisance to Eula but not to young children, who loved its smell of freshly ground coffee and shoe leather, and its promise of candy and soft drinks. In the early days before he got the red Coca Cola cooler in his store, and before the drink truck made regular runs to deliver goods to Endicott, Paul bought soft drinks in Rocky Mount and kept them in the cold water at the spring house. They proved to be a greater temptation than Edsel and his cousin Harold, thirsty ten-or-so year olds, could resist. They helped themselves to the drinks, prized open the tops, sipped half the refreshing treat, filled the bottles back up with spring water, reattached the cap on the diluted drink, and returned them to their place in the spring house. Some customers grumbled that "these here Cokes don't taste right." This apparently was one of the few times that Paul failed to catch on to monkey business by children and probably blamed the "no count" drinks on lack of quality control at the Coca Cola plant. The bad boys didn't confess to this misdeed until 2002, when Paul was no longer with us and they were safely in their 80s.

Investment in a store was an important way for Paul to put his shrewd business acumen to work and to get ahead in a part of the country with very few opportunities for financial success. In those days there were lots of country stores operating, at least one every mile or so. To be competitive Paul wanted to make sure his customers had easy access to his place of business. So he arranged to have the road over to Hurd's Branch rerouted, to bring potential patrons directly by his store, even though it meant traffic went right through his property, bisecting his farm, another irritant to Eula.

In addition to general merchandise, Paul sold gasoline from a single bubblehead pump in front of the store. We still have the bronze plaque from Shell Oil with an inscription congratulating him for 20 years (1930-50) in business with their company. He even had a "garage" to work on automobiles, actually two planks of wood—a car axle width apart—that stretched out over a hillside beside the yellow flat apple tree, that let a "mechanic," whoever that was (perhaps the car owner himself) have easy access to the underneath side of the car, and to change the oil or lubricate its parts, or to perform some other service. No need for a pneumatic lift when nature provided one!

The upper house and the store sat in the shadow of Chestnut Ridge. I don't remember exploring this area of the farm as a child and probably saw it for the first time in 1998 with my mother, Elva, and my Uncle Earl during a trip to the country. By then the chestnut trees were long gone, and there was only an open field with a few remnant apple trees and a magnificent view of the Appalachian Mountains—a keen reminder that we were in their foothills. In the days of healthy American Chestnut trees, in the 1910s before the blight had infested the Simms farm, they had a huge stand of those bountiful trees. Earl and Elva recalled that on one occasion, a powerful wind wrested the fruit from the trees and covered the ground with a carpet of chestnut burrs thick enough to walk on. During the years the trees thrived, the family gathered the chestnuts and sold them for 5 cents per pound, or whatever the market would bring. Chestnut wood was resistant to rot and weathering, which made it ideal material for fences. Paul used chestnut wood to construct a split rail fence across the Simms farm on the hillside above the chicken house.

Further along the ridge, beyond the Chestnut stand, Paul planted an orchard—an acre or two of apple trees (many of them pippins) but also a few cherries (sour and blackheart) and some damson plums, peaches, and pears. While we were surveying the former fruit orchard, Uncle Earl and my mother told me that those trees had made splendid jungle gyms and that they each had laid claim to their own personal trees, one that "belonged" to him and one that "belonged" to her.

Although there was a variety of fruit trees in the orchard, apples were "it," the main crop—so plentiful that they ate them in one form or another at almost every meal. They picked the best ones to eat raw, and others they canned, or cooked, or made into vinegar. To make vinegar, they saved apple cores, peelings, and rotten apples, and put them together in a large cask which they allowed to stand until "ripe." Then they turned the tap and drained off as much vinegar as they wanted. They gave away surplus apples to neighbors whom they invited to go to the orchard and help themselves. They included their tenants in this generous offer.

The tenants, and the tenant house, were an integral part of the Simms farm. The small house was down the road about an eighth of a mile from the store. Built by Paul and Eula around 1910, it was home for four or five different families over its 50 years—the Dixons, their widowed daughter Miss Bernie Griffey and her daughter Nannie Belle, Miss Griffey's brother Buck, the Gillespies, and then the Adkins—folks who helped Grandma and Grandpa with the mountains of work self-sufficient farmers had to do. Having resident help was almost a necessity, but it was also a symbol of success for a family prosperous enough to hire workers and to provide them with their own home.

The tenant house was a miniature farm and gave the residents a certain amount of independence. It had a barn for a cow or two, a plot for a vegetable garden, and space to raise a few chickens, dogs and cats. In the early days the exterior of the house was unpainted. The tenants decorated the interior with pages cut from magazines, newspapers, and catalogues which made an inexpensive wallpaper.

In the isolation of early to mid 20th century Franklin County, and with the goodness of Paul and Eula, these families became more than workers; they became friends, and their children became the friends of the Simms children. Miss Bernie Griffey, a widow, and her daughter Nannie Belle, Earl's great pal, were among the first families to occupy the tenant house; then her brother, Buck Dixon, with his several children moved in with Miss Bernie after his wife died. Buck and the children had to sleep in the barn. Eventually he remarried, left Miss Bernie and went to live in Callaway with his bride. Buck's young son was unhappy in the new house, and the little fellow, about 6 years old, walked all the way back to Miss Eula's house—ten long miles. He arrived dirty, exhausted, and snotty-nosed. Before taking him back home, she gave him a bath and fed him cobbler pie, or fried chicken, or pinto beans, or whatever she had on hand.

The most traumatic event in the life of the tenant house came with the next family—the Gillespies. Their little boy Uriah found some matches, figured out how to strike them, and accidentally set the house on fire. Frightened, he crawled under his bed and hid. Fortunately his little sister, Wilsie, "told on him," alerting her parents who went into the burning house and dragged the child out. Elva remembered Uriah's mother, Dilly, standing outside, the house in flames, crying helplessly. The fire was devastating; it destroyed the place, and Paul had to completely rebuild it. The new house emerged much nicer than the first. Over the years they enlarged it, added a porch across the front and painted it white.

One of the sad ironies of the Simms farm is that today the tenant house, a subordinate building to the main house, survives—part of an attractive, small, active farm with well-groomed yard, barn and fields. The Simms farm house is gone, burned down, the fields overgrown, the upper house unpainted and deteriorating, the far barn, nearly collapsed, the granary still standing, solo and naked, almost ashamed to have survived, abandoned by the other buildings which gave it meaning.

When Paul and Eula sold their farm in 1951, it was complete, thriving and flourishing, a work of art. They had spent almost 50 years building its buildings, cultivating its gardens and fields, creating a success—a place those of us who were fortunate to live and visit there return to often in our memories.

Notes for Chapter V, Over in the Country:

1. See "Settling the Ancestors," Note 53.

2. Edsel remembered that he was the one who had turned the building, which was already in place, into a chicken coup as part of a project for Future Farmers of American.

6

First Farmer of Endicott: Innovator

My Grandfather Paul Simms was a successful, nearly self-sufficient farmer. We, his children and grandchildren, are proud of his accomplishments, of his ingenuity, and his toughness. He was not perfect, but he worked hard at being the best he knew how to be.

In writing about his achievements I have included descriptions of some of the farming methods and equipment he used. I know little about such things and have relied on my mother and uncles who experienced farm life to explain them to me.

If Endicott, Virginia, had had a mayor, Paul Simms would have served in that post for most of the years he lived "over in the country"—perhaps alternating with his first cousin, Isaac Thomas Cannaday, or Old Man I.T. as he was generally and respectfully known.[1] A leader in his community, Paul was an ambitious, progressive farmer, a pioneer in the latest methods of agriculture, and, like Thomas Jefferson, a man willing to try almost anything, at least once. He was constantly searching for new and innovative farming techniques and machines which could help him become more efficient and successful, and pursuing promising financial ventures which could help him become more prosperous. We like to think of Paul Simms as the First Farmer of Endicott.

Paul kept himself informed about the latest agricultural discoveries by subscribing to magazines such as *The Progressive Farmer*, by conversations with other farmers at supply stores and cooperatives, by tuning in to the market reports on radio broadcasts from Roanoke, and by any source of farming news or information available to him. He learned from his own experience and by using his own good common sense.

Paul Simms who was known to chew on occasion

Paul's family could testify that he was a true researcher who was continually, persistently, and forever bringing home some piece of equipment or machine for a test run. He found most of these new products in Rocky Mount. One of his earliest purchases was a grain drill, a large, cumbersome, horse-drawn piece of equipment that he used for planting seeds. It had two hoppers, one for fertilizer and one for seed, each dispensed into the ground through separate tubes.

Paul also owned a horse-drawn mower and a hay rake. The mower had a long serrated blade he used to cut grass, weeds or hay; the hay rake had a claw-like wheel which he used to gather up the mown hay or grass and empty it into clumps once the claw was full. While he was operating the farm machinery, Paul often took his little children along for the ride. This delighted the youngsters, but terrified their mother who, always concerned about her darlings' safety, realized the possibility they could be hurt. As father, with son or daughter seated on his lap rode merrily away, she would yell, "Paul, you're going to kill that child." She was proved right about the dangers of farm machine rides when her son Earl had a serious mishap with the hay rake. By the time he was a teenager Earl was skilled enough to manage the hay rake and the team of horses, Stormer and Darby. One day during hay-making season, Earl was riding the hay rake. Just as the horses pulling the rake started down a hill, the metal tongue that connected the rake to the horses broke. Earl was thrown forward and fell in front of the machine; he got caught up in the tines when the horses bolted, still harnessed to the rake. They dragged Earl only a short distance before Paul, who was working nearby, rescued him. He was able to grab the reins and stop the horses. Earl's encounter with the claw left him with a scar on the back of his shoulder, (but no permanent pain or injury) and a great story to tell—one he did enjoy telling. In fact, in is last years he retold the story of the hay rake accident almost daily.[2]

Once Paul and his crew (sons and hired hands) cut the hay, they mounded a portion of it around poles and packed it tightly into haystacks. They pitch-forked the remainder of the hay onto a wagon and took it to the far barn where Paul kept his baling machine, one of the only balers in their part of the country. They fed the hay into the machine's hopper, which compressed it into a rectangular bale. The baler then spit out the hay bale and the men hand-tied it with wire. At first Paul used horses walking in a circle to power this labor-saving piece of equipment, but later he had gasoline engines that did the job.

Paul also had a corn planter, a hand-held box-like contraption about 4' high. It dispensed grains of corn through a cylinder into a plowed furrow when Paul, or Earl, or Edsel, or whoever was the operator released an interior mechanism. The worker then covered the seed with dirt using his feet. Edsel said, "It beat the heck out of doing it by hand."

Another of Paul's farming aids was a corn sheller. This clever little machine stripped dried corn from cobs. The operator placed an ear of corn into the sheller, turned a crank to rotate the device, which had hundreds of small projections to knock off the kernels from the cob. The sheller was helpful, but it required a worker to turn the handle. For this chore, Paul sometimes hired cheap unskilled labor, like his little girl Betty and his grandson Keith, Betty's slightly older nephew. He paid the pair ten cents each to shell a bushel of corn. The children took turns turning the crank on the sheller. By the end of an hour they had produced a single bushel of corn, earned 20 cents, and had had enough of exhausting farm work.

Up-to-date machines and equipment were important to any farmer, but Paul knew that the best labor-saving devices harnessed the power of kerosene, carbide, a Delco battery system, and eventually, electricity. Once he discovered the advantages of electrical energy, Paul said, "No matter what the cost, electricity is the cheapest labor I have ever had in my life."

Long before the Rural Electrification Administration (REA) found its way to the back woods of Franklin County, the Simms family, like everyone else, used kerosene lamps for light. These lamps varied in size and design; they had a metal or glass receptacle at their base for the kerosene, a cotton wick saturated with the fuel, a knob to adjust the length of the wick and a glass globe or chimney to cover the flame. To keep the flame burning bluer, thus hotter and cleaner, they trimmed the wick every day. To keep the light bright, they cleaned the chimneys once a week. This was a job for the little hands of children. Scrubbing chimney lamps made them aware of the importance of the hot, blue flame because a yellow flame left soot from unburned carbon on the inside of the chimney and made more work for them. Elva found washing the lamp globes awkward work; sometimes the wet glass slipped out of her hands and broke.

For some reason, Eula thought her children were careless with her beloved dishes and anything else that would break—dropping a dish was a switching offense. The children had their own defense—a hole under the house where they hid broken dishes and lamp globes. On one occasion Eula and Paul discovered a shattered lamp chimney. They cross-examined the most likely suspect—Elva, whom we know would have stashed the evidence under the house if she had been guilty. She declared over and over that she was innocent, but her parents refused to believe her. Finally they told her that if she would just confess, they would not punish her. So she settled, admitted her "guilt," even though she was blameless "this time," and was, thus, delivered from the switch.

Kerosene lamps became less important once Paul discovered more modern methods of producing light. First, he bought a generator fueled by carbide, and later he replaced it with a Delco system, basically a generator powered by 16 batteries, each yielding two volts. The 32 volts supplied enough energy to operate the ceiling lights in the house. Paul housed the Delco system inside a small concrete building with a slanting roof, tucked into the hillside across from the granary.

Eventually all of these means of lighting gave way to one of the greatest discoveries of the twentieth century, electricity produced and marketed by the Rural Electric Authority. When this magical new power came to the country, it changed the farmer's life forever. It did not arrive on the Simms farm without a struggle, however.

Appalachian Power Company had the contract with REA to install power lines in Franklin County. The company set up poles and strung wires along the main highways, including Route 40 and Runnett Bag Creek Road, at no charge to customers who lived there. When they reached the access road to the Simms property, the power company balked. It must have decided that area was too remote for free service and tried to charge Paul and Eula a fee based on the number of poles and the amount of wire needed to string the electric line the quarter-mile to their house.

Paul was having none of that. The utility company had to run its lines across several pieces of his property to continue their work along Runnett Bag Creek Road, and he had no intention of granting a right-of-way for Appalachian Power to traverse his land until it waived the fee to run the line to his house. Paul had to travel to the office of Appalachian Power in Roanoke to facilitate this deal. Either the employees in the office in Rocky Mount would not cooperate, or they did not have the authority to make the arrangement. Needless to say, Paul got his electric line installed free of charge. One component of the legislation that established REA that Paul didn't know about was the three-customer rule. If three paying customers lived along a power line, the REA paid for the installation. On Paul and Eula's route, in addition to their house, were the home of his brother and sister-in-law, Gale and Ruth Simms, and his tenant house. So he actually didn't need the leverage the right-of-way gave him. Appalachian Power installed the line as far as his house. Later it extended the line beyond their property to their neighbors on Hurd's Branch.

With electricity charging into their house, Paul could try all sorts of inventions and gadgets—many to assist his wife. He bought an electric churn which she never really liked; she thought that it did not work nearly as well as the old hand and arm-killing churn. He bought her an electric stove, but she refused to give up her beloved top-of-the-line, wood-burning Home Comfort cook stove. She did, however, keep and use them both—and a refrigerator which she came to accept and perhaps even love. Before the electric refrigerator they owned one which ran on kerosene, the first of its kind in their part of the country. It was a curiosity which attracted their neighbors who stopped in to see the amazing machine. No one could believe that you could use heat to make cold. "Feel of it. It's ice in July."

Always looking for ways to improve life on the farm, Paul devised a system to bring water into the kitchen. He laid one-inch pipe to a spring, a quarter mile up the Bitty Hill, and relied on gravity to move water down the ridge into the house. Paul took a certain pride in his ingenuity, and was astonished that his neighbor and friend Cannie Shively did not share his enthusiasm for indoor plumbing. When Paul asked him why he didn't do the same thing—pipe water into his own house—Cannie replied, in what we can only hope was a smart-aleck remark: "It won't do to let the women get too lazy." (Where's my gun?)[3]

Water on tap, modern machines and new sources of energy were only a few of Paul's innovations. With Eula's help he also experimented with growing different varieties of crops such as alfalfa, lespedeza, hybrid apples, and out-of-the-ordinary animals like turkeys, ducks, and bees.

For a short time in the 1910s, Paul and Eula took up raising turkeys. They had a male gobbler and several hens which they allowed to roam freely around the farm. Earl and Elva remembered that the turkeys were secretive parents; the hen hid her nest, actually covered it up, when she was laying eggs. She must have known with her turkey intuition that she needed to protect her future babies from predators and dangers like the Simms' breakfast table. It became the children's job to find the turkey's hideout; they surreptitiously followed the mother turkey to her nest which she had secreted on a hillside beyond the kitchen garden near a rock outcropping. Later, when the hen wasn't "home" the children used a dipper to keep human scent away from the nest and "stole" an egg. If the turkey had detected the aroma of little boys and girls around her unborn babies, she would not have returned to the nest. Earl and Elva replaced the purloined egg, which was about 1½ times the size of a chicken's, with an artificial one made of glass, and covered it up with leaves. (What kind of a mother couldn't tell the difference?)

The turkeys may have been more trouble than they were worth. One night, for some reason, perhaps because she was attracted to the light inside the house, one of the hens flew into the kitchen window, smashed the glass and shattered it into a million pieces, caused instant death for herself, and startled the family who were forced to eat turkey dinners for a week. On another occasion, the turkey gobbler attacked Elva. The male turkey

Bitty Hill School class picture 1913.
First row: (left to right) Nola Wright, Elva Simms, Amy Simms, Lizzie Dixon, May Dixon, Macey Spencer, Ethel James, Teacher Miss Lizzie Gussler. Second row: Wright boy, Earl Simms, Roy James, George (?) Spencer, Jeff Trail, Ed Shively. Third row: Delma Simms, Nora Wright, Bessie Simms, Beulah Spencer (Macey's sister), Nannie Belle Scott.

was quite proud of his "beauty." He strutted around the farm with his red waddle bobbing, his wings stretched out, and his glorious, shiny, black hind feathers on display. The vain creature must have thought Elva, ready for school and decked out in a red fake fur coat, was competition for the love of the hens. She, too, was proud of her new outfit which her Grandmother Ophelia had made for her favorite grandchild. The turkey gobbler became incensed and attacked the innocent little girl. Drawn to the red fur, and jealous of another beauty on the farm, he spurred her with his claws and beat her with his wings. The assault scared the child to death, but her parents rescued her, shooed the turkey away, and sent her on to school.

The stylish little red coat, which was unlike anything the other little girls in the country wore, continued to cause problems. At school on classroom picture day, the teacher, Miss Lizzy Gussler, took it upon herself to put Elva's precious red coat on one of the children, little Macey Spencer, who wasn't dressed very well. Elva was so furious that when the picture arrived from the photographer, she took it home and poked a hole in Macey's mouth with a straight pin, and for good measure, stabbed another pinhole in Macey's sister, Beulah's, mouth. We still have that photograph from Elva's first year in the one-room schoolhouse and can see her sour expression, clear evidence of her displeasure. We can also see Macey wearing the trouble-making coat, with a black hole where her mouth should be.

Turkey-raising was one of Paul's short-lived undertakings, one which did not work out. But that failure did not deter him from trying his hand at raising another kind of fowl—ducks. Paul and Eula always had chickens on their farm, but ducks were a little out of the ordinary for them. These little feathered animals had the great advantage of being self-sufficient; they did not require special food. They found their nourishment in the creek and on the ground. During this experiment, one of the mother ducks abandoned her eggs or maybe she had died. Eula solved the problem by providing the future ducklings an adoptive mother; she smuggled the duck eggs under a setting hen. When the baby ducks hatched out, they followed their natural instinct, and waddled down to the branch and jumped into the water, which drove the mother hen to distraction. She assumed, quite naturally, that they were her baby chicks. The ducklings swam and paddled around in the water, enjoying themselves in their natural environment. All the while the mother hen was going berserk, running up and down the stream bank, clucking and squawking at her strange little baby chicks, trying to get them to come out of the water, which was no place for sane chickens.

As if turkeys and ducks weren't enough, (not to mention the usual pigs, horses, cows, and chickens), Paul also raised bees for at least 20 years. All of his children remembered helping in one way or another with the beekeeping business. In the life cycle of bees, April and May are the months they are on the move. The swarm, with the queen bee, leaves the hive for a new location which scout bees find for them. The swarm normally alights first in a temporary location, forms a ball of 12 or more inches, and remains in that temporary location for a day or two before departing to the permanent home, usually a hollow tree, unless a beekeeper captures the swarm and provides a new "residence" for it in his apiary. Elva remembered that she tapped on the bee gums to coax the swarm into the family's square-shaped hives.

One year she took over full responsibility of tending the bees and the five or six gums, which at that time were on the road to the tenant house.

She wore special sting-proof equipment—round head gear with netting down to the shoulders, mask and gloves—and was allowed to keep all the money from the sale of the honey that season.[4]

It was a beekeeping incident that caused Betty (the baby of the family) to receive the only whipping from her father that she could remember. (None of the other children had trouble recalling countless thrashings.) She was about six years old when her father asked her to watch out for the swarm and to be sure to follow it to its new location. He knew by the time of year, and by examining the hive for queen larvae, that the swarm was ready to migrate. He could not be there to keep an eye on the swarm himself. So he engaged Betty to be his bee-minder and even offered to pay her the handsome sum of 25 cents for doing the little job. When he returned he asked her, "Where have the bees gone, Betty?" "They are still in the hive, Daddy." But they weren't still in the hive. Betty had gotten distracted and not noticed that the bees had moved. For her negligence, she received that one-time spanking and, of course, no cash reward.

Paul—with Eula's help, not that she had much choice—tried his hand at raising unusual "crops" such as bees and various fowl, but their mainstay was livestock and grain, the same as any farmer. They owned a few beef cattle, some hogs, and dairy cows, only two or three, but those cows were very demanding.

Milking. Twice a day. Every day. A dairy cow was essential, a godsend, a burden, a ball and chain. The animal provided that most basic food, a nutritious liquid which could be drunk "straight," or with enormous effort converted into butter or cottage cheese. She had the added advantage of making babies.

Paul rose early every morning of his working life. The first one up, he started the fires in the cookstove and in the main room fireplace, grabbed the spotlessly clean milking pails, and headed to the barn. Eula got up soon after the kitchen had warmed a bit, ready to prepare one of her hardy and scrumptious country breakfasts. She told me that she had decided, even before she was married, that she was not going to be the one who climbed out of bed and made the fires in a cold house. She had seen her mother do that and was determined that when she had her own household, things would be different. That was one small triumph for Eula, one of her few rebellious acts.

On most mornings, milking was uneventful, but on one morning Old June, a Jersey cow that gave especially creamy, rich milk, felt a bit rebellious herself, and took it into her head to kick over the bucket full of freshly squeezed milk. This made Paul so furious that he picked up a rock and threw it directly at the unruly animal. Fortunately for them both, he did not hit Old June in a vulnerable spot or wound her seriously. The Simms family kept several milk cows, all of them affectionately named. In addition to Old June, they had Old Pansy and Old Pet and others we can't remember. Earl said, "If you have to spend a lot of time with animals and you have to drive them, it is better to give them names."

With so few dairy cows, they had to maintain a delicate balance between those giving milk and those that had gone "dry" and provided no milk for the family. Sometimes my grandparents encouraged a cow to stop producing milk, and sometimes they had nothing to do with it; she stopped naturally when she became fertile, or went into "season" as they called it. Then they pastured a cow, maybe Old June, with a "worthy" bull, and if all went as planned, she became pregnant and some months later produced a calf, usually in the spring of the year. For a short time after the birth, the mother's milk was unusable for humans. They allowed the calf to "run" with its mother, nursing when it was hungry, until the baby was mature enough to eat on its own. Then they separated mother and child and took over the milking. Even during the time the calf was nursing, they had to strip the milk from the mother cow, that is, take any milk the baby calf didn't need.

Sometimes the cycle didn't work or failed, and there wasn't enough milk for the family. When this happened to the Simms or the Rakes families, they helped each other by trading milk. If the Rakes were in need, Earl would haul a week's supply of milk to their farm, riding one of the horses, either Stormer or Darby, carrying six half-gallon jars, loaded into saddle bags, three jars on each side. If one of the Simms' cows went dry and they needed more milk, Earl brought milk back from the Rakes' farm.

Processing raw milk required skillful and careful handling to avoid the bacteria which grew readily on improperly cleaned vessels. The Simms family took great care to keep all utensils, crocks, cloths—everything involved in the preparation of the milk—sterile. Immediately after milking the cows, Paul or Eula carried the raw milk in pails to the spring house, with its dank, moist earthy smell, and cold water flowing out of the north-facing mountain. There, they took down clean crocks from a shelf, rinsed them in scalding water (brought from the house), placed a cloth, similar to cheese cloth but thicker, over a metal cone-shaped strainer, and poured milk through the cloth into crocks which varied in size from one to five gallons. After straining the milk, they rinsed the cloth in cold water, washed it in soapy water, and rinsed it again. They scrubbed empty crocks in hot water and put them on a shelf to dry in the sun. They designated a portion of the whole milk for drinking—some of it they took to the farm house, some they left in crocks standing in the spring house trough, covered with a cloth, where the cream rose to the top. Once or twice a week Eula skimmed off the cream, allowed it to thicken into a clabber, and churned it into butter. The residue, or leftover milk from the clabber called blue john (our revered skim milk), was considered too thin and tasteless for human consumption, so it was fed to the pigs. The milk left from churning was buttermilk—the family's Sunday night treat, often served with cornbread. (A sour pleasure now lost on most of us city folks.) The Simms never allowed milk to go to waste; any they were unable to drink, they gave to their animals.

Paul wanted to make sure his children learned the proper procedure for processing raw milk. "Come on, Edsel, I want to show you how to take care of the milk," he said to his young son, as he prepared to give the boy a memorable farming lesson. Paul brought a pail of scalding water from home to the spring house and stressed to his little boy the importance of keeping the utensils thoroughly clean. He went about the business of straining the milk. Edsel didn't dare say a word when he saw his father make the mistake of pouring the fresh milk in with the hot water. When Paul looked around and asked, "What's become of my hot water?" Edsel had to tell him, "You put the milk in with it, Papa." Paul's response was, "Don't tell your Ma." Edsel obviously told someone because we all know about his milk straining lesson.

In addition to the dairy cows, the backbone of any self-sufficient farm, Paul and Eula had a few beef cattle, a steer or two—one of which they occasionally slaughtered in the fall of the year. A single animal would provide more beef than the family could eat. So, when word got around that Paul was killing a steer, the neighbors would gather and buy the extra meat. Uncle Mitch Cannaday, the local butcher, told one customer who complained that he was getting too many bones, "When you buy land you buy stones, and when you buy beef, you buy bones." Eula preserved the freshly butchered beef by cutting it into servings, boiled it, ladled the meat into jars or cans, along with a generous helping of pot liquor, and finally, sealed the containers. According to her children, that canned beef was a favorite food they enjoyed throughout the year.

The fall was butchering season, not only for beef cows but for hogs, as well. They fattened up the hogs by feeding them a mixture of daisy midlins, used dishwater, blue john and slops—any leftover food. Nothing went to waste on the farm, and the pigs were not picky eaters. The method of killing the animal was particularly gruesome. Paul stuck it in the throat with a knife, the dying hog emitted a piercing squeal so penetrating and pitiful that children covered their ears when they heard it. He then hung it up to allow the blood to drain out of its body. Once the hog was free of blood, he dunked the carcass into a vat of scalding water to make scraping off the hair easier, and then he carved it up. Uncle Gale cured the hams and the bacon, and Eula made sausage from ground muscle tissue.

During the times I visited over in the country, the pig sties were tucked away, down an embankment on the road to the tenant house almost out of sight, but not out of hearing and smelling. During "my mother Elva's little girlhood," the sties were farther away from the house, under a cherry tree. She remembered the "confluence" of the pig pens and the cherry tree for very good reason; they were a source of considerable discomfort to her. Toward the end of cherry growing season, the last of the good sweet cherries clung to the end of a branch of the tree. Elva noticed the tempting fruit and decided it was worth the risk of climbing up to get it. Up the tree, and out on the limb, she inched her way toward the cherries, when all of a sudden, she slipped and fell off the branch, smack dab into the nasty pig trough. Unharmed, but filthy dirty, she snuck around the house and up to her room, cleaned herself off and changed into another dress—one exactly like the one she had been wearing, both made by her grandmother. What luck! The twin dress allowed Elva to escape any other unpleasant consequences, always a possibility, from her dip in the pig pen.

If her spill had happened in the autumn, it would likely have gone unnoticed. Her parents were completely occupied with the relentless round of regular work, animal slaughtering, and the arrival of the threshing machine. The Cannaday brothers, Virgil and Hanford, owned the huge machine that separated the wheat from the husk. They were the same two men who owned and operated the local sawmill and, in fact, used the same engine to run both pieces of equipment. All of the farmers in the community who grew wheat used the Cannadays' thresher. No one could afford or needed to own his own machine, so they cooperated by sharing in the work and in the expense.

Elva remembered seeing the threshing machine come up to their house being pulled by horses. It was so enormous that it filled up the entire roadway, with men holding ropes tied to the machine on either side to keep it from tipping over. They guided the behemoth over to the far barn to thresh the wheat Paul and his helpers had cut and stored there. The threshing operation required a horde of men, most of the Simms neighbors, to complete the work. Paul greeted the men, pitched in by bringing wheat to the thresher, and directed them in any way they needed directing. One memorable fall day, Paul was away on a trip with his sister Mollie, exploring Civil War battlefield sites, when the threshing machine and all its company arrived. Even though the crew no doubt knew exactly where to go and what to do, it fell to Eula, the perfect helpmate, the woman who could rise to any occasion—something Paul certainly knew—to welcome the men, to tend to their needs, and to keep them well-fed. As was so often the case over in the country, she could count on the able assistance of her female neighbors to cook for those hard-working, hungry "hands." She probably grumbled about being stranded with the full responsibility of man's work and woman's work, but what self-respecting person wouldn't? I can imagine what she must have thought: "Paul's done gone off and left me to deal with all those men and the thresher, on top of the store, and the milking, and the cleaning, and cooking and everything else I have to do—his work and mine, too."

Paul took the threshed grain to the mill at Endicott, where the operator further processed the grain into flour. The mill owner was Paul's cousin, I.T. Cannaday. Besides the mill, Cannaday ran a large general store, the post office, a saw mill, and a rolling mill, a regular country mall. Cousin Tanny, the name Paul called his Cannaday kinsman, made a profit from the mills by taking a toll, 10% was the standard amount, as his payment. When I.T. opened his rolling mill, his witty sister Floridy Adkins teased her successful brother by asking, "So Tanny, are you going to charge on the halves?" For those of us who need a translation, Floridy was poking fun at I.T. by asking him if he was going to take half the milled goods from his client as his share, an amount that would have been grossly unfair.

After they harvested and threshed the grain and had it ground into flour, they used the husks for mattress ticking. They wasted nothing.

In addition to corn and wheat, Paul grew a "miracle" crop which provided more food for his animals, one that he did not have to be sown every year—alfalfa, a fast growing, deep rooted perennial plant which could be cut four times a year and added nitrogen to enrich the soil. It was a farmer's dream and delighted my grandfather to have a plant that worked hard for him. After he discovered alfalfa, he did not cultivate any other fodder crops.

With Paul's love of invention and the latest new "toys," it may seem odd that he never owned a tractor, but that was for very good reason. Many of his fields were at a slant, and a tractor would have been both impractical and dangerous. He continued to use the old-fashioned horses and plows to cultivate his fields and a slide, a wagon on wooden runners, much like a sleigh, for hauling.

Paul may not have owned a tractor, but he certainly owned an automobile, and he bought it as soon as he could. He purchased his first car, a new 1917 Model T Ford, from his brother-in-law Samp Snead who had bought it in Roanoke. The person most fascinated by the new motor car was probably not Paul, but his 12-year old son, Earl. The youngster quickly mastered the complicated starter mechanism and driving technique. Without much traffic on the back country roads, and no requirements to have a license, Earl became the family's chauffeur, the chief driver. Elva was determined not to be left out; she also wanted to drive the family's new vehicle. Several years younger than Earl, perhaps less mechanical, and apparently without anyone's permission, she cranked up the Model T, climbed up into the seat behind the steering wheel, and managed to navigate the machine from under the granary shed where it was "garaged." She accelerated, turned the steering wheel to the right, but failed to straighten up, and continued to drive in a circle until she bumped into the granary. It was just a little nudge, but enough of an accident to frighten Elva into giving up driving until she was 17.

Some time after Earl and Elva learned the art of driving, Edsel had his own adventure with the Model T. He was only nine or ten years old, but eager to have a turn at the steering wheel, but "they" wouldn't let him; "they" thought he was too little. He surprised them all. One day "they" looked down at the bottom land and saw the car, which by this time was being kept under the canning shed, moving very, very slowly, just creeping along, all by itself, no driver in sight, or so it seemed. But there was a driver. It was Edsel, so small that his head was barely visible above the steering wheel. It was amazing that he could operate the Model T at all, but he certainly showed "them" that he could.

Eventually all the children became proficient at driving and had their turns at the wheel. On Sundays, however, Paul was the driver-in-charge, and that was the time, after all the family was "aboard," dressed and ready for church, that he decided to whisk-broom the automobile free of dirt, to spruce it up for the ride to church. He managed to stir up dust particles which flew everywhere, landing on the passengers dressed in their best Sunday clothes, irritating mother and children, who coughed and fussed about the last-minute cleaning.

On the way to church, Paul stopped the car to pick up as many people walking to the monthly preaching at Long Branch Church as he could stuff into the automobile—a half dozen or so. Some sat on laps, some rode on the running board, holding on to the inside of the open windows. One of the benefits of having extra passengers was that there were willing hands to pitch in and push if the car got stuck in mud, which it often did or if it had any trouble climbing Long Branch Hill, which it usually did. Those rides were filled with laughter, cooperation, and appreciation—a splendid way to begin a religious service.

The automobile, this new means of transportation, brought a comfort and ease in travel, and a more efficient, faster way to market, but it was not without problems. The early rubber tires, for instance, were a constant nuisance. Not long after he bought the Ford car, Paul invested in a Ford truck. Those new motorized wagons were a welcome convenience, but they had solid rubber tires and no inner tubes. The tires were smooth and slick and had absolutely no tread, thus no traction on wet hills, a particular problem over in the country. Most of the roads were unpaved, and any time it rained, the tires spun, and the vehicle got stuck. It required men to push and sometimes horses to pull—an indignity for the horses—which now had to stand aside, to give way to the faster, flashier motor cars and trucks.

The next improvement were tires with inner tubes and tread, which provided better traction in muddy hillside conditions, but had the annoying habit of blowing out and going flat, requiring a hand pump and a patch to get the vehicle back on the road. During a trip Paul and his brother Jim took to Mountain Lake in Giles County, only 60 miles or so from the farm, they had five blow-outs—which meant five stops and five flat tire repairs.

Earl had a problem with the new truck that was more serious than slick or flat tires. He was almost squashed flat between the truck and a wagon. Preparing to drive the truck, he went through all the normal start-up maneuvers; he set the emergency brake, pulled down the throttle (perhaps a bit too far), got out and turned the hand crank in the front of the truck. Suddenly the emergency brake failed, and the truck began to move forward on its own, threatening to smash Earl into the wagon directly behind him. He immediately pulled the choke, located on the front of the truck, full out. His quick action stopped the vehicle and saved him from serious injury. Earl did seem to have near misses with machines, first the hay rake, then the Ford truck, and probably other lucky escapes we don't know about.

My grandfather was a modern man. Nothing new came down the road that he didn't catch a ride on it and give it a trial run. From the latest in farm equipment and methods to the labor saving power of electricity and the convenience of an automobile and a pickup truck, he was at the forefront of technological innovation and experimentation in Southwest Virginia.

Notes for Chapter VI, First Farmer of Endicott: Innovator:

1. Paul's mother, Lucinda Cannaday Simms was a sister of Charles Cannaday, I.T. Cannaday's father. 'Old Man' I.T. was my other grandfather.

2. Earl died in 2002 at the age of 96.

3. My cousins Judy Simms Strawn and Betty Jane Simms Hagan whose other grandparents were Floridy and Cannie Shively told me that the women in that household cooked and served food to the men, then stood behind them like servants while they ate. Only after the men had finished eating did the women and girls sit down to their meal after which they cleaned up the dishes.

4. When working on this story my mother quoted an old rhyme about bees making honey: "A swarm in May was worth a stack of hay; a swarm in July was not worth a dead fly." In May the hive was filled with honey but not in July because there wasn't enough time to develop a thriving hive.

7

First Farmer of Endicott: Entrepreneur

In addition to being a pioneering farmer, Paul Simms was also an innovative businessman who undertook many and varied commercial ventures. He had an instinct for wise investments and seized on opportunities that came his way—anything he thought was sensible and safe and would advance him and his family financially. Over the years he canned tomatoes for the government, ran a general store, owned and operated a school bus for the county, traded livestock in markets in Rocky Mount and Roanoke; he invested in real estate in Salem and Roanoke, many miles from his home. In Roanoke he owned the building that housed Goode's Grocery Store, which he rented to his half sister Bessie and her husband John Goode. Along with Vance Snead, and one or two others, he owned the River Jack, an unusual combination of gas station, restaurant, and night club. In Salem he and son Earl co-owned a large apple orchard on the edge of town.

Like all "great" entrepreneurs, Paul sometimes made mistakes. One such misadventure was the cannery, one of his first business undertakings. During World War I the federal government asked farmers to help in the war effort by growing, canning, and selling tomatoes to increase the supply of food. This was a patriotic undertaking, but it was business, too, and Paul decided to answer the nation's call to service. He built a cannery, a shed-like building, down near the spring house and gave over a sizeable patch of new ground—rich, acidic soil—on the north slope of his farm, for the sole purpose of raising "government tomatoes."

Once the tomatoes were ripe and ready for harvesting, everyone pitched in to help in the "war effort." Paul and Eula, of course, the children (Earl and Elva), the tenant family (Miss Bernie Griffith and her daughter Nanny Belle), neighbors like Cleve Trail, as well as the school teacher, Miss Lizzie Gussler, who was boarding with the family at the time, and no doubt many others—including the cousins who spent as much of their summer vacations with the Simms family as their parents would allow. The large crew picked the tomatoes, put them into boxes and loaded them onto a slide. They hitched up the horses that pulled the slide down the hill to the cannery shed. Next, a smaller crew processed the tomatoes by dipping them into hot water, making it easy to peel off the skins, then cutting them up into manageable chunks and spooning the ripe red fruit and its juice into tin cans. Several members of the team soldered the tops on the small, round, opening of the now full cans and placed them in a vat of boiling water. As the final touch, they glued on a label with a picture of a big, fat red tomato and the notation: 16 ounces. There was the problem. Paul and the canning team did not think to weigh each can to make sure it had the advertised pound of tomatoes. They just filled each one to capacity, but that was not good enough. The weight of the tomatoes fell short; they were rejected because they were not up to federal regulation snuff. Paul was never able to sell the uncertified tomatoes to Uncle Sam, but he did sell them in his own store and to local merchants and friends.

Miss Lizzie Gussler

While the cannery operation was still functioning, there was trouble in the field. Several of the laborers fell into conflict: Miss Lizzy versus Earl and Elva. Apparently Miss Lizzy, the teacher living with them at the time, was gullible, and the children, who were ten and twelve and no longer her students, recognized this weakness and delighted in teasing the poor young woman. Miss Bernie Griffith, the family's tenant, encouraged this mischief. One day when they were all out working in the tomato patch,

Earl and Elva went too far with their taunts and torments of Miss Lizzy. They didn't remember what they said—the final straw, the insult that set her off—but they sure could remember her basket full of tomatoes sailing across the field, hurled in a fury, red fruit flying everywhere. Miss Lizzy, her face ablaze with anger, had had enough of those bratty children. She took off to the house, got on the telephone and called her brother to come get her. She quit.[1]

An unhappy teacher and the disgruntled Feds made Paul's cannery business a losing operation all around. But it was only a side-line to his most successful financial undertaking—his general store, a going and growing concern for 30 years (more or less), from 1918 to 1951.

Over in the country some enterprising soul had a small, general store every other mile or two, which seemed excessive to me, but I was only eight or so, and that was 1949. Earlier on in the century having a store "handy," within easy walking or horse-riding distance, was important to the people living in the community, so they could get the supplies they needed without traveling long distances over terrible roads and wasting time and energy. Operating a store was one of the few ways that a farmer in an isolated part of the state could bring in some extra cash and improve his financial position.[2] Paul Simms was not going to miss out on this opportunity.

He began his shop-keeping modestly. He set up a few shelves and a counter in a portion of the granary, used a cigar box for the money, bought an iron safe and placed bars across the window for security.

Once Paul took it into his head to have his own general store, he did everything he could to make it a success. Around 1930 he moved the store into the front half of the newly constructed upper house and took on what I assume was the politically and physically difficult and expensive task of having a road moved so that it passed right beside the store, making it more convenient for his customers. At one time, his cousin I.T. Cannaday held the position of Superintendent of Roads, which no doubt would have facilitated any bureaucratic hassles Paul might have encountered, if, in fact, I.T. was in charge when Paul requested the change. Even though Cannaday had a store, the biggest one in the community, he probably would not have given a second thought to competition from his cousin's dinky little business, two or three miles away. I.T.'s store, unlike Paul's, had a sign, and a false front like the ones in old westerns, and an uncovered platform or porch with nail kegs where men sat and gossiped. This drove Dr. Morris, the woman who had come to St. John's Episcopal Church as a medical missionary, crazy; she told the lazy men to get off the nail kegs and go to work. When they asked her what she thought they should do, she told them in no uncertain terms to "Go out in the woods, build yourselves a still, and make some corn liquor."

The road to the Hurd's Branch neighborhood originally crossed Runnett Bag Creek, followed a small stream as far as Uncle Gale's house, made a sharp turn left or south to a steep climb up the Ivy Hill to a breath-taking view of the valley below, the mountains above, and continued on to the far part of their community. That road required especially strong horses to pull the incline, which was a good reason to reroute the road, and no doubt the argument Paul used to persuade authorities to favor the alteration.

In those days the road to the Simms farm was only a lane off the main road before it started its treacherous ascent over to Hurd's Branch, and ended peacefully at their house. Paul's new road followed the original one as far as Uncle Gale's, but it did not cross the little creek; instead it kept going straight to the Simms' farm, where it cut between the main house and the bottom land, climbed up the other side of Ivy Hill, and meandered on back to Hurd's Branch. Not everyone was thrilled by the rerouting. Certainly not Eula, who hated having traffic whip by her house, creating noise, dirt and possible harm to her children, nor did her friend and neighbor Floridy Shively, who lived at the far end of Hurd's Branch. She was afraid of the hairpin curve at the top of the hill, which was part of the new road, and she got out of the car and walked, rather than risk her life when they got to the dreaded drop-off.

In his store Paul carried general merchandise, the sorts of goods his neighbors couldn't grow themselves or come by easily, freshly ground coffee, work boots and coveralls, candy, soft drinks, seeds, animal feed, and sugar. Great quantities of sugar. Ocassionally he was able to buy a large stalk of bananas, a rare treat that sold out quickly. Customers also bought cans of pork and beans, and sardines, which they opened and ate in the store with saltine crackers and vinegar over a piece of linoleum on the counter. The management provided the spoon.

From the very beginning Paul operated on credit and barter. His customers often paid their bills with farm produce—eggs and butter, or with animals (chickens, turkeys, baby pigs, even calves). At first he sold those bartered goods for cash to a Mr. Greer from Floyd who subsequently sold them at the farmers' market in Roanoke. But it wasn't long before Paul was in a position to take the produce and animals to market himself, cutting out the middle man and increasing his profit.

My Grandfather didn't always wait for people who owed him money to come to him with payment. He followed the value of livestock in the Roanoke newspaper and the noon farm news report on the radio. When the price was favorable, he would call on customers in debt to him and offer to take baby pigs or calves, for instance, to pay off their accounts, an arrangement which suited them just fine. Paul loaded the livestock into his truck, hauled it to market, and stopped by the bank in Rocky Mount on the way home.

Occasionally Paul's business plan ran into a snag. One day when he had the truck loaded with pigs, ready for a trip to Roanoke, the driver of the school bus he owned, operated, and leased to Franklin County did not show up for work—sick perhaps. Paul had a dilemma—he needed to be in two places at once: driving the bus full of children to school and delivering the truck full of baby pigs to market. He solved the problem by "persuading"—there was no saying "no" to this determined man—his reluctant 16 year old daughter Betty to drive the truck to Ferrum. The pretty, self-conscious, high school teenager was equally determined not to show-up in the school parking lot in a truck filled with squealing pigs. Fortunately her father had been a little vague about the place they were to meet—in Ferrum—though they both knew he expected to find his truck at the high school. Betty left the vehicle with its embarrassing cargo behind DeHarts Store in the center of town and walked up the hill to school. After class she received a well-deserved verbal whipping from her father who spelled out in detail his tight schedule and the inconvenience she had caused him. He had had to drive the bus all over Endicott picking up and dropping off children at their schools, then, when he got to Ferrum, he had to hunt up his truck-load of pigs—that took 30 minutes and would have taken longer if the little porkers hadn't been making enough noise for him to locate them in downtown Ferrum. Then he had to rush to Roanoke, sell the piglets, and return to Ferrum in time to drive the bus on the return route. But it was all worth it to Betty. Anything—even a tongue-lashing from her angry father—was better than the humiliation of an unpleasant arrival at high school. She didn't mind driving the empty truck home.

The town of Ferrum was important to the residents of Endicott and the other neighboring communities, not only for its public high school and its private, Methodist-run Ferrum Training School, but also for the Norfolk and Southern Railroad depot. The train was a connection to the "outside world" for people who lived off the beaten path. It took them to other parts of the state and the country, and brought in supplies to stores like Paul's.

Paul had a WalMart-like mentality. He purchased commodities (such as sugar) in large quantity because he could pay less per item. The merchandise arrived by rail at the Ferrum station. The train dropped off a freight car loaded with goods belonging to Paul, and left it on a side track. He had a grace period of several days to unload his cargo before he was charged demurrage, a fee I bet he never paid. Paul owned a small storage building in Ferrum, his packhouse, where he could unload and stash the supplies that arrived by train. With a packhouse, he could order goods in bulk and leave everything there until it suited him to take the merchandise to his store in Endicott.

The store, second only to the Ivy Hill swing, was a child's paradise, especially for me and the other grandchildren, who, unlike their parents, never had to mind the shop—only to enjoy its treasures. By the 1940s Grandpa had softened and allowed his grandchildren to buy goodies from the store at a significant discount. I remember that the hardest decision I had to make was which drink to pick from the red Coca Cola chest cooler—Grapette, chocolate milk, or Coke? Which candy to choose—Mr. Tom's Peanut Butter Delights, a Hershey bar with or without almonds, a Moon Pie, or an oatmeal cookie sandwich with vanilla icing?

In the summer of 1946 or 1947 Edsel's little boy, Buck, a bright-eyed four or five year old, adorable, even if his ears did poke out a bit, spent a few days with his Simms' grandparents. Every day during the visit, Buck walked up to the store, penny in hand, and after careful consideration purchased a candy bar from his grandfather, who then gave his little grandson "change" of another penny. The last day of his visit, Buck went shopping at the store, as usual, with a coin in his sweaty little hand, picked out his treat and paid for it. But when he got to the door to leave, he realized something was wrong. "Grandpa, you forgot to give me my change." Later that same summer Buck, back home in Radford, went to Red Burrough's market with his father and tried to buy a candy bar for a penny. Red told him, "Son, you can't get candy for one cent, it costs a nickel." Buck was stunned. "I know better," he said, "I can buy a Hershey bar from my grandpa's store for a penny and get change back."

Buck Simms, Edsel's son, c1948

Sweets were not so easy to come by in the early years of the 1940s, during World War II, with sugar rationing in effect. It was during those days that Edsel was in Endicott helping out in the store. He waited on a customer who made a purchase with a large bill ($5 or $10 dollars). Without enough cash in the money drawer to make change, Edsel had to go to the safe. When he dialed the combination lock and opened the door, he found no money at all, only a safe full of chewing gum. In fact there was no room for money. He found the cash stashed next to the safe in a galvanized bucket, covered with a burlap cloth. This peculiar arrangement protected the rare sweet from Edsel's 14-year old sister, Betty. Her parents knew that she wouldn't bother the money, but they weren't so sure she wouldn't "steal" the chewing gum and share it with her friends.

Without a doubt, the general store was Paul's most prosperous venture, but my CEO grandfather was not satisfied with only one financial achievement; he wanted more. One, which brought in extra cash for the family and helped the local community as well, was his investment in the school bus. Paul owned and operated the bus and leased it to Franklin County. His contract required him to provide the bus and driver, gasoline and maintenance, and the county to pay him $150 per month for this service. In 1936, the approximate date of the agreement, teachers earned $100 per month, $50 less than the school bus owner.

That arrangement may sound like an easy undertaking—a slick deal—but it wasn't. Paul had to buy the bus in stages, first the chassis which consisted of a truck bed, an engine, and a steering wheel. He then purchased a body frame and seats for $600 from a manufacturer in North Carolina, who agreed to install them on the chassis. He enlisted his son Edsel to drive the naked chassis the 250 miles to Wilson, North Carolina for the installation.[3] In preparation for the trip, Edsel, who was 20-years old, built a seat over the gas tank and persuaded his friend Zera Gillespie to go along with him to keep him company. The young men drove the "topless" bus to the eastern North Carolina city and spent the night while the company converted the truck into a bus. Once the body was attached and the seats installed, they drove the completed bus home. It appeared to Edsel that the vehicle with its new additions had grown into a monster, wider than the highway. Even though he and Zera were riding in an enclosed vehicle with protection from the elements, the trip seemed endless, and they wondered if they would ever be safely home.

Paul usually hired a man to drive the bus route, which took about an hour from the time he left the Simms' garage, drove all over the hills and hollows collecting youngsters and deposited them at the Endicott School and Ferrum High School. When the regular driver was sick or couldn't be there, Edsel, or on occasion, Paul took over. The first time Paul drove the school bus, he had a problem with children misbehaving. He asked them to sit down and be quiet. When they did not mind him, Paul jammed on the brakes, stopped the bus in the middle of the road, cranked open the door, ordered the disobedient students off his bus, and forced the boys to walk several miles home. After that original demonstration of discipline, Mr. Paul never again had any trouble with unruly riders. In fact he evoked enough fear and respect that the Simms house was safe even at Halloween—no windows soaped, no outhouses overturned.

My grandfather's bus was another of the farm's attractions for my cousins and me. We loved to climb aboard the vehicle (which he kept parked in the granary), sit in the long, bench seats and pretend to be going to school.

Another of my grandfather's financial investments was in the Salem orchard. He had experimented with horticulture in his own orchard and learned to produce hybrid apples, improving a basic apple such as the

Rome by using grafts.[4] I remember a small apple that grew on a tree over the hillside by the kitchen, a yellow flat—golden, sweet, juicy and gone in four bites. To my taste, it was the most delicious apple God and man ever devised.

The success of his orchard on the Chestnut Ridge encouraged Paul to branch out and invest in another one in Salem, far afield of Hurd's Branch. His son Earl, who was living in Roanoke and working in real estate at the time, found the property and suggested that the two go into partnership. The Salem orchard was a large grove of apple trees which needed many hands to help at picking time. Paul could supply a work force from the country to bring in the harvest. Even with friends and neighbors available to help harvest his apple crop, Paul soon realized that the orchard business was a losing proposition, and, as they had agreed, he sold his share to Earl for the same price he had paid for it.

Salem retained its appeal to my grandparents who in 1951 sold their home-place, the marvelous Franklin County farm, and moved to a house they built on land they owned, only a mile or so from the orchard property.[5] Even in retirement, my grandparents remained attached to farm life. In back of their new red brick house they built a barn for a cow, and plowed up a plot to grow vegetables. Those farming remnants must have been Grandpa's "brainstorm" because Grandma, in another of her very few rebellious acts, refused to churn butter or to can vegetables ever again. Like the cannery tomatoes, Grandpa was able to sell the extra milk and garden produce, this time to his new neighbors on Upland Drive. It was no doubt hard for him to stop doing what had always been essential in his life.

Eventually Paul grew to enjoy the modern conveniences in his home in Salem. He was reminded of one of the hardships he had left behind when he returned to Hurd's Branch to visit with his friend Cannie Shively. Later back home he said, "I about froze to death over there." My Grandfather had become accustomed to the comfort of central heat.

He certainly deserved a few easy years in retirement. He had worked long and hard to be the best, most progressive, most successful farmer in his part of the world, a direction he had determined for himself when he was a young man working in West Virginia. We know beyond all doubt that during his life in Franklin County Paul Simms was the 'First Farmer of Endicott.'[6]

Family gathering at Paul and Eula's new home, c1951.
Back row: (left to right) Edsel Simms, Russell Cannaday, George Hayes, Keith Simms, Paul Simms. Middle row: Elva S. Cannaday, Eula P. Simms, Betty S. Hayes, Sylvia S. Simms, Irene Simms, Virginia Simms. Front row: Becky Cannaday, Judy Simms, Kenneth Cannaday, Buck Simms, Betty Jane Simms.
Missing: Earl Simms-probably the photographer.

Notes for Chapter VII, First Farmer of Endicott: Entrepreneur:

1. I have that same tomato basket resting quietly in the entryway to my house.

2. The other way, in Franklin County, as the whole world knows, was by making moonshine, but Paul had nothing to do with that "trade," at least not directly.

3. Edsel wasn't sure how much his father paid for the chassis.

4. My mother explained to me that most good eating apples require cross breeding. Her father created a hybrid tree by making a cut into a good basic apple tree such as a Rome, then split the cut section about ten inches and spliced the graft inside the cut. Finally he taped and sealed the splice with wax, which allowed the graft to grow as part of the original tree. He often had several grafts on one tree.

5. The orchard property now grows houses.

6. He lived for 13 years at 67 Upland Drive before he died in 1964 at the age of 86.

8
Eula

My Grandmother and Grandfather were a hard-working, two person team, but she was the one who made their house hum.

Eula Simms could rise to any occasion. Her husband knew that, and relied on her resourcefulness and ability to manage the family, the farm, and the store when he was away on business or pleasure (something he believed in more than she did). Not only that, he knew she could handle any medical emergency with the instinct and skill of a trained nurse.

The two of them turned hospitality into an art form. The welcome mat was always out. They invited anyone in the vicinity at meal time to "come on in, it's on the table." Their house teemed with life, young people, their own four children (who began arriving in the first year of their marriage in 1905, the last in 1929), cousins and grandchildren who came for holidays, Sundays, and long summertime visits. Over the years Paul and Eula boarded school teachers, housed scores of friends and kinfolk during religious "Association" meetings and, when necessary, provided shelter for displaced relatives.

In addition to the demands of tending to their farm and business, our grandparents were vital members of their community, caring for their friends and neighbors. If anyone was in trouble with the law, or suffering from an illness, or down on his luck, the Simms took them food and clothing and extended them additional credit in the store. If there was a death in the neighborhood, Paul and Eula helped prepare for the funeral. People in that isolated part of Virginia had to rely on themselves and one another for just about everything. There was no 911 to dial in an emergency, not even a telephone to dial it in the early days of the twentieth century, nor was there a doctor handy. The nearest doctor was in Floyd, an arduous ten or so miles away, up and over the Blue Ridge Mountains by way of Cannaday's Gap, until one set up a practice in Ferrum, an easier hour's buggy ride away. Everyone on Hurd's Branch and in Endicott knew they could depend on Eula and Paul Simms if they were in need.

In the early days of their married life, Eula got an example of her husband's self-reliance and determination when he walked into their small log cabin followed closely by his horse. He was getting ready for a trip and noticed that the animal had thrown a shoe and needed some blacksmithing. It was freezing cold and snowing outside—too awful for the barn, I guess, or maybe there wasn't a barn in the winter of 1905—so Paul brought the horse into the house, re-shod him right there and rode off, undeterred, to Ferrum—or some distant place, on some unstoppable mission, leaving his bride slack-jawed with amazement; she couldn't believe her eyes.

Paul was determined and resourceful, but no more than his wife. Once when they were living in that same log cabin, Eula was home alone with Earl who was just a baby, wearing what all babies wore in those days, a long dress. Something happened outside that demanded her attention. Either she had to go milk the cows or she had to rescue an animal in trouble; whatever it was, she couldn't take the baby along with her. With no crib, playpen, or safe place to stash the crawling infant, and with a fire ablaze in the fireplace, she had to think quickly. She solved her dilemma by putting a table leg on little Earl's dress to keep him safe and out of danger while she tended to the emergency.

A less dramatic example of this woman's cleverness was the way she entertained her baby while she went about her duties. She coated his hands with honey and gave him a chicken feather to play with. Wonder if he giggled with delight or screamed with frustration?

She called on that same quick-thinking constantly, particularly in her capacity as family nurse. She may have acquired her medical training from her father, or she may have been a natural, instinctive nurse. This was (and is) a precious skill under any circumstances, but especially for a woman living many miles from a "real" doctor.

When one of her children was sick, Eula was very compassionate. She knew just how to treat an ailing child to make her comfortable and feel better. (Unlike Paul whose idea of medicine was a bottle of iodine. He used that burning, stinging stuff for all occasions—scratches, stings, scrapes.) My mother told me it was almost "worth" it to be sick because her mother allowed her to stay in bed, fluffed her pillows and smoothed her sheets, brought her meals of hot tea and soup to the bed on a tray, warmed her head with cloths, applied Vaporub to her croupy chest, and murmured comforting words children love to hear. "Don't fan around," her mother would say to a son or daughter who was not feeling well. Whatever the illness, she knew or figured out the best remedy. Her general "case load" was bad colds, stomach upsets, and other ordinary ailments, but on at least one occasion, Eula needed all her emergency medical know-how to care for her stricken daughter.

It was after supper, late one fall or winter evening in 1914 or 1915, cold enough for a little girl to wear an extra pair of stockings. The four of them, Eula and Paul, Earl and Elva, were sitting by the fire in their new house, the grown-ups playing checkers and Elva begging for a turn. Paul finally told her to come on over and play. She was so excited that she carelessly ran across the hearth too close to the fireplace and the kettle of boiling hot water hanging beside it. She caught her dress on the handle and knocked it over. Scalding water spilled over her left leg.

Paul and Eula flew into action. He tried to rip off Elva's knitted hose, but couldn't get them to tear, so he found a pair of scissors and cut off the double layer of stockings. Eula saturated sterile cloths she kept on hand for emergencies with linseed oil, and wrapped the bandages and soothing balm around Elva's leg. Earl, alarmed by his parents' fear and his sister's painful sobs, slipped off into the pantry, out of sight, and cried.

The next morning, Paul saddled his horse and rode ten miles up the mountain to Floyd in bitter weather to fetch the "local" doctor, Dr. Thurmond. When the two men arrived back at the farmhouse, the doctor examined the young patient and told Eula that she had administered the best possible "medicine" for her child's burned leg, exactly what he would have prescribed. Elva stayed home from school for quite some time. Her leg eventually healed without infection or complication, but not without scars and discolored skin which she has borne all her life. I remember noticing my mother's strange leg long before I knew the story of "the scalding."

Maybe it was to lighten the mood of this tale of suffering, but the telling of it was almost always accompanied by a description of Dr. Thurmond, who had a scar of his own. The good doctor had a harelip which made him speak with a lisp, an impediment which did not escape a child's notice nor her imitation. Like most country doctors of his time, Dr. Thurmond made house calls, riding his horse all over Floyd County. He did not normally come to Endicott unless there was an emergency, an epidemic or a serious outbreak of illness such as flu.

At the end of an exhausting day in Franklin County, the dead-tired doctor was seated on his horse and ready for the hour long ride home when one last patient showed up and pleaded for relief from the pain of an aching tooth. Dr. Thurmond, still astride his horse, leaned down and took a look inside the gaping mouth, reached into his bag for his tooth-pullers, clapped them around the problem tooth, held onto the reins of his horse and spurred him into a rapid giddy-up—a quick solution to a simple problem for a weary physician; he pulled the tooth on his way home.

A few years after the scalding, Earl had a little accident of his own. Eula was in the kitchen preparing a meal when she heard a shriek for help coming from the wood pile outside the screen door, up the hill a bit. She rushed to the door and her heart stopped when she saw her young son covered in blood. "Oh, Lord-a-mercy"—her verbal response in any emergency. She wiped her hands on her apron, which she was rarely without, and grabbed up cloth bandages. It appeared that Earl had sliced into a major artery in his leg while chopping wood and that he was in danger of bleeding to death.

Earl knew the minute he saw his mother's reaction to his bloody leg that he was in big trouble; his accident was a charade, a harmless prank, a lark gone wrong. He had grown weary of the relentless farm chores and had gotten a bit lazy, (normal behavior for a young boy.) Earl had decided to take a "holiday," a break from his every evening task of chopping wood and cutting up kindling. That evening he went to the wood pile as usual, took a few hacks with the axe, and then put his plan into action. He poured blackberry juice, which he had found on the counter in the kitchen, all down his legs. He then let out the howl which had so alarmed his poor mother and set her into action.

It didn't take Eula long to realize that Earl was just fine—no doubt his speedy flight on healthy legs convinced her—and that he was due for something more stringent than bandages, iodine and comforting words. His punishment was swift and sure.

Earl wasn't the only child to feign illness, although his act was not as innocent as his little sister Betty's. She was in first grade at the Biddie Hill School. Early that year she and Old Buddy, her canine companion (and the best dog in the world), arrived a little late for the beginning of the school day. The teacher had rung the bell and closed the door; all the other students were inside, seated and singing. Betty was shy. Rather than face the embarrassment of opening the door and going inside the schoolhouse, all eyes staring at her, she decided it would be much better just to walk back down the hill and go home.

At home, she slipped into the front guest room, crawled under the bedspread and pulled the covers up over her head. She was pretty sure she would go undetected and "be safe" there until school was over; after all, her mother rarely went into that room, no more than once a week. But Eula picked that day to clean the guest room. What a surprise for her to see a pair of little girl's shoes under the bed and a lump under the counterpane. When Eula asked Betty what in the world she was doing there in the bed and not in school, Betty claimed to be sick to her stomach. Whether Eula was suspicious that her daughter, who always came to her for sympathy when she was ill, was playing hooky or whether she thought the little girl was really sick, she decided that a dose of castor oil—the foulest-tasting medicine imaginable—would be the cure for either problem. This proved to be an important lesson to Betty; she learned to be much more devious in the future.

With years of nursing experience, Eula was not easily fooled by children or by disease, but my brother Ken was a rare exception. Kenneth, as he was called then, was born in 1946, a good year for sickly children. And Kenneth was that. He was ill so often that his Grandmother Eula said in confidence to other family members, "I don't think Elva will raise that child." She feared that Kenneth would not live long. In one of his early years, he turned gray with disease. When Eula saw him in this condition, she

Kenneth Simms Cannaday, 1950

knew that he was desperately ill and told her frightened daughter Elva to get him to a doctor. Of course Elva had taken him to the local doctor in Martinsville several times, but her mother's warning prodded her to seek out a specialist, a pediatrician, Dr. Newman, in Danville. He immediately diagnosed pneumonia, ordered the child to the hospital and prescribed a blood transfusion and the new wonder drug penicillin.

After the miracle cure, Kenneth recovered and grew strong and healthy, enough that by the time he was four years old, his mother allowed him to visit his grandmother and grandfather on the farm all by himself. While he was there, Grandma decided to give the little city boy a farm education. She took him to the hen house to see the clucking chickens, pecking and pooping all over the place. Not only that, she took that opportunity to combine a visit to the hen house with preparations for supper and chopped off a chicken's head. Kenneth watched in horror as the headless animal ran hither and yon until she fell over dead. "This is where your eggs and fried chicken legs come from, Kenneth," she explained. She took him to the barn to see the cow with the enormous teats and showed him cow pies to avoid—"This is where your milk and butter come from." She took him to the pen to see pigs snorting and covered with mud—"This is where your bacon and ham come from, Kenneth." This educational experience had a profound effect on my little brother, who came home and announced to Mother that he was never again going to eat eggs or meat, or ever again going to drink milk. Mother must have inherited some of her own mother's quick-thinking. She solved the predicament of the problem-eater with a little imaginative fibbing. She told Kenneth that the milk she served him came from milkweed, his eggs from eggplant and his meat from the Beechnut tree. And Grandma continued the "trickery" with her own food nomenclature. She assured Kenneth that he was eating "certified" food as opposed to farm products—certified tomatoes, for example, and that his eggs were jingled, not scrambled—which he didn't like. He was, after all, only 4 or 5 years old.

On his next trip over in the country, Kenneth took home more trouble than food aversions. With Kenneth at his side Grandpa set out a rabbit trap, but snared an opossum instead. Opossums with their razor sharp teeth, pink eyes, and long skinny, hairless tails are not cute or appealing in any way, but Kenneth, with a will of iron, insisted on taking the critter back home as a pet. Reluctantly, Mother agreed. So a wild animal came to live under a washtub in the back yard of our Villa Heights house in Martinsville. Kenneth fed Mr. Opossum and brought his little friends over to see the strange, ugly creature. It soon became more than Mother could stand. She was worried to death that the animal might bite a child, so she left the washtub ajar overnight, and Kenneth's pet escaped. He was sad but eventually recovered from his disappointing loss, or so we thought. When Mother confessed many years later to having set the poor, trapped creature free, Kenneth responded in feigned fury, "Mother, I can't believe you let him go. I loved that opossum."

In spite of her own medical abilities, Eula was a little intimidated by Nannie Hash, one of the local, self-declared healing specialists. Nannie was insistent, confident, and overbearing—sure that her herbal remedies were the best cure for any ailment. One of those cure-alls was her infamous wormseed concoction. Wormseed was a bitter-tasting plant loaded with seeds, which Nannie combined with molasses to make it somewhat more palatable. When she heard (probably from Eula at church) that Elva was at home sick, suffering with intestinal troubles, Nannie insisted that Eula give her a dose of her special brew. Several days later, Nannie asked Eula if she had given Elva her wormseed "medicine." Eula was able to answer truthfully "yes" she had. Naturally Nannie wanted to know, "Did it help? Is she any better? Would you like another dose?" Finally, Eula confessed, "Elva did not take the wormseed cure very well. In fact, she spit it out." Mrs. Hash was disgusted and told Eula, "You should have scraped it up and made her take it again." At this point in telling the Nannie Hash and the wormseed story, Earl noted that Nannie and John Goode Hash had lost several of their children and suggested, facetiously, that they might have had too much of Nannie's wormseed cure.

The death of children was a common occurrence for families over in the country, particularly in the early part of the 20th century. Paul lost two of his young brothers; Eula lost a baby sister. During the world-wide flu epidemic of 1918, which reached even into the remote villages of Franklin County, people of all ages died. Paul and Eula inflicted a self-imposed quarantine on themselves during that dreadful time to avoid what they called the sleeping sickness. Fortunately, they remained healthy and did what they could for their infected neighbors. They took food and left it by front gates or outside front doors; they did not go inside, nor did they welcome company at their own house, in what was almost an unnatural act for them. During that period of isolation, the children stayed home from school. Earl remembered that he and his father spent that time building a fence using wood from the then plentiful chestnut trees to enclose one portion of the farm.

Before the flu epidemic, an outbreak of typhoid fever had struck people who lived up the creek, but not the Simms family. To avoid further occurrences of this disease, public health authorities sent nurses to inoculate residents in the Appalachian Mountain communities such as Endicott. Everyone in the Hurd's Branch neighborhood, including Paul and Eula and the children, went down to the main road along Runnett Bag Creek and lined up for their vaccinations.

There was, of course, no escaping death, whether from flu or typhoid fever or tuberculosis or old age. Before funeral homes became common, family and friends in the neighborhood cared for their dead. In the Hurd's Branch community, Paul and Eula were often the first ones to arrive at the home of a grieving family. It must have been comforting to them to have the Simmses there to help them in the most practical ways. Paul would drive his pickup truck to Callaway, a mountain-top village 10 or15 miles away, buy a coffin with his own money and haul it back home. During the funeral, which was usually a graveside service, Paul would pass the hat to pay for the casket and the other burial expenses.

Lera, Uncle Jim's wife, often took charge of preparing the corpse for burial. She bathed and dressed the body, sometimes with Eula's help. Elva accompanied her mother on one of those occasions and watched as her aunt cleaned the body. She and her mother noticed that Lera was not doing a very thorough job. Eula looked over at Elva with a show of disapproval at the way her sister-in-law was slighting the corpse, not up to Eula's high standards.

They didn't call it a wake, but some people did stay up with the body the night before the funeral. During one of those vigils, someone—probably Jim and/or Gale, (Paul's brothers)—took the cadaver, which had become stiff with rigor mortis, out of the coffin and stood him up in a corner. We can only assume that none of the family members was present for this morbid prank.[1]

Assisting with funerals was only one of the ways Paul and Eula helped people in their community. They were a regular social service agency. If a man was in trouble with the law—in jail for moonshining, say—Miss Eula and Mr. Paul made sure the man's family back home had enough to eat and warm clothes to wear. If a family became impoverished or fell into serious debt, Paul extended them credit in the store.

They opened their home to school teachers, providing them room and board. Some of the teachers who boarded with them were Miss Ethel Wade and sisters Miss Lindy and Miss Lizzy Gussler. The young women taught at the nearby one-room, primary school—the Bitty Hill School. Earl, even when he was an old man, remembered with great fondness his first teacher Miss Lindy, holding his hand as they walked to school up the bluff which overlooked the Simms farm. The teachers received $30 a month for their services and paid $10 to Paul and Eula for room and board, so keeping the teachers wasn't strictly an act of charity. In addition, Miss Wade and her school teacher friend Miss Emily Northcross, who boarded with the Rakes family and taught at the Dry Hill School, filled the house with music, playing the dark mahogany organ in the parlor and singing hymns and popular songs on Sunday evenings after supper.

Paul and Eula loved company, even though it was extra work for her. Guests broke the loneliness of country living and the monotony of work, and brought news and gossip from the outside world. Besides, there was bountiful food and beds everywhere—in the three bedrooms of the main house, on the sleeping porch, in the upper house, and pallets for small children. The Simms farm with its big welcome and its big outdoors of freedom was THE place for cousins—Rubye, Hugh, Neza, Warren, for grandchildren—Keith, Judy, Buck, Betty Jane, Kenneth and me, and for many other friends and relatives to come in the summer. (Eula's sister Effie Snead counted 13 beds that she made up one morning after a family gathering).

On occasion the Simms provided a bed and a good meal to the traveling doctor or a minister. They kept a multitude of guests during religious gatherings such as Association Meetings. They accommodated as many "worshippers" as possible with beds in the houses, and gave the rest straw ticks and sent them to the barn. They (mostly Paul, but Eula reluctantly went along) provided shelter for less desirable relations, who loved to drink too much and were invited out by their wives.

They "took in" beloved relatives for long periods of time. Gooder Rakes, Eula's father came to live with them for most of one year—about 1931—after his wife Ophelia died, and before his unfortunate second marriage to Sally Willy. Grandma Thomas, Eula's mother's mother, stayed several months at a time. She was especially welcome company, a favorite guest both to her granddaughter and to her great grandchildren. Grandma Thomas was an old woman, a widow, forced to give up housekeeping and become a gypsy who spent time with various relatives. But she had her pride and wanted to be a useful member of the household; she remained with a family only as long as there was work for her to do. She had no intention of becoming a burden. She minded the children and entertained them with riddles. "What's black and white and read all over? A newspaper." She took on all the handwork that needed attention. Once all the "holey" socks were darned, the ripped clothes mended, the linens

Four generations-Eula, Gooder Rakes, Keith Simms, Earl Simms, 1941

patched, every scrap of material pieced into a quilt, and her repertoire of jokes exhausted, she moved on to another relative.

I never knew this great-great grandmother, nor have I seen her picture, if one exists.[2] I do, however, have one of her quilts. It is a log cabin design, an exquisite example of that familiar pattern, with tiny rectangular blocks of reds, blacks, whites, and a few blues—a pleasing arrangement with strong contrasting colors. My mother could look at that old quilt and remember the clothes from which the quilt was made. It is a treasure, worn with age and years of use, now in retirement, to be admired for its contribution to our family's history, and for its beauty and craftsmanship.

Grandma Thomas lived a long life, too long, eventually suffering her worst fear. She went blind and became bedridden; she had outlived her usefulness—so she thought. She prayed that God would let her die.

In the old days, over in the country, life could be harsh for women like our Grandmother Thomas. Most women exhausted themselves with physical labor. Eula certainly did, and she condemned anyone—man, woman, or child—who did not work hard as "sorry"—the most derogatory thing she could say about anyone—a lazy, good for nothing. She would turn down her mouth in pure disgust when describing such a useless lowlife. That was something none of us ever wanted to be: "Sorry."

Eula not only worked hard, she worked well, or as her daughter Elva would say, she was a perfectionist who never took shortcuts, particularly in her handwork. It did not matter how long a project took, it had to be perfect. Elva remembered that her mother was meticulous in making clothes for her, so careful that she, Elva, almost outgrew the dresses before her mother could complete them.

Eula was an expert seamstress, but the kitchen was her queen-dom; there she reigned supreme. She was a fabulous cook and served up the world's best fried chicken and fresh green beans boiled for hours in fat back and sugar until they were limp with flavor. In the springtime, she made a salad of green onions and just picked lettuce that she "wilted" with a dressing of hot bacon grease and vinegar. In fall she created mouth-watering creamed corn—she double cut the kernels from the ears, scraped the juice from the cob, added a bit of milk, sugar, salt, and pepper. She prepared a "good" breakfast every morning, some combination of eggs, bacon, sausage and gravy, fried apples, pancakes, oatmeal, made-from-scratch biscuits.

Eula in her garden

Paul was a biscuit critic, often breaking open Eula's freshly baked hot bread, inhaling its aroma and declaring that it had "too much sody." (A woman of restraint, she never struck him after one of these proclamations, as far as I know). On occasion Paul made the biscuits, but by his own recipe. He purposely left out the shortening which produced surprisingly good bread as long as it was hot, but once it was cold, it was as tough as hard tack. They both made hoe cake, one large round of sweet biscuit dough, baked in a black, cast iron skillet, torn apart and served with butter and syrup. None of these foods would score high on today's health-o-meter, but they were prepared in the country way, and after the hours and hours of labor they put in on the farm, my Grandparents deserved wonderful food.

Eula's children long remembered their mother standing over her prized Home Comfort cookstove. Hers was the deluxe model, the Rolls Royce of wood burning stoves. It was designed to take full advantage of heat from the firebox located in the front of the stove. That one fire was the source of heat for the oven, the top of the range, the warming chamber and the large, attached cylinder used to heat water for washing dishes and bathing. Not one single BTU escaped without double or triple use. The stove top had four round burners with removable lids and a slot in each for a metal lifter. She used the lifter to pry up the metal covers and place the pots that fit snugly into the spaces down into the stove. As the heat was exhausted through a pipe, it traveled through the warming closet above the stove.

With no thermostat to control the temperature, but with a lot of experience and some guess-work, my Grandmother played that Home Comfort stove like a one-woman band. She orchestrated meal preparation by moving pots and pans around from hotter to warmer spots on the top of the stove or in the oven or the warming chamber, depending on how much heat the beans, the corn, the fried chicken needed. She covered cooking pots with cooked pots of food to make everything come out at the right temperature at meal time, or to "hold" dinner until everyone could get to the table.

It was the custom in the country to serve the main meal at midday. If there were "hands" working on the farm, as there often were in the summer and fall, she, along with help which she usually had, fed them a man-sized hot meal at noontime. At night she generally served a cold supper of left-overs. "Let's eat up these scraps," she would say.

Nothing was easy about housekeeping over in the country. Food was a real challenge—growing it, of course, and then preserving it—every summer. August, the hottest month of the year, when most of the vegetables were ripe and ready, was canning time—hot, steamy work with vats of water bubbling away on the wood stove. When it was complete, the result was beautiful—shelves and shelves of colorful canned goods— green beans, red tomatoes, yellow corn, orange pickled peaches, cucumber pickles, bread and butter pickles, chow chow, relish, damson preserves, strawberry jam, blackberry jelly, fruits, and all the vegetables they grew and preserved, a store-house of goods. And every visitor, especially women guests, got an obligatory tour of the pantry, a chance to admire the rows of mason jars filled with produce. Eula and all farm women were rightfully proud of the food they had "put up" for the year. Having that enormous chore done eased somewhat the work involved in preparing three meals a day.

There was still much to do in addition to getting food on the table. Eula always had someone around to help her with cleaning and general housework; sometimes her maids were young girls. May Midkiff or Mammie Simms, Uncle Jim's daughter, or one of Lou Shively's daughters lived in for a while. The girls washed dishes, swept and scrubbed floors, whatever Eula needed them to do. And, of course, she expected her own children to work as hard as anyone else. The most difficult job was doing the laundry; this weekly task required a specialist, a laundry woman—Mrs. Boyd or Lula Wagoner, a woman wonderful with children. I remember loving Lula and even walking across the Bitty Hill, holding her hand, going home with her for a visit. Lula or Mrs. Boyd would make a fire outside under an enormous black pot, a cauldron, filled with water and dirty clothes or linens. They sorted out the whites and boiled them with soap powder; the other colors they scrubbed on a wash board. Then they rinsed everything in a tub of warm water and wrung out as much of the water as possible from the heavy-as-lead coveralls, from the sheets, the other clothes and underwear by hand and hung them to dry on the clothes line. They had a few "modern" aids, a wash board to scrub out stubborn dirt, and, eventually, a wringer (a hand-crank with two rollers and a tub). The women fed saturated garments into the rollers and turned the crank which squeezed out the excess water.

Earl, Elva, and Edsel Simms at home, c1923

Lula or Mrs. Boyd came to work every Monday or Tuesday morning. One day Mrs. Boyd did not show up, and Eula was sick in bed. Earl and Elva were small children, but they wanted to help their mother and decided to do the laundry for her as a surprise. They had observed Mrs. Boyd at work and knew what to do. They made a fire outside under the large black pot, gathered up the dirty clothes and put them all together in the boiling water. But they overlooked one step in the process, they forgot to separate the whites from the darks; they lumped everything together. As the clothes and linens bubbled and boiled, the colors bled into the whites, turning everything an unfortunate gray. Earl and Elva's good intentions had gone awry, but mercifully they were spared the switch. They weren't even scolded, just corrected.

Eula always had some form of assistance with the housework, but she still had too much to do—there was "no let up," as Edsel put it. And once Paul became a businessman as well as a successful farmer, she was tied even "tighter" to the farm. She had to run things and deal with any problem that might arise while he was away, like the arrival of the harvesting machine and its company of workers and tending to the store and its customers, if somewhat reluctantly.

Paul's trips took him to markets in Roanoke or Rocky Mount, to his packhouse in Ferrum, or occasionally on a vacation, one of them a two week tour of Civil War sites with his married sister Mollie Simms Denison, an Oklahoman, who came "back home" for a visit with her Franklin County family.[3] Eula stayed home. She preferred it that way.

On one rare occasion, Paul and Eula left home together for a short vacation to Natural Bridge, proclaimed the Eighth Wonder of the World by the local tourist industry. They spent the day and brought home a memento, a photograph of the Virginia landmark, which hung in their house for the rest of their lives. While they were away, all was not as it should have been back home. The farm and whoever was tending it managed just fine. It was their teen-aged daughter, Elva, who "sinned." She and her friend Glendola Thomas, with whom she was staying while Mama and Papa were away, got drunk, or at least quite tipsy, by overindulging in brandied peaches, resulting in uncontrollable giggling and upset stomachs. Neither set of parents ever knew of their daughters' outrageous behavior. This was a latter day confession—Elva was over 90 when she told on herself.

As far as Eula was concerned, trip-taking and driving were for others. She was a home-body, uncomfortable away from her farm and routine. She never learned to drive or gained the kind of independence that women today consider a birthright. As a younger woman she rode on horseback, but did not adapt to the modern automobile, which made horses obsolete as a means of travel. I don't remember seeing a horse in the Simms barn, but I do remember how displeased she was when I told her about my own horseback riding class in college. I was intimidated and a little afraid of the horses which sensed my apprehension and either ran away with me clinging to their manes, or stood absolutely still refusing to budge while I pounded their sides with my heels.

Eula found her entertainment at home on the farm. My grandmother loved the hour or so after supper when all the chores of the day were done. On chilly nights, she often made hot chocolate, popped corn over the fire, and gathered everyone around to play checkers or double six dominoes, her own specialty, a game at which she was a champion. I remember how the trail of dominoes made intricate designs of black and white spotted rectangles as they stretched down the long length of the family table.

Her other favorite past-time was reading; she read anything she could get her hands on. She ordered books for her children—the Rover Boys mysteries, Robert Louis Stevenson's *Treasure Island,* the Horatio Alger series, *Black Beauty,* and she borrowed other children's classics from Aunt Ruth's bookshelf at school. She subscribed to *Comfort Magazine* a monthly periodical for homemakers that had dress patterns, recipes and a "Cubby Bear" story she read to her children and her grandchildren. Unfortunately, there was never enough opportunity for reading when she lived on the farm; she had to steal time for such pleasures.

Eula appreciated books, but she did not approve of reading all the time, which was what she thought her daughter Betty wanted to do. Betty would sneak read—under the covers at night with a flashlight. She never offered an explanation when her father wondered about the short life of his batteries, but she did occasionally get caught by her mother. When Eula had to get up at night to let Sweet Pea the cat, in or out, she would notice the beam of light from upstairs. "Turn out that light and go to sleep," she called up the stairs to Betty.

Eula was a strict mother, quick with the switch when called for. She was what we would consider puritanical—no bad language, drinking or smoking by the girls and no off-color jokes by Earl.[4] She was a worrier, concerned that her loved ones would get hurt by not being careful. She often turned her anger on Paul, whom she was sure was going to kill one of her children or grandchildren by taking them for rides on the mowing machine or pushing them too high on the Ivy Hill swing. My grandmother believed in the goodness of food—eating aplenty, making sure every visitor, whether friend or relation, had at least one meal and took home something from her well-stocked pantry. She knew how to comfort and care for anyone sick or dying. When my father was desperately ill, near the end of his life and having trouble breathing because of the cancer in his lungs, she climbed into bed with him and held his head in her arms to comfort him. I will never forget that strong, decisive, caring act by a normally modest woman. Once her work-day was done and there was no one or no thing to fuss about or worry over, she could relax and enjoy herself with laughter and a good game of dominoes. She did the best she could and was the best she knew how to be for her husband, her children, her parents, her in-laws, her grandchildren, her friends, and her community. And she was not "sorry," not one single day in her long life.[5]

Notes for Chapter VIII, Eula:

1. Earl told me this story. Elva said that she never heard such a thing. Perhaps the men spared the womenfolk the knowledge of this disrespectful treatment of the deceased because they knew the women would condemn such insensitivity.

2. There is a tintype, black and faded, which may be a portrait of Grandma Thomas when she was a young woman, seated, holding a baby, perhaps her daughter, Ophelia, on her lap.

3. Mollie left (or ran away from) home around 1894, when she was in her late teens, and went to Missouri to stay with relatives, Aunt Julia Griffith's family—the same ones she and Paul had lived with when their mother died. She met and married Frank Denison in 1897, and the adventuring young couple moved to Oklahoma territory and settled in Okema, a name they gave their first son. Mollie's visit in about 1925 was one of the few times she ever came "back."

4. After moving to Upland Drive, Earl called often to check on her. During one of those calls, he mentioned that he was having a little trouble sleeping, then decided to entertain her with one of his dirty jokes. She let him have it: "No wonder you are having trouble sleeping with such a filthy mind and mouth."

5. Eula Rakes Simms died in 1982 at the age of 96.

9

The Children: Earl and Elva

"A Hate/Love Relationship"

Sibling rivalry is a significant feature in most families… The two oldest Simms children, Earl and Elva, had a generous supply of this trait and were ingenious at creatively abusing each other.

Earl was only two years older than Elva, but as everyone knows, a child's years—like a dog's—are much longer than 12 months, and Earl took full advantage of his superior position in the birth order. I once said to my mother that she and her brother had a love/hate relationship. She corrected me and said, "No, we had a hate/love relationship." She and Earl feuded constantly until their dating years, when they lost their hostility and became friends. But before the peace, there was conflict. She remembered that her brother tormented her by making mental lists of her misdeeds, which he kept handy and ready to use to bribe her into doing his chores and to keep her at a disadvantage. As an old man Earl grew gentle and sweet; in our conversations he rarely spoke a harsh word about anyone, including his younger sister and her struggle to "get even" during their growing up years. She, on the other hand, had no trouble remembering being his victim, and retold her few triumphs with relish. He recalled her successes with a certain pleasure, almost glad that his little sister had gotten in a good lick every now and then. Of course they played and worked together. As children on a remote Virginia farm, they had no choice; they were stuck with each other. Their "real" friends were children who lived in the tenant house, or on farms up the creek or down the road, and the family's animals, especially the horses Stormer and Darby. Elva said that she loved them much more than she did Earl.

Earl and Elva, c1908

That boy did have a talent for driving his sister to distraction, and what better place than school to work his craft? Earl and Elva both attended the one-room Bitty Hill School. It was when she was in her first year, and he in his third that he found an effective way to infuriate her.

Elva was an adorable little girl with big brown eyes—her Grandpa Simms called her "Shiney Eyes" (and her Grandpa Rakes nicknamed her "Chinquapin")—and long thick dark hair braided with ribbons tied around the ends. She wore pretty dresses made by her mother and grandmother. It was no wonder that Roy James, another first grader, lost his heart to little Miss Shiney Eyes. Elva did not return his affection. In fact she could not stand the nasty red-headed boy. That was all Earl needed to know; he teased her relentlessly. If she hadn't despised Roy before, she sure did then.

Earl did not limit his harassment to taunts; he took his tomfoolery a step further. He offered Roy cash, a penny, to kiss his sweetheart Elva, an irresistible proposal for a fellow in love. During recess, with the entire class for an audience, Roy grabbed Elva and kissed her smack on the lips. She was disgusted and expressed her repulsion by wiping her mouth and picking up a rock and throwing it at the poor little boy. Earl fell over laughing. He had gotten his money's worth and the additional pleasure of telling Elva about the payoff. All she got was punished.

Earl and Elva, c1915

Well, not quite all. She got even. After the embarrassment of the unwanted kiss in the public arena of the school-yard, Elva was motivated to seek revenge on her deserving brother. Before long she hit on a clever plan. Quite by accident, she had discovered that the purple juice from pokeberry weeds burned like "mischief" when it got on skin. With this secret knowledge, she suggested to her big brother that they play Indian and use pokeberries to decorate their faces. He readily agreed, not suspecting any foul play. After they gathered an assortment of the "wild" fruit, Elva very carefully and purposely dallied and allowed Earl to mash up the pokeberries and apply his war paint. He covered his face completely with the purple juice which went to work, stinging his skin until he screamed in pain. Years later, whenever Elva told this story, she would get a look in her eye and say, "I can still see Earl running off down the hill through the barn lot, yelling, his arms flapping, in obvious and serious discomfort as he jumped into the cow pond for relief." In the retelling, she could not restrain her giggles at the memory of Earl's reaction to his misery. That was one for Elva.

Then it was Earl's turn to put Elva in her place, to assume his position as the alpha sibling. Once again it was at the Bitty Hill School yard, that splendid site for retaliation. On snowy days during the winter, the children loved to slide on the ice down the hill beside the school house. They would crouch down and glide over the 50 or so yards of the gentle slope to a level landing spot. Then they would climb back up the hillside for another turn. Naturally, Elva and Earl wanted to join in the play, but their father, Papa Paul, had forbidden them to "skate" on the ice because he was convinced it would ruin their good shoes. His word was law.

During recess all the other children were having a great time, slipping and sliding on the icy run. Elva weakened; she could not resist the fun. Before going on such a dangerous "mission," she looked carefully around for her big brother, knowing full-well what would happen if he caught her in the forbidden act. Relieved to see that Earl was nowhere in sight, she took her place in line for a glide down the ice. But when she trudged back up the hill, there he was, spying on her from inside the schoolhouse. He had been sure that she would yield to the temptation, and he set out to catch her by hiding below the window. Then, when he saw her disobeying their father's direct order, he raised himself up so that she could see him. Earl turned her in, and Elva got a lashing.

The rivalry continued long after they left Bitty Hill School and moved up to Trinity School, the next educational level for grades five to seven. Trinity was a one-room school house, sponsored by the Methodist Church and held in one of the mission's buildings. The school and church, located at the "corner" of Runnett Bag Creek Road and the Griffith Hill, were several walking miles from the Simms farm. The going and coming, sometimes on the frozen-over Runnett Bag Creek, always in the company of friends, was the best part of the school day. In those days teachers never cancelled school because of bad weather. On rare occasions when the temperature dropped well below freezing and the wind blew bitter cold, Paul took his children to school on horseback—Elva riding in front, Earl in back. When they came to an incline so steep and so slick with ice that even Old Stormer or Old Darby couldn't climb it with passengers on his back, they all had to dismount and go on foot to the top of the hill.

But school was school, and there were lessons to learn—for instance, how to write a proper letter. Earl's teacher instructed the class and gave her students the homework assignment of writing a formal letter. Earl wrote his pretend missive to his Aunt Effie and signed it "Love, your niece, Earl." (In our interview, he jokingly said it was probably because he couldn't spell nephew.) When he was called on to read his letter out loud to the class, the teacher pointed out his mistake. "No, Earl, you aren't a niece, you are a nephew." If that wasn't humiliating enough, the correction took place with his younger sister present and all ears. Elva stored up his little error as ammunition for some future skirmish which was sure to come.

The opportunity arose—and not too long afterwards either. Earl and his friend Russell Cannaday were preparing to go for a Saturday afternoon hike. Elva wanted to join them, but they didn't want her tagging along. As the boys walked down the lane, Elva close behind, Earl turned around and shot back at her, "You stay home. We are boys and girls can't go with us."

But Elva was ready for him. She replied with her own ready arrow, saying in the nastiest, sing-song voice she could muster, "Nieces can't either." I can see her there with her hands on her hips, her arms forming little wings, leaning forward with her face twisted, shouting her insult at the boys' backs, enormously pleased with her snappy come-back.

The conflict between brother and sister was constant , the children always fussing and fighting. Paul grew irritated with the continual bickering and decided to put an end to it once and for all. His solution was to have Earl and Elva kiss and make-up. Now, even though Paul ruled with an iron hand and his children lived in fear of him, there were some things even his determination and tough-mindedness could not overcome. The siblings did as they were told—gave each other a very reluctant kiss—but it did not change a thing, certainly not in their hearts, not for years to come.

Elva was convinced that Earl was the best loved, the favored child, that he got all the good stuff—like a bicycle. She remembered his going on bike rides with his friend Roy Thomas along the Runnett Bag River Road—one of the few long level places over in the country—jealous that she never had a two-wheeler or had even learned to ride one. Even more unjustly, Earl got an automobile from his parents as a graduation present from high school (Ferrum Training School), a reward for not drinking until he was 18. Elva, of course, did not drink a drop during her first 18 years (unless you count the over-indulgence in brandied peaches), but her good conduct did not earn an automobile. At some point, her father must have felt a pang of guilt that his daughter wasn't getting her fair share of stuff. He told her that he hadn't done anything for her so he was giving her a sewing machine. Thus, she did get something. Not only that, after Ferrum Training School she got to go to college for two years, an experience Earl never had. Even Elva will admit that her associate degree from Blackstone College and a sewing machine were equal to a bicycle and a car. She, in fact, wished that her brother had had a college education because she was sure, "it would have been good for him."

In spite of their conflicts, jealousy, bickering and teasings, and their general dislike of one another, the brother and sister managed to have many good times together. All summer they went bare-footed and played in the nearby branch which had its headwater there on their farm, (so they called it Simms Branch) and on the Ivy Hill, the rise of earth above the branch and the spring house. Below the spring house was a beech tree and farther down the waterway foxglove vines and orange touch-me-not wildflowers that attracted hummingbirds. In the creek the children constructed little flutter mills and caught crawdads. They threw pebbles at water snakes sunning themselves on the branch banks, and Earl tried to create a swimming hole by damming up a section of the creek, but his effort failed. In the woods they made whistles from willow branches and designed playhouses, using small white stones to outline rooms and for furniture on thick-piled moss carpets under the mountain laurel bushes.

The official day to go barefoot was May 10th, and not one day before, no matter what the weather. The official end to shoeless days was the first day of school—four months to toughen up shoe-softened feet, to wade in cool branch water, to enjoy the tickle of grass and the luxury of moss, and to brave iodine on cuts and the pain of stubbed toes. No one ever suffered snake bites, but that was no doubt because they—children and reptiles alike—were on the alert, aware and cautious of one another.

To their "playhouses" in the woods they brought dolls—Elva, as you might imagine, had quite a collection; Earl, on the other hand, had only one, but she was a well-loved playmate he named Dorothy. Dorothy was about 12 inches long with a delicate porcelain face, dressed in a long gown to cover her canvas body which was filled with sawdust. When Earl turned 12 and was preparing to go to boarding school, he sadly but wisely decided not to take Dorothy with him. He reluctantly gave her to Elva, and she joined his sister's family of dolls that already included Dorothy's twin.

In summer the children had their own garden in back of the house, below the granary and across the branch on a flat spot of land too small for Paul to plow and plant, but just right for children. Earl and Elva had their own separate plots. When their mother Eula planted seedlings—a tomato, an onion, a potato—her children planted the same things in their little gardens

Then came September, shoes and school, and the turn of the seasons—first to brisk autumn, then to frigid winter. Earl and Elva were sure that the Franklin County winters of their youths were far superior to current winters—confident that they had much more ice and snow and freezing temperatures. Their memories were sharpened by chilled walks to school through snow, and on Runnett Bag Creek, frozen in its tracks, and by life in a house without central heat. Winter meant union suits for everyone, even little girls. Elva said, "I hated to wear them, but mother made me." She had to pull her stockings up over the long underwear. Everyone at school knew by the sagging folds under the leggings that she was wearing longjohns. Only better-off folks could afford to look that foolish. The clothing was cumbersome, but at least it was engineered with a flap and buttons at strategic points to accommodate visits to the bathroom.[1]

Getting dressed and undressed in a cold farm house required ingenuity to protect bare body parts from exposure to raw air. To stay warm, the children usually got ready for bed downstairs in front of the fire that blazed in the kitchen. From time to time, or at least once, Earl and Elva had a contest to see who could get dressed first in the morning. She cunningly went to bed in her clothes to get a head start on brother Earl, who may have done the same thing. No one seemed to remember who actually won the competition, just that they had one.

In spite of their many disagreements, Earl and Elva did manage to have a little fun together, but they found their "real" friends elsewhere. Elva had two best girl friends—Amy Simms, (her Grandpa Simms' youngest daughter by his second wife) Elva's same-age aunt, who lived down the lane on an adjacent farm, and Glendola Thomas, daughter of Nanny and Sam Thomas who lived on Runnett Bag Creek Road between Grandpa Simms and Endicott. The girls were inseparable all through their school years, except when one of the three was on the "outs" with the other two, which was a regular occurrence. One day the best friends, who were fifth or sixth graders at the time, were walking home from Trinity School just after a rainstorm had left pools of water in the main road beside Runnett Bag Creek. Glendola was up ahead of the other two, mad at them for some girl's reason, her mouth stuck out in a pout. About half-way home at the driveway that led up to Uncle Jim's house, they came to a deep rut filled with muddy water. In a sudden rush of inspiration (the devil, no doubt, at work, although Elva gave credit to Amy) the two of them ran up beside Glendola, one on either side, picked up the startled girl and set her down in the mud puddle. She was furious, her dress soaked through and covered with dirt, but in time she forgave them because they continued to be friends through seventh grade, high school, Ferrum Training School and beyond.

Not that there weren't other unpleasant incidents, like Amy and her corn flakes. (Keep in mind that my mother Elva was a major source for these stories; I never got Amy or Glendola's versions.) It is hard to imagine these days that anything as ordinary and taste-free as corn flakes could be a cause for dissention, but in the 1910s the boxed cereal was a brand new product, a novelty. On her way to Miss Ora's Summer School, at St. John's Church, Amy bought some corn flakes at Old Man I.T. Cannaday's general store, the largest and most modern of any of the many little markets in those parts, the WalMart of Endicott.

She opened the box of treats and began to eat. Elva was walking to school with her and begged for a few bites, but Amy refused to share. This blistered Elva whose turn it was to listen to the devil. To get to Miss Ora's school, the girls took a short cut through the woods on a path in back of I.T.'s store to a crossing log over the Runnett Bag Creek, and on up a steep incline to the church. At the crossing log, Amy edged her way along and when she neared the vulnerable middle, Elva, who was at one end of the log, tried to knock her "friend" off by shaking it with all her might, a fair punishment, she thought, for Amy's blatant selfishness. The miller, Old Man Boyd, saw what was going on and yelled at Elva to "stop that right this minute! You'll push Amy into the creek," which, of course, was the idea. Amy did not suffer a fall, only a little fear that she would.

The girls got over their tiff and went on with summer school and summer play until the next occasion for "trouble." This time, it was during the regular school year at Trinity School. The school's hand water pump failed, and they needed drinking water for the students. The closest spring was at Miss Nancy Jane Cannaday's house across the road and on the other side of Runnett Bag Creek. Elva and Amy volunteered for water patrol. To get to Miss Nancy Jane's, the girls had to walk up the road to another one of the crossing logs which spanned the creek. The two of them, the brainstorming kin, decided that rather than travel all the way up to the log "bridge" they would take a short-cut across the creek by using the buckets for boots. They put one on each foot and marched through the shallow stream. This proved to be such a lark that they waded ole Runnett Bag back and forth over and over, before finally filling the pails with drinking water and bringing them back to school over the usual route. No one knew, they never told, and Elva was SURE that they rinsed the pails out thoroughly before filling them with drinking water for their classmates.

Elva loved her girl friends. Whether they were on the outs, in trouble, or at play, they remained best buddies. But all her friends weren't girls; she had a boy friend too, Gossie Scott. Elva and Gossie were "an item," as we say today. Their infatuation began at the Bitty Hill School, where Elva had another one of those embarrassing kissing scenes, but at least this time it was with a fellow she liked—a lot. She and Gossie were inside the classroom sitting on benches. Some of the benches were taller than others. Elva was perched on a higher one and Gossie on a lower. The love-birds were "air" kssing at one another when Amy (that devilish child), who was probably repulsed by their public display of affection, gave Elva an unexpected shove; she and Gossie made "contact," their two (or is it four?) lips touching. They were both amazed at what had happened, but it did not alter the course of their romance, which continued to flourish on into the next grades at the Trinity School. Elva did have some competition, however. Her cousin Elsie Brogan developed a crush on the charming Gossie, but he remained faithful to Elva. Apparently Earl did not tease his sister about this more serious boy friend, probably because he knew he couldn't make her mad; she might even enjoy the ribbing.

Earl had his own set of friends to pal around with: Cleve Trail, Gossie's brother, Artie Scott, Gossie (another reason to let the romance alone), Roy Thomas, and especially Nannie Belle Griffey, who lived with her mother Miss Bernie in the Simms tenant house. As youngsters Earl and Nannie Belle spent hours playing happily together, except for one unfortunate event. Earl and his friend Cleve, who lived one ridge over from the Simms farm, were on their way up the hollow to drive the cows "home" to the barn for the evening milking when they spied a hornet's nest attached to a tree branch by the side of the road. Being stupid boys, they threw rocks at the nest. Then to add drama to the occasion, Nannie Belle, unaware of any mischief, came skipping innocently down the road. When Earl and Cleve spotted her, they eased up a bit on the bee torture, ducked out of sight behind a hill—until Nannie Belle drew closer to the nest. Then the bad, little boys threw a barrage of rocks to arouse the hornets out of their home and stir them into an angry pitch. The incensed insects flew at Nannie Belle, buzzing around her face, hair, and head while she fought them off, her arms and hands flailing like windmills at the hornets.

In spite of it all, Earl said, he didn't think Nannie Belle got stung. Even if she had she must not have held it against him, or maybe she didn't know he was the cause of the attack. Anyway, she forgave him if she did. Not long after the hornet nest incident, she and Earl were at Grandpa and Grandma Simms house visiting his slightly older and much larger aunt, Delma. Somehow Earl, who had a talent for tormenting girls, had so enraged this intimidating relative—over what, who knows?—that she was beating him on the fanny, and he was trying to escape by climbing over the side-yard fence. Nannie Belle came to his rescue. She pulled Delma's hair to get her to leave her best friend alone. Many years (80 or 90) later, Earl said, "She was my good friend. I loved Nannie Belle, I guess."

Boys (and occasionally girls) do idiotic things—sometimes to others' disadvantage, sometimes to their own—like caving in to a sweet tooth. On one occasion Earl's friend Thurmond Thompson persuaded Earl to ride with him in the wagon to Ferrum to pick up supplies for Thurmond's father, Mr. Will Thompson's store. Mr. Will, notable in Elva's memory for serving as Sunday School Superintendent at Trinity Methodist Church and for his numerous gold teeth which tended to collect bread crumbs, had a large and thriving general store up Runnett Bag Creek. It was almost at the foot of Cannaday's Gap, at Laurel Bluff, next to Nowlin's Mill, the Laurel Bluff School, and the post office, before it was moved to a more central location at Endicott. At the warehouse in Ferrum, Thurmond and Earl loaded up the wagon with the goods Mr. Will had ordered, including wooden buckets filled with candy. On the trip home, bumping along over the long ten miles, Earl began to think about the delicious sweets in the back of the wagon and how much he would like to have a taste or two. The small buckets were divided into three compartments, one for chocolate candy, one for caramel candy, and one for coconut candy. It was the coconut section that Earl concentrated on, and before the trip was ended and the boys back at Mr. Will's store, he had eaten so much from the coconut triangle that he was sick as a dog. Earl reached the age of 96 without ever again eating another piece of coconut candy, coconut cream pie, coconut custard, or coconut of any sort. Whether Thurmond participated in the sugar splurge, Earl couldn't remember. He only recalled his own punishment for overindulging.

Children will be children, as they say. Earl and Elva had adventures with their friends, fussed with one another and sometimes misbehaved, but on one thing they agreed—they loved the farm animals, especially the horses, "Old Stormer" and "Old Darby." Both animals were studded males. Stormer was larger, stronger and pulled harder, but Darby was always ready to work and would sometimes bite Stormer on the neck to get him going.

When the horses weren't pulling a plow or a wagon or busy with some other farm task, they were available to give the children rides. I have heard that horses are quite smart, and I have heard that horses are quite dumb, but these two—smart or dumb—always protected the young people who rode them. The brother and sister were out for an afternoon's gallop, Elva riding Stormer bareback and Earl riding Darby, when they suddenly came to a steep drop off. Before she knew it, Elva slid over her horse's head, slick as butter and landed directly in front of his front hooves. Stormer somehow managed to stop dead in his tracks and avoid trampling the sweet little girl. "So you know I loved that horse," she told me.

Elva had another falling-off adventure with Stormer and Darby, only this time it was her awkward cousin Elsie Brogan who took the fall. The two girls were riding the horses, Elsie on Stormer and Elva on Darby, on their way from Elva's house in Endicott to Elsie's in Callaway. Along the way they took a side path to enjoy a mountain-top view, but the ride up the slope proved too steep for Elsie, and she fell off the back of the horse. She was unscathed but unhappy; she remounted and the girls arrived safely at the Brogan home. Elva and the horses spent the night with Elsie and her family. The next morning Elsie was telling her family about the trip home and complained—within Stormer's hearing—"that that hateful horse threw me off." With that—maybe a bee stung the animal or maybe he was indeed smart—Stormer picked up his big hind leg and kicked Elsie sharply in the shin. She began shaking her leg and shouting, "Oh, my leg is broke! My leg is broke!" Her father, Uncle Bob, told her in disgust: "Elsie, you dunce, if your leg was broke, you couldn't kick it like that."

Elsie may not have appreciated Old Stormer, but Elva and Earl loved their horse, in fact they loved all the animals that were essential parts of their farm family—even though they required feeding and watering and driving, if they were cows—Old June, Old Pansy, or Old Pet. Before they had Old Buddy—the best dog God ever created—Earl (and later Edsel) had to bring the cows in from the pastures where they spent the day, to get them to the milking gap, or to the barn. Earl was on one of those routine missions when he noticed a sizable hole near the path the cows generally took to the barn. He found a fence post—about 6 feet long—and plunked it down into the hole to prevent the cows from stepping in it, or maybe he did it because he was a ten year old boy. On the return trip, for a reason he never knew himself, Earl pulled up the stick and there wrapped around it was a big, fat snake. He had hit on a snake pit. Frightened by the unexpected strangeness of the squirming reptile—probably a harmless black snake—Earl immediately plunged the post with its slithering attachment back into the ground and ran as fast as he could for home, relieved to be back to the everyday business of bringing in the cows and gathering the evening's supply of wood and kindling.

Like the milk cows, the wood box had to be tended every day. Paul and the "hands" he hired harvested trees from the wood lots on the edges of the farm, trimmed the branches, and deposited the bulk wood in back of the house by the chopping block—ready to be sawn into large back logs for a long, slow burn or cut into smaller pieces for the cookstove or small chips for kindling.

Most evenings, Paul covered the hot coals in the kitchen fireplace with ashes. And in the mornings, uncovered the ashes and used the previous day's coals to start the new day's fire. Sometimes he doused the coals and extinguished the fire completely, which meant he had to start fresh the next day. Whatever his routine in the mornings, he had to have stove wood and kindling, and he expected Earl to keep the woodboxes filled.

One time, and only one time, Earl neglected to bring in the supply of firewood. He was fast asleep in his nice warm bed when his father roared into his room, shook him awake, and ordered him down the stairs and outside into the cold to gather the kindling and wood he had failed to bring in the night before. Earl said the experience of being frightened awake by his angry father and hauling wood in the dark and cold "helped his memory" from then on.

The children had long lists of chores they performed without pay, but there were a few tasks that earned wages, such as cracking nuts and catching flies. Flies were a big problem in the country, especially in the summer. The farm house of the early twentieth century was not sealed up tight as a drum, the way ours are today. It was open and airy; the screened doors kept busy with grown-ups and children running in and out on trips to the garden for a mess of greens for dinner, or from visits to the barnyard, or the spring-house, or play in the branch, or on the Ivy Hill. Flies were opportunistic. Every time a door or window opened, they rushed in and, with no manners at all, landed on any food they could find and helped themselves. The farm family fought back; they had fly minders—a sort of newspaper fan—fly swatters, and flypaper in several designs. There were coils of fly paper, yellow, sticky twists hung down from the ceiling—often directly over the kitchen table, making quite a "centerpiece"—to catch the nasty pests. That paper must have smelled mighty good to the flies because they flew right into it and stuck there. In addition to the coils there were sheets of fly paper, 12 inch by 8 inch rectangles, laid out on table tops and other surfaces to trap the insects.

Even so, flies escaped and remained a nuisance. The next line of defense was the children, mercenaries paid a penny for every ten flies they killed. The practice of hiring children to swat flies crossed the generations, from Earl and Elva, to Edsel and Betty, on down to me and my cousins, the grandchildren. When flies became scarce—maybe it was DDT, or extra fly paper, or too many troops on the prowl, or the end of fly season—enterprising children would open the doors and let the pests in, kill them, collect their penny rewards, and spend them on candy at Paul's store.

The bounty of the country provided "flies for profit," as well as chestnuts and walnuts—real cash crops. At one time, before the devastating chestnut blight of the early 20th century, the Simms farm had a huge stand of chestnut trees above the house—a place they called Chestnut Ridge. When those trees were ripe with fall fruit, the Simms children gathered chestnuts and sold them for five cents a pound. They used the money to buy school books and shoes.

Almost as plentiful as chestnuts "in their heyday" were walnut trees, a species with survival strategies far superior to the chestnut.[2] The early walnuts that the children collected from under the trees were covered with a green protective hull. They spread the walnuts out to dry and left them until the green coat swelled, turned black, and the outer casing was easier to remove. It almost fell away, but it left black stains all over their hands. Another layer remained; they still had to penetrate the shell exterior to get to the nut meat. To make a clean break, and to avoid crushing the precious interior kernel, Elva and Earl stood the walnut on end and whacked it with a small hammer. Walnut cracking and extracting were often the family's evening work and amusement. Some of the walnuts they kept and used for baking and for eating "raw," and some they sold for five cents a pound or whatever the going market rate was, usually to I.T. Cannaday for resale at his big as a Kmart store at Endicott.

Russell and Elva Simms Cannaday

Earning a little extra cash, whether from swatting flies or extracting walnut meats, became important to young people growing into adults. Earl and Elva had a group of teenaged friends, including May and Russell Cannaday (who had moved to Maryland but spent their summers "home" in the country), Gossie Scott (Elva's old flame) and Ethel James. The six friends had heard about a special light show, a beacon shining into the sky all the way from Charlottesville—at least 100 miles as the crow flies. The prospect of an extraordinary event like a great beam of light became a splendid excuse for an evening mountain-top picnic. The young folks packed baskets of food and at dusk, headed off up Stan Martin Mountain, the tallest of the mountains behind the Simms farm. The dating sextet—boys and girls of a certain age—going off together in the "middle of the night" did not set well with Paul. In an effort to keep his teenaged children "pure," he sent their little brother Edsel along as a chaperone. He, of course, was happy to be tagging after his big brother and sister and their friends. They, of course, were not at all happy to have the pesky little brat in their company. Edsel trailed them only as far as the tenant house before Earl tried to persuade him to "go on back home." That tactic didn't work, but Russell knew how to dispose of the unwanted boy. He offered Edsel a quarter to leave them alone. Edsel's dubious reply was: "Let me see your money!" Russell, good as his word, gave the boy the bribe and sent him "on back home." The teenagers never made it to the top of the mountain; a fence across the mountainside ridge put a stop to their ascent; nor did they see the extraordinary light from Charlottesville, but it really didn't matter. It was just an excuse for a coed outing.

After 13 years of friction Earl and Elva were at last leaving behind their combative, competitive, childish rivalry and growing into a friendship which lasted a lifetime. The inventive insults and attacks of their youth became amusing memories, something they could take out, talk over, and laugh about in their declining years.

Notes for Chapter IX, The Children: Earl and Elva:

1. In our talk about such things, Earl laughed and said that the long underwear was fart-proof.

2. Black walnut trees produce a toxic substance that inhibits growth of certain other plants under or near them.

10

The Children: Edsel and Betty

"There's never any let up."

These are some of the best-loved and best-remembered stories from Edsel and Betty's childhood.

By the time I was alive and paying attention, all the Simms "children" appeared to my little girl eyes to be a family of grown-ups, all of similar age. That perception was clearly an illusion. Earl, Elva, Edsel and Betty were adult siblings all right, but spread out in the birth order about as far apart as children could be and still remain brothers and sisters. First in line, Earl and Elva were born right after their parents were married, two years apart, 1905 and 1907. They had Papa and Mama to themselves for eight pugnacious years before their tow-headed little brother Edsel arrived. Then 14 years later, in 1929, in what must have been a mighty big surprise, their baby sister Betty was born.

In some ways Betty and Edsel were like only children, although they never thought of themselves that way. Until he was five years old Edsel had Elva for his reluctant babysitter. Beginning in 1920 she and Earl were away at Ferrum Training School for most of the year. By the time Betty was born, Earl was married, Elva was soon to be, and Edsel was home from boarding school only during vacations. Even so he proved to be a wonderful big brother who took time for Betty and taught her all kinds of useful things, like how to shoot a rifle.

No child, except Jesus, should be born on Christmas Eve. That was Edsel's inconvenient arrival day, December 24, 1915. Earlier that week Earl and Elva had been shuttled off to Otter Creek to stay with their Rakes grandparents, out from under foot, and not around to ask embarrassing questions. Under normal circumstances they loved to visit Gooder and Ophelia Rakes, but this was Christmas and not a normal time. It was the one day in the year children needed to be home, to be "good" and await the arrival of gifts, not babies (even though that was what got the whole Christmas thing going). On the evening of December 24th, the baby was born. It had begun to rain, so Grandpa Rakes put up the sides of his buggy as he prepared to drive his grandchildren over the Griffith Hill to their home on Hurd's Branch, to meet their new brother.

Things were different with a new baby in the house—even an adorable blonde boy—especially for Elva. Before his arrival, she only had Earl as her constant irritant, an obstacle to a problem-free life. Now she had another. Being a girl and at eight, old enough to qualify as a babysitter, she became Edsel's chief caretaker. Her mother expected her to rock the baby, feed the baby, watch out for the baby. When her girl friends expressed jealousy and wished that they had a baby in their house to play with and to rock, Elva suggested that it wasn't nearly as much fun as they thought. The novelty of "peddling" an infant in a cradle for hours on end soon became a mind-numbing bore.

Elva was a dependable keeper most of the time, but occasionally she became resentful of the responsibility or let down her guard. She once tried to cram spoonfuls of mashed potatoes into little Edsel's mouth faster than he could swallow. He almost choked to death before Eula heard the baby gagging and came to his rescue. Elva's most memorable babysitting lapse came when the unthinkable happened. Edsel "showed up missing." How much time passed before she noticed the elusive four-year old had vanished? It didn't matter. He was gone. Nowhere in sight. Everyone was upset. Eula was distraught. They looked everywhere for that little boy, calling his name: "Edsel, Edsel, where are you?" They searched the most dangerous places first—the branch, the barn yard, the woods. Then they looked all through the house—upstairs, the sleeping porch, downstairs, under beds, in the outhouse, the granary, out the path to the tenant house. No luck. Now, frightened to death, with one last place to look, Elva hur-

Edsel with his gun

ried down the lane toward the mailbox on the main road, about a quarter mile from home, looking with growing panic on both sides of the road, still calling his name. And, then, just as she came in sight of Arthur Snead's millet field which bordered Runnett Bag Creek, Elva noticed the tops of the grain moving very slowly, in a waving motion. It was Edsel. He had gone for a walk, done a little exploring, had an outing. He claimed that the first thing his big sister did when she discovered him was to whack him good on his fanny. She only remembered how relieved and happy she was to find him.

That wasn't the first or the last time that Edsel would be a problem child. He was still a little boy when he became infected with a nasty case of head lice. Eula was scrubbing his scalp with a home-made brew to rid him of the filthy infestation and picked off one of the little vermin to show him. Edsel looked at the tiny black bug and said, "Well, ain't it cute!"

Not all of his "sayings" were so amusing. Edsel was not much older when he mistakenly accused a perfectly innocent neighbor of a crime. He had overheard talk that a fellow "Boyd" had been "helping" himself to some of Paul's wood. So when Ike Boyd next stopped by the house Edsel made a wrong assumption and angrily demanded, "Why have you been stealing my dad's lumber?" Ike swelled up and replied in a gruff, outraged voice, "I didn't steal your dad's lumber." Edsel's embarrassed sister was there when it happened, and offered an immediate apology and explanation. The thief was a completely different Boyd.

Edsel could be explosive when something riled him up, but most of the time, in his general demeanor and in his work, he was slow, deliberate and thoughtful—a characteristic which expressed itself early on and lasted for a lifetime. Uncle Jim, one of Paul's younger brothers, stopped by the house on his way to somewhere up on Hurd's Branch and saw Edsel out chopping wood in the side yard. "Where's your Pa, Edsel?" Edsel didn't reply right away, in fact he didn't say a word. He paused with the axe on his shoulder, pondering where his father might be; he didn't want to give a wrong answer. Finally, after more time than he could spare for Edsel's thoughtful response, Uncle Jim said, "Never mind, son. I'll find out on my way back home."

Edsel was as deliberate about his chores as he was in his speech. His turtle's pace irritated his mother who was always on the run herself. She asked her young son why in the world he didn't work faster, complete his errands, and get them behind him. "Why rush?" he said. "When I finish one job, dad just finds two more for me to do. There's never any let up."

It must have seemed to Edsel that his life was an endless round of work, but that was not always the case. He found plenty of time for fun and mischief. What boy with spunk or sense of adventure could resist a challenging test of his balancing skills by walking the top of a fence? At one time the Simms farm house was enclosed on three sides by a white picket fence—installed when Earl and Elva were just old enough to hold a hammer and drive the stakes. Paul, or one of his workers, then attached supporting horizontal crosspieces, about a child's-foot width, several inches below the picket points. Eula, worried as usual about her child's safety, had specifically forbidden Edsel to walk on the fence, but he did it anyway. She must have been off somewhere on one of her many tasks—out of sight long enough for the little boy to get away with his acrobatics, unobserved—almost. He was found out in a most unusual way. After his high wire act, he tried to jump down to the ground, but the straps of his coveralls or maybe it was his suspenders—got snagged on the pickets. He hung there, vulnerable as a parachutist impaled on a tree limb, until his discovery, rescue, and inevitable whipping.

Edsel was not finished with finding ways to be bad. The next time he had an accomplice—his young cousin Rubye Snead, who was visiting from Roanoke. One day in late summer the two cousins, not yet teenagers, got an itch for watermelon growing in the garden, about ready for harvesting. Rubye and Edsel wandered among the vines in search of a ripe one, but couldn't tell from looking at the green outsides which melons were mature and ready for eating. So they took a peek inside by cutting small, square plugs in a number of the watermelons until they found one with bright red innards. The two of them knew this was not the best way to handle fruit because they very carefully turned the scarred melons to the ground to hide the evidence of their plunder.

Elva caught the culprits red-handed when she saw her brother and cousin hacking at the fruit and reported them to the mother "police." The crime didn't end with a purifying willow branch switching. Edsel, aided and abetted by Rubye, retaliated against his big sister tattletale who was preparing to go away to Blackstone College. Elva was packing the new clothes her mother had spent hours making for her. Edsel and Rubye attacked her brand new dresses with scissors by making tiny vertical cuts, barely noticeable, along the hem lines. He "did in" the flowered frock because he thought it the prettiest and the best, and let Rubye slice up the linen dress. Unfortunately they punished the wrong person—mother Eula, rather than sister Elva, because Eula had to make repairs on the damaged clothes. Justice prevailed however. Edsel got a double whipping, one for plugging the watermelons and one for damaging the dresses; Rubye, being younger and a visitor, escaped the switch.

As a small lad Edsel did seem trouble-bound or at least those are the stories we remember from repeated tellings. But he was a generous little boy who shared his bicycle with all the neighborhood fellows, who all took turns learning to ride one of the few two-wheelers on Hurd's Branch. He also gave the family immeasurable pleasure. It was Edsel who imagined and engineered the erection of the better-than-ice-cream swing on the Ivy Hill. It was Edsel who taught Betty to be a sharp-shooter; and it was Edsel who selected Old Buddy from a bag-full of pups. He knew the minute he saw the tan and white collie-mixed puppy, the first one to bound out of the sack, that he was "it." Mr. Brammer had brought a litter of doggies by the house in hopes of "selling" one to the Simmses. Paul, Uncle Jim, Grandpa Rakes, and Edsel were all there out in the front yard, when Brammer stopped by and turned the irresistible puppies loose. Edsel, almost a puppy himself at 7 or 8, fell in love with the prettiest of the lot, Buddy, and could not be persuaded even to consider any of the other dogs. Paul suggested that he look them all over before deciding, but Edsel stubbornly stuck with his lucky first pick. So Buddy came into the Simms family and won every single heart.

The dog, besides being a great companion, (which was and still is the generally accepted rule and first principle of being a dog), took on additional responsibilities—herding the cows and, later, guarding baby sister Betty. Paul trained Old Buddy to herd Old June and Old Pansy; he relied on the dog's natural Collie instincts to round-up and drive the cows from the pasture to the barn. On the command "go get the cows," the Lassie-like dog took off for the distant pasture, barked the cows to their feet if they were lying down, and nipped at their heels to head them in the direction of the barn. He soon learned to avoid the kicks the grazing, lazing animals tried to inflict on the annoying dog. Old Buddy was always obedient, responding immediately to his master's orders, except on one memorable occasion. Paul gave the command to bring home the cows, and Old Buddy started out for the pasture, but then had second thoughts. He returned and laid down, testing his owner's seriousness. It was never wise to question a direct order from Paul Simms, whether by child or by dog. For the only time anyone ever knew, Paul whipped him. After that Buddy never again refused to hustle after the cows.

Old Buddy

Sometimes Buddy, being a round'em up breed of canine, tried to race the occasional automobile which sped by the farm house. He lost out on the chase with Montague Adkins who accidentally whacked him with his car. The dog took that hit personally and never forgave Montague or his car; he growled at the man and his vehicle whenever they drove by or whenever Montague stopped in at the store or for a visit. Even so, Old Buddy was the sweetest and the best dog God ever created—any of the Simms children and their parents would tell you that. Elva and Earl loved Buddy; they were 16 or so when Edsel adopted him. Little Betty probably considered him a furry brother. By the time she was born, the dog was an established member of the family, middle-aged as dogs go. And he certainly considered her "his" in some instinctive animal kind-of-way. When she grew into her toddler years, the dog became her guardian. He would not let her wander outside the fence gate and nosed her back into the front yard if she tried to escape. Betty never "showed up missing." Buddy wouldn't allow it.

When she was ready for school, Old Buddy was too. He padded along with her each morning up the hillside to the Bitty Hill School. At the end of the school day, with no bell to warn him, (somehow he was able to tell time, Eula said), Buddy was outside the school house door waiting to see her safely home.

Edsel on the porch swing

When Edsel was working to install the wondrous child's swing up on the Ivy Hill, risking his neck by climbing the tall-as-a-mountain tree, and hauling up the heavy metal chain, Old Buddy—the faithful friend—was there, resting under the shade of laurel bushes, watching out for his master.

I guess all dog stories end the same. This one is no exception.

Buddy grew old—he was 13—and sick. When Paul found him in the woods, lying down, suffering from some unknown illness, he knew what had to be done. Paul was able to do almost anything he had to in this life—whether it was cleaning out a well or digging an outhouse, shoeing a horse, sticking a pig, whipping a disobedient child, killing a rattlesnake, riding to Ferrum in a snowstorm, tending to funeral arrangements for a neighbor—but he could not bring himself to put Old Buddy down. For that he asked his brother Jim.

At the time Betty was a little girl of seven or eight. She did not understand what was happening when she found her mother in the front parlor sobbing, the first time she had ever seen her cry. Eula had heard the sound of the rifle and knew that Jim had shot Old Buddy. They told the children that their dog had died, which of course he had, quickly and mercifully with a bullet in his head.

Edsel did a good thing and got well-deserved credit for selecting Old Buddy and bringing him into the family. He also got high marks from his

14 years younger sister, Betty, who said that Edsel was a wonderful big brother.

Betty was such a late in life child that she never remembered seeing her father with anything other than a full head of white hair, except for the one time he put color back on it. The dye bled all over the pillowcase and exasperated Eula—such vanity causing her such trouble. Paul was 50 when Betty was born and quite pleased with his new baby girl; Eula was 42 and mortified by this late "gift," born at what people then considered late middle-age. She, in fact, told Elva when she discovered that she was pregnant, that having a baby at her age was almost a disgrace. Once the sweet child arrived, however, the embarrassment vanished.

Elva was living at home and on hand to help her mother with the baby. By 1929 she had completed her associate degree from Blackstone College and was teaching at the Bitty Hill School. She was there when Betty was born and recalled that early May morning when her father anxiously left the house at dawn to fetch Nurse Annie, the English missionary mid-wife who was living with Miss Ora at St. John's Episcopal Church. When Paul returned home with Nurse Annie, she put the obviously nervous Papa to use: "Mr. Simms, get me some hot water in here." Next thing they knew the baby had arrived without Eula uttering a peep. She had been determined that she would not cry out or say a word during the birthing of the baby.

The parents decided to name the infant for Paul's mother, Lucinda Elizabeth, whom everyone had called Betty. Paul insisted that his little girl only needed the name Betty because that was what they called his mother; he saw no need for the use of a full-fledged name like Elizabeth which he considered wasteful, superfluous. A practical man, he even thought his own last name had too many m's. He often signed his name Sims, rather than the extra mm-ed Simms. After all, you couldn't hear that additional "m," so why use it? Paul won. Betty was named plain old Betty—almost. Her mother did not think that name was quite sufficient and she tacked on another, Iris, a name Betty could have happily done without. In fact, if you ever wanted to see smoke pour out of her ears, nose, and mouth, just put the two names together and call her "Betty Iris." She wasn't the only one dissatisfied with her name. Elva was stuck with Althea as her first name, but she shed it as soon as possible. Nor was she all that crazy about the name Elva which had been suggested to her mother by Beulah Spencer, (one of Cousin Green's daughters), who was staying with Eula to help out when Althea Elva was born. Somehow Elva acquired the nickname Ebb, a pet name used almost exclusively by her immediate family. Betty and Elva weren't the only malcontents; Eula didn't like her name either. She confessed her secret to Edsel when she was an old lady. He asked her why she never told anyone, and she said, "No one ever asked me."

Names were important to the Simms children, as was their place in the family line-up, neither of which they could do anything about. Betty was much younger than her sister and bothers and had a special relationship with her big brother Edsel who was still at home during some of her little girl years. He gave her the pet name "JaBonnie" which was from a popular song he liked. He "allowed" her to tickle his back for 30 minutes at a time, and paid her with comic strips from the Sunday paper. (I am sure he did not intend to take advantage of an adoring little sister.) But Edsel had rewards for JaBonnie more wonderful than the funnies.

It was for Betty that Edsel devised the Ivy Hill swing. I have written in the chapter, "Over in the Country," about this marvel of ingenuity which, once installed, endured without a single adjustment or hitch for the next 20 years. That swing of swings, that joy ride of joy rides, became a gift not just for Betty, but for every child, (including me and Edsel's children) who ever spent time at the Simms farm.

It was for Betty that Edsel spent one summer as a rifle instructor. She could not have been more than ten years old; maybe she was even younger. He didn't intend to teach her on the sly—it was a summer pastime, a new skill for her to acquire, something fun to do. Betty loved games and took to the handling and firing the .22 rifle with the same skill and enthusiasm she had for other sports, such as croquet and badminton. The rifle was a relatively small weapon, weighed no more than five pounds, and had very little recoil. Edsel had her practice by shooting at tin cans he set up on fence posts and at snakes innocently sunning themselves on rocks in the creek bed. He made sure to warn her about the danger of a ricochet—a sophisticated new word she loved to turn over in her brain—from bullets bouncing against hard surfaces, especially rocks in the branch or on the side of the hill.

For some reason, Paul and Earl (who was married and living in Roanoke at the time), were unaware that Edsel had been teaching his baby sister to fire a rifle. One weekend late that same summer, when the family had gathered at the farm for Sunday dinner, the men decided to have a shooting match. To make it a fair competition, they all used the same .22. In those days and in that place, most females—and certainly not little ones—did not handle weapons. It was a man thing. So when Betty wanted to join the men in the competition, Paul and Earl laughed and told her to go on back home and play with her dolls. When Edsel, slyly suggested that they give her a chance, they objected, "She can't shoot." But he insisted. "Oh, come on, let her have a chance. What's the harm?" So they relented and decided to let Betty have a turn. Imagine their amazement when she knew how to hold the weapon, got off a good shot, and hit the bull's eye. In fact, she out-gunned her father and both of her brothers. They could not believe that this girl, their daughter and sister, was a deadeye. For Betty it was one of her finest childhood moments. Later she said that she was sure that she was never able to impress the men in the family so thoroughly again. Of course Edsel shared in her triumph, and surely all of them were proud of her.

Long before Betty won the family rifle championship, before she was even on the scene, rifle practice was a regular entertainment for the Simms men. Edsel remembered that it was almost a daily recreation in warm weather. They had a shooting gallery of tin cans which they lined up along the fence post on the hillside, about 100 yards above the back side of the house, in front of a pine thicket. Of course Eula hated the whole dangerous game, and warned anyone leaving the safe confines of the house to use the outhouse to watch out for the gun-slingers, even though the men were cautiously aiming and firing their weapon in the opposite direction from the john. With so much practice, both brothers and father were fine marksmen, which made Betty's achievement that much more remarkable. Years later Edsel said, "I was a good shot at one time, but I got over it."

The brothers sometimes used their rifles for a sport other than blasting apart tin cans; sometimes they went hunting for small game—squirrels, rabbits, opossums. On one inelegant occasion Earl fired at a squirrel but only wounded him. The crippled animal tried to escape by running up a tree, but the brothers grabbed him. The desperate creature jumped on Edsel and bit the living daylights out of him, leaving a scar that he claimed late in life that he still had. Earl knocked the squirrel off his brother's shoulder and pounded the unfortunate critter to death.[1]

Squirrels, rabbits, and opossums were about the only game available to southwest Virginians in early twentieth century Appalachia. Earl, Edsel, and Elva did not remember ever seeing wild turkeys, beaver, or bear, nor, even deer, a sure sign of the devastating toll on the once animal and tree rich land taken by deforestation. The loss of forests to settlement by pioneers like our ancestors, from the timbering industry which denuded the land, and from the blight that wiped out the once plentiful chestnut trees, destroyed the animals' habitat.

Thus hunting for the Simms men was reduced to a minor sidelight, not a serious endeavor. It was a game, a sport consisting, for the most part, of firing at inanimate objects. Still, it was an achievement for a mere "girl" not only to be able to handle a .22 safely, but to shoot the "eyes" out of the target.

Betty did love the challenge of competition in most any game, whether it was cards, or checkers, or gun-slinging, but her specialty was croquet. She was a crackerjack player and had almost everything she needed for that sport, a croquet set with wickets, balls, and mallets, a nice level lawn area, and plenty of time. There was one missing ingredient—a ready opponent, someone to "beat." Always on the lookout for a competitor, Betty often coaxed the mailman off his horse for a game or two. By the time he arrived at the Simms house, he was at the end of his route and ready for some relaxation, so he was easily talked into a round of lawn ball with the charming little girl. Despite her size and age, Betty was determined and skilled and usually won.

As the only child at home, Betty didn't have anyone to get in trouble with, except her nephew Keith when he was there to aid and abet, but generally she had to manage that feat all by herself. On those occasions, she often ran afoul of her mother. In one of her little girl tantrums, Betty threw her dolls down the steps, not a very smart move so close to Christmastime. Eula was quick to warn her daughter that Santa would know about such ugly behavior, her disrespect for her old toys, and for that he might not bring her anything new that year. In fact, she added, "Santa might just stuff your stockings with switches and ashes." She made Christmas morning an anxious time for bad, little Miss Betty when she tiptoed down the stairs and peeped around the corner into the front room to see if her stockings were filled with the dreaded switches and ashes. But, as he always did, Santa came through with new dolls and toys.

As Betty grew older, she grew wiser and a little devious. She knew that her mother, for some inexplicable reason, did not believe that a child could unintentionally break anything—a glass, a dish, a lamp. One time, when Betty was practicing her dancing—prancing and spinning around the parlor—she accidentally knocked over a lamp and it shattered. Cleverly she put Sweet Pea, the dearly loved cat, into the room, closed the door, and said nothing. The "bad" cat got the blame and no one got punished.

That time Betty held her tongue, but she wasn't always as circumspect. One of those unfortunate occasions occurred when Eula asked her daughter to mind the store. That was a two-handed job. On one hand, it was boring because there were so few customers to wait on, but on the other hand, it was a chance for undisturbed reading, a pastime the often lonely child loved. No sooner had Betty swept the store floor, straightened up, and settled in with her book, than her mother appeared at the door. Certain that Eula had something more for her to do, some way to upset her reading plans, and before she could get the words back in her mouth, Betty blurted out, "You get out of here." As soon as she saw her mother's face, she apologized, but it was too late. A great silence descended over the farm house for several punishing days.

In 1942, the sassy 13-year old was ready for high school. Like the other Simms children, Betty was enrolled in Ferrum Training School, but unlike the others, she flamed out, and quit after only two weeks. When her father came to school to take her to the dentist, his little girl dissolved into tears, confessing to him how miserable she was. That tough old guy melted and brought his "baby" back home. It was awfully quiet in the Simms home without any children there—the first time in 37 years. Besides Betty had an educational option her siblings never had, a public high school at Ferrum High School. Unlike Ferrum Training School, it was free. She exercised that option and missed out on the excellent education her brothers and sister received at Ferrum Training School.

Betty was a bit wicked but she was also witty and charming, and grew into a beautiful young woman. And she thought I was adorable. We loved one another to death. When she was home from college during her winter breaks and I was visiting, she allowed me to be her bed-fellow. I considered this a special treat, even though I knew I was being used for a noble purpose, to warm up the ice cold sheets for my cunning aunt, who came to bed later than I did and scooted me over to the frigid side of the bed.

Betty was more like my sister than my aunt; after all, we were closer in age than she and her actual sister, my mother. I was sure I would grow up to be just like her—pretty and confident with hundreds of boys in love with me, that I would be witty and entertaining, and go off to college. Well, I did go to college, and I do have a good sense of humor—I'm still working on the other part.

Betty Simms spraying the author with a hose. c1944

In my efforts to emulate my glamorous aunt, I tried out her make up—smearing "paint" all over my face—and squirting on her *Evening in Paris* perfume in the cobalt blue little bottle. And with a devious streak of my own, I read her voluminous collection of love letters, which she kept unlocked and stashed away in clear sight inside her closet. I will never forget the sad day after Betty became engaged to George Hayes and decided to "clean house." I watched with horror from the sleeping porch while she stood over a stump near the spring house and burned all that great reading material. I thought to myself, "How can she do this to me?" That was the first time I realized that Betty wasn't perfect.

Of course, neither Betty nor Edsel was perfect. They both caused their parents anguish—showing up missing, reading on the sly, breaking perfectly good lamps, ruining perfectly good fruit. In many ways the brother and sister were opposites. Edsel was serious, deliberate, and hardworking; Betty was witty, fun-loving, and a little spoiled. In spite of differences in their age and personality, the two of them had a warm and loving relationship.

Notes for Chapter X, The Children: Edsel and Betty:

1. In the interview during the retelling of this story the discussion diverged to the treatment of injured animals. There were six of us there—Edsel, Elva, Edsel's daughter Judy Strawn, Earl's grandson Paul Keith Simms and me gathered around Uncle Earl's bed, who at the time was 95, and spent most of his day in bed. Listening to this tale about the injured squirrel, Paul Keith remarked that the moral to the story was "Don't mess with an angry squirrel." Then the conversation moved on to the subject of killing wounded animals as the kindest cure. Judy said, "If you drive along and hit a rabbit, you have to stop your car, back up and run over it again to be sure it is good and dead." Elva said that she was certain her brothers would have finished off the squirrel and not allowed it to be crippled without "doing something about it." She then told about her own efforts in animal kindness. How she took the half-dead birds her cat, Gandhi the Hun, dragged into the house, back outside and beat the poor little things over their heads with rocks to put them out of their misery. After those stories Paul Keith came up with another moral. He sure as heck didn't want to show up hurt around any of these family members!

11a
Earl and Elva at Ferrum Training School

Boarding school. Sounds like an option for over-privileged teenagers. Beginning in 1914 there was such an option in a remote section of the Blue Ridge Mountains of Virginia, but it was designed for young people without advantage, or in fact, without any other alternative for a high school education. That was when Ferrum Training School (FTS), located in the town of Ferrum in the depths of Franklin County, opened its doors to any young person who wanted to continue beyond the ninth grade.

Earl and Elva Simms were among the fortunate "country" children who took advantage of this opportunity. They remembered their days at Ferrum with affection and in exquisite detail. They could tell you the layout of the campus, the location of their rooms, the names of their roommates and friends, their teachers and the classes they taught. They recalled the rules, the work requirements, embarrassing incidents, hair and dress styles, dining room manners, the food, Dr. Benjamin Beckham, the social life, student entrepreneurs, and the honor system—impressions which remained vivid in their minds all their lives.

The minute they drove up to the campus, in the fall of 1920 for Earl, who was 14, and 1921 for Elva, who was 13, members of the two literary societies, the Beckhams and the Athenians, greeted all new students with pleas to join their clubs. "Be a Beckham" or "Be an Athenian," they urged. The Beckham team must have been more persuasive to Earl and Elva because they both selected this group. The societies were rival organizations that competed throughout the school year in debates and public speaking—important features of Ferrum life. The origin of the debating

Ferrum Training School, c1925

clubs can be traced to the Southern collegiate experience before the Civil War. Their purpose was to prepare young men to be effective lawyers and congressmen, skilled in the fine art of oratory. The Ferrum clubs were following in that old, established tradition.

After her encounter with the debating society representatives, Elva received her dormitory assignment from staff members who had set up tables on the front lawn. She walked along the main pathway of the campus with its buildings laid out single file facing west. She passed by the faculty residences of the assistant principal, Mr. James Batten, and the president, Dr. Benjamin Beckham with Mrs. Beckham's rose garden separating the two houses; she continued on by John Wesley Hall, (the boy's dormitory), the Administration building that housed classrooms, book store and offices, and finally she came to Centennary Hall, the girl's dormitory which had rooms on the three main floors and the dining hall in the downstairs daylight basement. Her first room was on the third floor, a dormer room, the second from the right when facing the building.

The boys' dormitory, John Wesley Hall, was the first building erected on the campus. The design for Wesley Hall set the pattern for both dormitories; they were large, handsome red brick structures, each with a flight of stairs leading to a covered front porch and dormers on the top floor.

The Simms children's initial experience away from home affected each of them differently. Earl was homesick; he missed his family and his mother's cooking. He sent the biscuits, made of coarsely ground whole wheat, served in the dining hall home to his parents to demonstrate that the food they had to eat was simply awful. Elva on the other hand enjoyed Ferrum from her very first day. She found a congenial group of friends and relatives—her first cousin Wilma Brogan and half-aunt Delma Simms—to help her navigate through the new school, and brother Earl had already been there a year when she entered. She was a picky eater with a small appetite and didn't miss the pleasures of her mother's kitchen the way Earl did, nor did she miss the household drudgeries that were hers back in Endicott.

Even though Earl soon adjusted to the new environment, settling in, making friends and a place for himself, picking up the affectionate nickname "Chink"—his fellow students thought his high cheekbones, (a feature he inherited from his mother), made him look like a Chinaman—he continued to dread returning to FTS after the summer vacations, but Elva couldn't wait to get back to school.

During Earl's first or second year at Ferrum, the older boys thought he was ripe for a little joke, so they took him out on a snipe hunt. But they misjudged Earl's cleverness, probably because he was small for his age. The boys accompanied him deep into the woods, handed him a burlap bag, and instructed him to hold it at an angle so they could drive the snipes into it. They left him there alone and pretended to go off in search of the critters, no doubt giggling to themselves. Earl said that he was "kindly on" to what was happening and wanted to make the trick backfire. He left the bag there, open and ready to receive a snipe, crept out of the woods and back to school, but not back to his room. Instead he crawled into the upper bunk bed in his friend Jim Keith's room. The older fellows stayed out all night searching for Earl, all the while he was snug in bed. They didn't find him until the next morning when they went in to breakfast, and there he was.

After choosing their debating clubs, getting settled in their rooms, acquainted with their roommates, matriculating, and registering for classes, Earl and Elva along with all the other students received their work assignments. Unlike most boarding schools, Ferrum required all students to work at chores around the school and on the farm—to run the school and to help pay for their education.

The actual cost for one year, including tuition, room, and board was $200, but students were charged $100 or less, depending on need. FTS opened its doors to any young person who wanted to attend, and provided generous scholarships to any students who needed financial assistance. The Honorable E. Lee Trinkle, governor of Virginia (1922-1926) stated, "Through the work program, it was possible for a student to pay the entire cost of attending Ferrum. Given the opportunity, the latent ability of the under-privileged student of the southern mountains broke forth into the greatest piece of work accomplished by any institution in Virginia."[1] In spite of the splendid opportunity the school offered, most of the children Elva and Earl grew up with did not continue their education beyond the eighth grade.

"We have no idlers," said Dr. Beckham, "everyone works at Ferrum."[2] All students participated, so work on campus was an accepted and unifying feature of the school. Students spent the equivalent of one day a week (two hours a day) at various tasks around school or on the farm. Miss Ames was in charge of assigning and organizing duties for the girls, Mr. Burke (or was it Mr. Cook?), for the boys. Except for the early morning breakfast routine, each student kept the same assignment for an entire semester.

Naturally the girls worked in the kitchen, helping the beloved cook Mrs. Harnsberger with preparing and serving the food, as well as with cleaning up after the meals. The girls reported for breakfast duty at 4 a.m. Because of the demands of the job, after a two-week stint, they were compensated with a month free from all work. For the other meals, the girls alternated between lunch and dinner for two weeks at a time. Girls also cleaned the classrooms daily, swept the halls, and scrubbed the bathrooms. Elva remembered that one of the girls on her floor, in charge of the large bathroom, with its open toilet area and enclosed shower stalls, took pride in keeping it spotless. Perhaps it was the novelty of having an indoor facility that motivated her! One of the unique features of FTS bathrooms was self-flushing toilets. The seats remained in an upright position until needed. The action of pulling down the seats opened a valve and released water for flushing when the seats sprang back up.

The boys did the manual labor, emptying the trash, making the fires, and shoveling coal for the boiler, which was in the administration build-

Elva Simms, c1925

ing—located between the girls and boys dormitories. A local business delivered the coal by horse and wagon unloading it in a heap behind the administration building. This one furnace heated the main building and the two dormitories. The steam it generated traveled through exterior pipes, which were connected to the buildings and elevated high enough for students to walk under.

Another of the boys' responsibilities was taking care of the farm under the direction of the farm manager, Mr. Scott. He had the young men feed and tend to the animals, milk the cows in the dairy, plant crops in the spring and harvest them in late summer and early fall. Clayton Brooks, one of Earl's roommates, worked regularly on the dairy farm, returning to their dormitory room every evening with manure saturating his shoes. In self defense, Earl and his other roommate put Clayton's boots on the roof outside their window.

Most students went home for summer vacation, but some returned for two to four weeks to earn extra money. Elva spent one summer session working in the school's cannery, processing vegetables and fruits for use in the cafeteria during the following year. While there she and the other student workers slept in the dormitories and ate in the dining hall.

In addition to general farm labor, the boys gathered rocks from the fields, stacked them in piles, loaded them into wagons, and hauled them to construction sites. The new school needed raw materials for its vigorous building program. By the early 1920s, after only six years in operation, Ferrum had completed construction of six buildings on campus: the administration building, (later named Beckham Hall); the boys' dormitory, (John Wesley Hall); the president's house; White Cottage, (additional housing for boys); Centenary Hall, (the girls' dormitory which also housed two separate dining halls—one for the boys and one for the girls, later named Roberts Hall); several outbuildings (barns and the cannery); and by 1925, a new place of worship, Schoolfield Memorial Chapel.

Students earned their way working around the campus and on the farm, but the most important business at Ferrum, as at any school, was education. Elva said proudly that the quality of instruction at Ferrum was excellent, much better than most public high schools in western Virginia at that time. Radford College professors said that they could recognize Ferrum graduates because they were well prepared for college work. Elva went from Ferrum to Blackstone, a Methodist college located in the heart of Virginia, where she earned an associate degree and a teaching certificate. Earl went on to become a successful businessman in the Roanoke Valley. The thinking in the Simms family was that the girls needed a college education more than the boys, because they would probably become teachers or nurses, professions that required additional study. The boys would become farmers, an occupation in which they could earn a "PhD" right at home.

The course of instruction at Ferrum was standard high school fare—domestic science, agriculture, music; English with Miss Ames; French and Latin with Miss Lottie Garrett, who became so emotional when she read *Les Miserables* in French and translated it for her class that she had her students crying right along with her; science with Dr. Frank Hurt;[3] and math with the incompetent Mr. Matthews. It was the only class Elva ever failed, but she had a lot of company. Thirty-nine other students in the class also failed; the only two who passed were repeaters. There was not a formal physical education course, but every day, around four in the afternoon, the girls took long walks accompanied by one of the female teachers. Ferrum was surrounded by 200 acres of green rolling hills and had many inviting places to walk. Cook's Knob, a small mountain near campus, was a favorite destination for the girls' constitutionals.

Any child, including Earl and Elva, who attended Ferrum Training School in the years between 1914 and 1934 knew, admired and respected Dr. Benjamin Moore Beckham, the school's first president. During Ferrum's struggling early years, he was the school's guiding light. He provided the missionary zeal necessary to help found the school, and once established, the spiritual leadership, the financial development, and all the other contributions of a school president. Before coming to Ferrum, Dr. Beckham, an ordained minister, was in charge of the Danville district of the Methodist Episcopal Church, South. In 1909 the Women's Mission

Society of the church asked him to establish and lead a coeducational high school in western Virginia. Even though he had no experience in school administration, he accepted the challenge of providing a Christian education for children in the isolated mountains of the southern Blue Ridge.[4]

Dr. Beckham and his teachers carefully organized the school day around academics, work and religion. He required students to attend church on Sunday and a 30-minute chapel service, which he conducted, every day. He was aware of the temptations that afflicted young people, particularly those growing up in Franklin County, the "moonshine capital of the world." He concluded almost every talk with a lecture on the evils of drink, using charts and graphs to emphasize his points. Mr. James Batten, the handsome chaplain and assistant principal, led the Sunday service and taught the compulsory Bible classes.

In the first years of the school's existence, the entire student body was able to worship together at St. James Methodist Church, the small Federal style church in the town of Ferrum. But as the school grew, students had to attend St. James in shifts. Dr. Beckham, unhappy with the divided sessions, began holding Sunday services in the auditorium on the top floor of the administration building. He considered this a temporary and unsatisfactory arrangement for a church-related school, and took as his next challenge the erection of a chapel on campus, large enough for all of "his" students. The construction of Schoolfield Memorial Chapel was a major accomplishment for Dr. Beckham, who was responsible for every aspect of the new building—raising the money, designing the building, and supervising the construction. Elva often said, "I can still see him standing there, admiring and watching the building of his chapel." In 1925 her class was the first to graduate in the new chapel. Today a modern church has replaced Schoolfield Memorial Chapel. Named Schoolfield Hall, it is also home to Sale Theater.

Ferrum administrators took seriously their responsibility to guide the ethics and morals of the students. The faculty and staff, concerned equally about honor and scandal, had rules to cover both. The honor system was simple and straight-forward: no one would lie, cheat or steal. Students signed a pledge that they had neither given nor received help on a test or an assignment. So far as Earl and Elva knew, no one every cheated; they honored their promise.

In contrast the rules to protect students and the school from scandal were endless, or so they seemed to students, and governed every facet of social life. There were rules for dress, rules for work and meals, and rules about contact with the opposite sex. Administrators posted the latest edicts in each dormitory, numbered 1 through 12, and updated them regularly.

The dress code stressed simplicity and modesty: "Fine clothes are out of taste at this school... Simplicity is at all times to be desired as the Bible commands."[5] The requirements for girls' clothes determined sleeves to be below the elbow and skirts to be below the knee. Eula, not aware of this particular regulation, sent her daughter a dress with short sleeves—an illegal garment. Elva got a demerit for wearing the dress, but thought she should send the bad mark home to her mother. None of this would have been a problem the year before when all students wore uniforms, but the school had dispensed with them by 1921, the year Elva came to Ferrum.

The rules required boys to wear coats to dinner. Earl wrote home that all the boys rebelled one hot spring day by wearing shirts only. For this show of rebellion the administrators penalized the young men with demerits and additional work. To retaliate, the boys appeared the next night in their winter overcoats. We might ask whom they thought they were punishing.

Because the school was coeducational, Dr. Beckham was most concerned about contact between the sexes—trying desperately and futilely to prevent any. Ferrum Training School dictated that scholarship and study were the most important part of student life. A rule stated, "Whenever a student yields to the temptation of 'falling in love,' there is always the distinct loss in the matter of studies."[6] In spite of policies, multiple rules, regulations, and vigilance by administration and faculty, the young people at Ferrum found ways to communicate and even to fall in love. The major path of communication between the sexes was an intricate network—their version of the information highway—the center of which was the kitchen. There, boys who shoveled coal met girls who helped with meals. Less secure sites were classrooms, where passing notes was more easily detected by ever-watchful teachers. Earl and Elva participated in this message swap. He passed notes to Millie Gilbert, his girl friend from Patrick County; her brother Odum was one of his roommates during his last year at Ferrum. Elva's most embarrassing note came from an unintended "postage." Her first year, as a ninth grader, she had a crush on an older boy, Ruben Shepherd, with whom she had been carrying on an eye-flirtation. Following the example of her young aunt and roommate, Delma Simms, who was always sending and receiving "love letters" from one or another of her many boy friends, Elva decided that she wanted to join the fun. She wrote as passionate a love note as her naïve mind could imagine to Ruben, never intending to send it; instead, she threw it into the waste basket. When the boys came to collect the trash, they found the note and delivered it to Ruben. Elva was mortified when she discovered this treachery. Not only did she suffer the torture of teasing by her classmates, she also fell out of love with Ruben. She even came to despise him, especially when he continued to flirt with her.

Once a month or so, the school officials held "socials" (actually restricted-dating) and allowed the teenaged boys and girls to walk together side by side, sometimes even holding hands—but only in designated areas and under the suspicious gaze of the faculty. The administrators limited the socials to campus walks, and under no circumstances did they permit dancing. At all other times, the staff kept the sexes apart, except during class. They established a clear, if imaginary, dividing line at the administration building. Beyond that point girls could not walk down toward the boys' dormitory, and boys could not walk up toward the girls' dormitory.

The barrier between the sexes was not absolute; the administrators allowed a few exceptions, some for classes and some for entrepreneurial purposes. Elva and the girls who took music lessons had to cross the "sexual" border to go to the basement of the boys' dormitory, where the pianos were kept, to practice and take lessons. Earl, on the other hand, crossed over to the female side to conduct business. He set up a shop on the steps outside the girls' dormitory where he sold candy. Using his father's license (and his permission), Earl purchased merchandise at a discount from Hurt's store in Ferrum. He took another boy with him to help lug his wares back to school, and in payment gave his assistant a free piece of candy. He sold chewing gum and candy to the girls at his "store" on the steps and to the boys out of a trunk in his room.

There were, of course, consequences for breaking the rules, an elaborate system of demerits which a miscreant could reduce with additional work. Elva said there were so many rules it was almost impossible to avoid breaking them. While she was at FTS, her first cousin Fred Brogan was the chief offender; he broke every rule and usually got caught, or because of his reputation, blamed for any unsolved "crime." His most famous violation was setting off dynamite 100 feet in front of the boys' dormitory. With such dangerous escapades, it was no wonder that Fred spent most of his time at Ferrum expunging his demerits. Elsie Brogan, his older sister, however, was little Miss Perfect, rarely collecting any demerits at all.

Elva was fortunate to have her half-aunt Delma Simms for her first roommate. Delma was a year or two older than Elva and experienced at dormitory living, because she had spent two years boarding at Radford High School before transferring to Ferrum. Elva's father Paul drove the two girls to Ferrum for their first day. As they were leaving, Eula called to Delma, "watch out for my little girl." Delma honored the charge by instructing her niece about the school's rules and regulations and helping her to settle into the routine of life away from home. Elva's second year roommates were her girlhood best friends Glendola Thomas and Amy Simms, Delma's sister. Her third and fourth year roommates were Gertie Ross and her beloved cousin Wilma Brogan, Fred and Elsie's sister.

Like everything else at Ferrum, there were rules for proper behavior in the dining room. They required all students to stand until Miss Ames, at the faculty table, tapped her bell and asked someone to say the blessing. Only then did she nod her head, allowing the hungry youngsters to sit down and begin eating. Elva and five of her friends and relations: Wilma, Elsie, Delma, Mildred Elliott, and one other girl ate together at the same table for an entire year. Provoked by the long wait for sustenance and to mock the niceties of the dining system, the girls created an informal eating club, called themselves "The Grabbing Six" and adopted the motto: "Root pig or die".

Elva, her roommates, and her friends across-the-hall often had midnight feasts, inspired by boxes of goodies from home or shopping trips into Ferrum. The late-night parties were against the law. Bedtime was 10 p.m.; but after bed check, the friends would gather in one of their rooms for the festivities. Their parties usually went undetected, but one night a neighboring girl, excluded and jealous, reported the troublemakers to Miss Ames and Miss Tony, the hall proctor, who walked in on the revelers and punished them with the surprise visit and, of course, more demerits.

Girls, even in backwater Virginia in the early 1920s, wanted to keep up with current fashion. It was the era of major change in hairstyles—the new look was the bob, a very short, boyish cut. Before this time, most of the young girls arrived at Ferrum wearing their hair long and pulled back in buns against the back of their heads. As for Elva, she had never cut her hair and wore pigtails; her mother had brushed and plaited her hair every day of her life. But she was growing up and wanted to participate in the new rage. To avoid trouble with Miss Tony and the school "cops," she asked Delma to help her gain her mother's permission for the haircut. In what must have been a dramatic scene, her friend Georgia Nicely cut off 13-years worth of Elva's thick dark brown hair, and in the process acquired a giant blister on her right thumb. On Elva's next visit home, she was anxious about her parents' reaction to her new look. She needn't have worried—they both thought their daughter looked adorable with her bob.

After the original shearing, Lawson Cabiness, a handsome student with blue eyes and black hair, became the regular barber for Elva and the other girls. He set up shop in one of the downstairs reception rooms of the girls' dormitory, brought his clippers and scissors, and provided his service at regular times during the week—charging 15 to 25 cents for each cut. He used his earnings to help pay his way through school. The enterprising boy went on to college and medical school, and eventually practiced medicine in Roanoke.

Among Earl's friends and roommates were Ted Richardson, who later became the manager of the school's dairy farm, Claytor Brooks, famous for his smelly boots and flat nose, and Jim Keith, his senior roommate, best friend and namesake of his only son.

As good friends often do, Jim and Earl "covered" for one another on several occasions. Jim had provided shelter for Earl when he was the intended victim of the senior boys' snipe hunt. Earl protected his friend Jim on another occasion, one that came close to causing them both serious trouble and the Beckham family grave embarrassment, if not disgrace.

The boys had heard from their male classmates that a local black family had a particularly tasty apple cider for sale. Jim and Earl left campus with directions to the "merchant's" house and plans to purchase the homemade brew. Unfortunately, the family had sold out of cider, but they did have moonshine. Earl and Jim did not resist; they bought the white lighnin'—even though it violated Ferrum's prohibition against alcohol.

On their walk back to school, Jim took several swigs from the jug. Earl, however, did not sample the liquor because he had made a promise to his father that he would not drink until after he graduated; in exchange his dad would buy him a horse and saddle. Jim, under no such pledge, became tipsy and began to stagger. The friends arrived at school just in time to have themselves counted present during roll call before dinner. Earl's trial was not yet over. He had to save his intoxicated friend from detection. Jim fell over on Earl who had to hold him upright during the blessing. Once they were seated, Earl had to kick Jim under the table repeatedly to keep his friend from putting his head down and going to sleep. Everyone knew Dr. Beckham was opposed to drinking and how he made that opposition clear almost every day during his chapel talks. If he had discovered that Jim had been drinking, he would have expelled him. But he may have found it awkward because Jim was Mrs. Beckham's nephew. Fortunately, Jim went undetected and Beckham was spared the unpleasant duty of expelling his wife's relative.

Students in their last year received senior privileges. They could study in the privacy of their rooms instead of in the classrooms during study hall; senior boys and girls could play tennis together. Elva and Wilma had a regular tennis date with Ed Derby and Albert Lynch every morning before breakfast. The boys pitched a pebble against the screen of their dormitory window—first floor, second room from the end—to let the girls know they were there and would meet them on the tennis court. This was one of Elva's happiest memories of her high school years.

After graduation Earl and Elva went in different directions. Earl kept his promise to his father not to drink until he was 18, and as a reward received $400 rather than the horse and saddle Paul had promised him in return. He used his graduation prize toward the purchase of a little black Ford roadster and drove his friend Jim Keith home to Norfolk, Jim's hometown. There the young men took the train to Virginia Beach and went swimming in the ocean—exciting firsts for the new graduate.

Elva went to college. She was influenced in her decision by a persuasive speech given by an administrator from Blackstone Junior College who had come to Ferrum Training School to encourage the senior girls to continue their education at Blackstone, a Methodist college for women. Elva was also inspired to look beyond Ferrum by her friend Mildred Elliot who said, "I'm not going to stop with a high school degree."[7] To pay for her first year at Blackstone, Elva received a scholarship, worked on campus and borrowed $200 from the ever-affluent Earl. Her second year was easier because her father paid her way. She earned an associate degree in 1927, at that time, that was all she needed to teach in the public schools.

The Simms young adults, along with hundreds of others, went on to successful and fulfilling lives made possible by the splendid education they received at Ferrum Training School. From 1917, the first graduating class until 1925, (Elva's class of 40, the largest to date) there were 143 graduates—the majority of whom went on to college.[8] Their high school prepared them for advanced education and adulthood, and gave them four happy and satisfying years—not to mention a rich supply of stories to share with us all.

Addendum: From the very beginning Ferrum Training School was run by hard-working, highly-qualified trustees and administrators who dedicated themselves to its success. After they founded Ferrum, they continued their educational mission, by establishing elementary schools in remote areas of Franklin, Floyd, and Patrick counties, and at Syria in Madison County to serve as feeder institutions. These schools satisfied the dual purpose of educating younger children and providing a steady supply of students to their high school. (The Simms children's feeder school was at Trinity Church in Endicott, located on the Griffith Hill, ten miles from Ferrum.) In 1926, aware of a shift in the state's attitude toward public education, the Board recognized a threat to their boarding school at Ferrum. Virginia, which until that time had been willing to leave the responsibility for primary and secondary education to the church, began establishing high schools in the parts of the state it had previously neglected. To survive and continue to thrive, the Methodist Church administrators expanded Ferrum into a junior college, retaining the high school and adding a two year business degree. The junior college experiment lasted from 1927 to 1929, was discontinued when it proved too expensive. It was reestablished in 1940. In 1949 Ferrum dropped the high school program and became a junior college. In 1971 it grew to its current status as a four year college.

The trustees and the Methodist Church have been justifiably proud of their accomplishment in the hills of Virginia. Dr. Beckham, who retired from FTS in 1934, wrote, "I am glad that I came to Ferrum and am thankful for the thousands of young people I have been able to help to better living, because most of them would not have had the chance they have had if Ferrum had not been."[9]

Notes for Chapter XI, A, Earl and Elva at Ferrum Training School:

1. Hurt, Frank Benjamin, *A History of Ferrum College, 1914 – 1974, An Uncommon Challenge*, Roanoke, VA, The Stone Printing Co., June 1977, p. 33.

2. Ibid., p. 46.

3. Dr. Hurt wrote *A History of Ferrum College.*

4. The need for educational opportunity in southwest Virginia was obvious. In 1910 within the counties of Patrick, Henry and Franklin only 1,400 of 9,400 children of high school age were enrolled in school. Hurt, *A History of Ferrum College*, p. 12.

5. Ibid., p. 36.

6. Ibid., p. 37.

7. Mildred became a nurse. Another friend from Franklin County, Beatrice Goode, went to Longwood College and earned a teacher's certificate.

8. Hurt, *A History of Ferrum College*, p. 61.

9. Ibid., p. 63.

11b
Edsel at Ferrum Training School

Edsel Simms was a model student at Ferrum Training School, graduating second in his class, and earning very few demerits. He said, "I didn't break many rules, but I did bend a few."

It wasn't easy for the young teenager, only 13 in the fall of 1929—his first year at Ferrum. His older brother and sister had graduated and gone on with their lives, but they had no doubt filled their young brother's ears with tales about their time at Ferrum and warned him about what to expect, especially about the endless rules and regulations he would encounter. Edsel appeared to adjust to boarding school life immediately. He made friends with his roommate Charles Cherry, who was from Richmond, and he already knew his other roommate Stewart Edwards, a boy from Long Branch, only several miles from his home. Among his other friends were Glenn Rakes, also from Endicott, and Edward Rudder, who had come to Ferrum all the way from California. But when Edsel, always a private person who kept his emotions locked inside, returned to campus after Christmas vacation, he became homesick and hid in the attic of the boys' dormitory so that no one would know how lonely and sad he was.

Working at Ferrum, on campus and on the school's farm, was a requirement for all students. Edsel's first assignment was at the dairy barn. Even at 13 he had more experience milking cows and farm work in general than most of the other boys. In fact, he taught Teddy Richardson, the man who had been one of his brother Earl's roommates and was now in charge of the dairy operation, an important lesson. Edsel told Teddy that his dad had drilled into him that the first step in milking a cow was to clean her bag, but Teddy said he considered that a waste of time because the milk was going to be strained and that would take care of any dirt. Before long, however, Edsel overheard Teddy instructing the new boys in the 'art of milking.' "As a sanitary measure you must be sure to clean the cow's udder before you begin milking her."

Some of Edsel's best Ferrum stories came from his friendship with the boys from Cuba. Missionaries from the Methodist Church had "invaded" Cuba, converted some families to the Protestant religion, and persuaded parents to send a few of their sons to attend high school at Ferrum. President Beckham introduced the young boys from Cuba and proudly announced that they were the first students to pay full tuition; that meant that they were exempt from chores.

The Cubans, who spoke little or no English, lived in the dormitory near Edsel. He realized that the foreigners needed someone to assist them in adjusting to life in this strange new place, so he befriended them. He escorted the boys to the annual school picnic held on Cook's Knob, and when one of them got lost on his way back to school, Edsel joined in the search to find him. (A local farmer rescued the frightened boy. When the student showed the man his room key with the Ferrum Training School label, he knew where to send him.) To demonstrate their appreciation for all Edsel's kindnesses, the Cubans gave him a few Spanish lessons so that he would have an advantage over the other students once classes began. Unfortunately, they taught him words he didn't understand. On the first day of class when the teacher, Senorita Lolita, also from Cuba, asked if anyone knew any Spanish words, the normally shy Edsel quickly raised his hand and jumped up to show off his new skill in the language. He realized soon after he began speaking that something was terribly wrong; he could tell by the expression on Senorita Lolita's face which was glowing red. She pointed to her young countrymen and gave them a look of disgust. They had taught Edsel to curse like a sailor; he had asked his teacher to kiss him in an inappropriate place.

At the end of the school year, Edsel took his Cuban friends to the Ferrum train station to begin their long journey home. He knew that he would need a large vehicle to haul the boys' footlockers and other luggage. His first choice was the school truck, but it was unavailable, tied up with farm work, so he resorted to the school's horse and wagon. Edsel loaded up his Cuban friends' year's worth of gear and hitched up the slightly frisky horse which was unaccustomed to the restraints of bit and bridle. As he drove the wagon across the railroad tracks toward the station, the horse bolted. Edsel did the best he could; he tried to run the horse into the station, but the animal reared up, broke the check line and headed up the bank to the right of the depot. Edsel jumped from the seat in the wagon onto the single tree which connected the horse to the vehicle, then onto the horse. He grabbed the bridle and stopped the animal. Frightened almost to death the Cuban boys screamed in Spanish, and this time Edsel understood exactly what they said. He saw the boys off safely with a fine story to tell about their trip home from Virginia.

After Edsel graduated, his sister Elva came home from Maryland, where she was living at the time, to help him apply for a scholarship to Roanoke College. He won the scholarship and stayed at the college for a year, but, much to Elva's disappointment, he transferred back to Ferrum Training School to take a business degree the school had begun offering.

Back at Ferrum, Edsel had signed up for a business course with Miss Lilla Payne and had arrived in class ahead of time. The elderly teacher needed help hanging a chart and asked Edsel to lend her a hand. While he was up on the ladder, Miss Payne walked between him and the wall, and he accidentally dropped the chart on her head. He watched in horror as her head fell off. That was what he thought happened. Actually, he had only knocked off her wig. She hastily picked up the hairpiece, put it back on her bald head, but managed to get it on crooked. "Now look what you've done," she fussed at Edsel. He apologized profusely and helped her straighten the wig. Mercifully the classroom was empty at the time, but somehow the story got around.

Edsel's one misdeed during his second stint at Ferrum was one he cooked up with another older student, Clarence Howe. The two of them decided to spice up the Junior-Senior prom by spiking the punch. Edsel borrowed his father's car, and he and Clarence drove to Roanoke and bought a gallon of gin. The mischief-makers snuck most of the booze into the pineapple juice punch at the party, but it became so diluted that the only effect it had was on the old maid school teachers who came down with a serious case of the giggles. Clarence and Edsel didn't want the teachers to have all the fun and reserved a fifth for themselves.

Edsel did bend a rule or two while he was at school. More importantly, he excelled in the classroom, worked diligently around campus and on the farm and had many loyal friends during his student years at Ferrum.

12

Religion and Education Over in the Country

"Don't Learn 'A' "

Over in the country in the early part of the twentieth century, religion and education—church and school—were often linked, not so much into a blend of those two crucial elements of society as a mixture of place. Church and school often occupied the same physical space and were operated and supported by the same organization.

Well-meaning missionaries from the Methodist and Episcopal churches came to the Blue Ridge Mountains to establish mission churches right along side schools—a double whammy of good for the isolated peoples of Southwest Virginia. In the Endicott area of Franklin County, the Methodists founded Trinity Methodist Church and School on a hillside at the base of the Griffith Hill, along Runnett Bag Creek Road. The Episcopalians established St. John's-in-the-Mountains Church and School on a bluff southwest of Endicott "proper," along Route 40.

Not all the local schools were associated with churches. In addition to Trinity and St. John's, there were at least four one-and two-room schools: Laurel Bluff located at the extreme western edge of Endicott, at the foot of the roller-coaster ride of a road called Cannaday's Gap; Sandy Level, south of St. John's; Dry Hill, above Otter Creek, near Grandpa Rakes; and our family's beloved Bitty Hill School, on a ridge overlooking the Simms farm. The Simms family was, in fact, the founders of that one-room school. Paul contributed a portion of their land and the materials for its construction, and his brother Gale planned and built the new little place of learning, plain and simple as it was. All four of the Simms children, as well as hundreds of others in the Hurd's Branch neighborhood, attended Bitty Hill primary school during the approximately 23 years of its life (1913—1936). The Simms' family also boarded the teachers, including Miss Lizzie and Miss Lindy Gussler, and then provided their own daughter Elva to be one of the teachers at Bitty Hill, soon after she graduated from Blackstone Junior College. (I don't know this for certain, but I suspect her father used his influence to arrange for her employment.)

School children at Miss Ora's school, which was also St. John's Episcopal Church

"Miss Elvie," as her students called her, had sole responsibility for educating 15 to 20 children who ranged in age from six to twelve. The classroom was a traditional design with student desks on either side of a center aisle, a large teacher's desk and blackboard at the front, and a potbellied stove in the middle of the room. Like the teachers before her, Elva made the fires on cold fall and winter mornings. Someone else ("probably Dad," she said in remembering those years) supplied wood for the stove. She began the school day at 9 a.m. by ringing a hand bell, taught until 3 p.m., with a short recess in the middle of the morning, and an hour at noon for lunch and play.

The building had no running water or indoor plumbing, but the school "system" furnished bathroom facilities across the road, boys outhouse in front, girls in the back, and water from the Simms spring house. Children took turns fighting over the privilege of walking the well-worn path, down the embankment to the spring, and missing school long enough to fetch ice-cold water up the hill for drinking and washing up.

Elva's first year of teaching was fraught with difficulties. For one thing she was admonished by school administrators for not cashing her monthly paychecks. As a new college graduate, only 20 years old, Elva boarded at home and had very few living expenses. When pay day came, the young teacher stashed her $85 check in her underwear drawer for safe keeping. After several months of this "banking" method, Elva received a plea from the school board to please cash her checks because the outstanding monies were causing havoc with the board's accounting system.

For another thing, she was accused by her little brother Edsel's teacher of writing his homework papers. He had begun sixth grade at Trinity School with Elizabeth Hedgepath as his teacher. She could not believe that Edsel's homework, which must have been mighty good, was his own and said, "I have no intention of grading Elva Simms' work." This accusation insulted and infuriated the honorable Edsel, who certainly wrote his own papers, as well as his sister and their parents. They all decided it would be best if he withdrew from Trinity School and enrolled in Bitty Hill, where he became one of Elva's students and a classmate of one of her most memorable and challenging pupils—Charlie Adkins.

Edsel remembered Charlie well. "Oh, yes, he and I threw rocks at one another, regular," Edsel chuckled. "He actually hit me once, then he apologized profusely." So, obviously, that was just a mischievous game, but Charlie was "bad" in serious ways. Edsel claimed that Charlie built himself a still when he was only12-years old and that he carried a gun to school—something Elva didn't know and even doubted.

Her primary concern was teaching this bright, but obstinate, undisciplined young fellow, who showed up at school only when he felt like it, to speak proper English. Among his grammatical errors, Charlie insisted on saying "If I was" instead of "If I were." After repeated oral corrections and no success, Elva gave him an assignment to write seven or eight sentences using the phrase "If I were." Charlie did the work, but the sentences he turned in were not quite what Elva had in mind: "If I were a horse, I would throw you," "If I were a mule I would kick you," "If I were a bull, I would butt you," "If I were a rooster, I would flog you." The teacher thought that she had to give the student an "E" for excellent. After all, he had written his assignment correctly. One of Charlie's classmates objected: "If I were you, Miss Elvie, I would give him a whooping." Charlie Adkins continued to have a troubled life, which ended all too soon in a gun battle.

Charlie was not the only one of her students who did not value his education and was reluctant to attend school. She also had to cope with Dillie Underwood and her son, Joe.[1] One of Elva's administrative duties was to turn in attendance records to a central office in Rocky Mount. She reported that Joe Underwood had attended school on the first day but not a single day after that. The school board followed up with a letter to Dillie, scolding her for not sending her son to class. This enraged Dillie, who lived not too far up Hurd's Branch from the Simms farm. She flew down the hill, prepared to attack her boy's teacher for turning him in, and siccing the authorities on her. Fortunately, Paul saw her coming and could tell by her expression that something was terribly wrong. When he heard how angry she was at his daughter, he headed her off and took her up to the store to cool her down and gave her a piece of candy. Dillie could not understand why anyone cared whether or not she sent her boy to school. After all, she said, "he can't larn anyway." Afterwards she did send Joe to school, and Elva said that he was actually very bright and "larned" just fine. He was just a little lazy and didn't want to bother with school.

Elva's favorite story of an underachiever was about a Whitlock boy who lived with his family and younger brother out on Route 40 beyond St. John's Church. When the younger boy was getting ready for his very first day of school, the older Whitlock fellow gave his little brother this sage advice: "For heaven's sake, kid, don't ever learn A, cause then they'll just make you learn B."

In the mid 1930s the school board built the modern Endicott School along Route 40 between Long Branch and St. John's. The days of the one- and two-room school houses came to an end; Bitty Hill, Laurel Bluff, St. John's and Trinity Schools and all the others in a five or so mile radius closed their doors. My grandfather's "busline" went into operation, collecting youngsters from neighboring hilltops and hollows and delivering them to the new consolidated primary school. The Endicott School had four classrooms and four teachers; one taught the first and second grade, Elva had the third and fourth graders, Mrs. Scott, (formerly Miss Hedgepath), taught fifth and sixth graders, and Miss Thompson served double duty as principal and seventh grade teacher.

The Endicott School

During her educational career, Elva taught at Bitty Hill, at St. John's, (often referred to as Miss Ora's) at Laurel Bluff, and at the Endicott School. Over the years she had difficult students and difficult situations, but none more challenging than her first assignment at the Endicott School. The youngsters arrived with varying degrees of preparation. Elva was dismayed to find that a few of her third graders had a very limited number of words in their reading vocabulary and that many couldn't read a lick. She had the awesome task of teaching those nine-and ten-year olds how to read, starting from scratch. Her supervisor, Mrs. Young, who was from Rocky Mount, realized Elva had a monumental task; she gave her some basic instruction in teaching remedial reading and hoped for the best. Remarkably, by June, in just one school year, Elva had taught all her students to read at the third grade level. Her supervisor was so astonished by Elva's achievement that she brought in her own supervisor from Richmond to hear the children read. It was a proud moment for everyone. Elva said, modestly, "I just did what Mrs. Young told me to do, and it worked."

Elva wasn't the only Simms at the Endicott School; her little sister Betty was also there, as a fifth grade student. Normally Betty would have been assigned to Elizabeth Hedgepath Scott's class, but Elva, worried that Elizabeth would be unfair to her little sister, just as she had been to her little brother, Edsel, interceded and had Betty placed in her own classroom. Betty skipped a grade and went into Miss Thompson's class the next year, avoiding the problem teacher.

Betty said that the only trouble with having Elva as her teacher was to remember to call her "Miss Elva" instead of "Sister." Elva was concerned about proper decorum in the classroom, among the students, and during visits from her supervisor. Not too many years after this, when Betty was in high school, she stopped calling Elva "Sister," considering the name too childish, in favor of "Ebb," the family's pet name for her.

Elva Simms was one of the most successful teachers over in the country during the 1930s and her ability did not go unnoticed by others. None other than the Superintendent of Schools recognized her as the best teacher in Franklin County. There was no official acknowledgement, but Mr. Superintendent told Otha James, who was on the school board and had a son in her class, that Elva Simms was the best teacher he had in the county. Otha told Miss Ora who suggested that the Superintendent actually meant the best teacher in their community. "Oh, no," Otha said, "he meant the best teacher in the county." That news eventually got to the teacher herself. It took Miss Elva 60 years before she told her daughter of this honor, and even then she thought she was bragging too much.

Several other outstanding teachers had great influence on the hundreds of young people who lived in Endicott, particularly Ruth Watson Simms and Miss Ora Harrison. Ruth Watson became Aunt Ruth to us when she married Paul's half brother, Gale Simms, whom she met when he gallantly offered her his seat during a church service. She was an especially capable woman, a school-marm Johnny Appleseed, who established schools all over the surrounding counties, an agent or a missionary for the Methodist Church, both before she was married and after. One of her earliest missions was in Endicott where she was a founding mother of the Trinity School, next to and part of Trinity Methodist Church.

Before her marriage to Uncle Gale, Ruth Watson lived above the Trinity School with another teacher, the notoriously lazy Cousin Sally Cannaday. According to the two young girls who lived with the teachers and helped them with chores around the house—Elsie Brogan, (cousin of the Simms' kids), and Esther Berkeley—Cousin Sally was so lethargic that she wouldn't even rock herself; as a joke the girls got on either side of her chair and pushed it for her.

After Aunt Ruth married Uncle Gale, the couple left Franklin County to set up mission schools in various places, and like military service, spent two years in each location. One of those was Old Pole Bridge in Patrick County, near Saltville. While they were there, Uncle Gale contracted pleurisy and was admitted to the local hospital where they inserted a tube in his side to drain the excess fluid. When he woke the next day, he inexplicably felt severe pain in his leg. From that day forward Uncle Gale was in pain and had a limp. Twenty-five years later while he was in Roanoke Memorial Hospital in preparation for a bladder operation, his doctors took a routine x-ray and discovered that the man had had a broken hip which had gone unset all those years. No doubt he had fallen when he was unconscious in the hospital in Saltville and never knew what happened; no one bothered to tell him.

After their tour of duty in Saltville, Ruth and Gale returned to Endicott where they settled. Over the next 20 years Aunt Ruth taught in most of the local one-room schools—Trinity, Bitty Hill and Laurel Bluff. She taught all the Simms children—Earl, Elva, Edsel, and Betty. Uncle Gale had several careers, he was a carpenter and a revenue agent.

Ruth and Gale rarely lived in one place for very long. They occupied Paul and Eula's tenant house, had their own house just down the road from the Simms farm, and in the 1950s moved into the J. R. Simms homeplace on Runnett Bag Creek Road. They had three children: Celeste, named for a stop on the organ, was never married and became a teacher in Roanoke; Archer Gale, named for his father, was a soldier who fought in and survived WWII and Korea without a scratch, but fell down the stairs back home and broke his neck; and Mary Elizabeth, a special child, who was about Betty's age and one of her playmates. This little cousin had a speech impediment so severe that only her immediate family could understand her. When she went to school, the other children, naturally and cruelly, teased the shy child until she refused to return. Aunt Ruth kept her safe at home and home-schooled her. Mary Elizabeth spent time alone in the woods around her house where she developed a love and knowledge of the natural world. Eventually she learned to speak clearly, married, had a son and lived a normal life.

Aunt Ruth was a notable teacher, but a shockingly shabby housekeeper. She kept piles and piles of magazines and papers stacked up around the house. Once when she was trying to locate a particular article for someone, she remarked: "I know it is here somewhere near the top." Instead of washing dishes, she wiped them off and turned them over, ready for the next meal.

The other prominent teacher over in the country was Miss Ora Harrison, a woman who dedicated her life to that community. She came to

Lucy Cannaday and Miss Ora Harrison, c1920

Endicott from the "other side" of Rocky Mount in 1908 at the age of 26 to teach at the Sandy Level School in the western part of the county, off Route 40. She remained in Endicott until she retired in 1954.

In 1914 she moved from Sandy Level to the new mission school at St. John's Episcopal Church built on twenty-eight acres of land given by I. T. and Lucy Cannaday along with their encouragement, influence, and money. I. T. had grown fond of the Episcopal Church in Rocky Mount when he visited with his friend Judge Lee, a nephew of R.E. Lee. Miss Ora boarded with the Cannadays, who became her friends and patrons, and she taught all their children—Zera, Harry, Ted, Charles, May and Russell.

Like Trinity, St. John's did double duty; it served as a church and a school. A traveling minister conducted religious services on the second Sunday of the month in the exquisite little stone church, and Miss Ora directed Sunday school every Sunday. In fact she rarely allowed the upstairs rooms of the church to remain idle. She kept those rooms hopping all year with Sunday School, regular school and summer school in June, July and August, supposedly for children who had to miss school during planting and harvesting months. But anyone could attend—Elva and Earl, the Brogan children, Amy, Delma, the Cannadays—all went, even though they never missed a day of regular school except for illness. No one wanted to be left out. If school was in session, their parents made sure that their children attended. The St. John's "campus" grew to include a comfortable country house for Miss Ora and her associate Miss Maude Beheler, another Rocky Mount native, a small craft house over the garage where Miss Maude taught local women to weave, a primitive tennis court, a dating spot for Elva and Russell, and a small cemetery surrounded by an iron fence.[2]

After several decades of teaching her beloved mountain children,

Miss Ora had to make several serious and difficult adjustments. In the early 1920s her benefactors and good friends, I.T. and Lucy Cannaday, moved away from the country to a large dairy farm in Sparks, Maryland, a tony area north of Baltimore. They were moving "up" in the world. Even so, Miss Lucy, a wonderfully good-natured person, never adjusted to life "up North." For many summers after the move, she and some of the children returned to their cherished Endicott home. Miss Jenny, I.T.'s mother, did not move to Maryland with the others, and continued to live in the Cannaday country house all year. Miss Ora got to see the Cannadays then, but it was never the same.[3]

The other major change in her life came with the opening of the Endicott School in 1936; it meant the closing of St. John's, affectionately known as Miss Ora's school. She and Miss Maude had to adapt. They turned their enormous store of energy to running the church mission. Miss Ora and Miss Maude were still at work in the late 40s when I went with my family to visit, occasionally attending Vacation Bible School or church on the Sundays the minister held services. In my mind, Miss Ora was a small, active woman with white, whispy hair. She pulled it back to stay out of her eyes, but stray straight bits escaped and got into her face. Maybe it was the hair, or maybe it was the way she held her mouth over her teeth, (which were no doubt false), that made me think that she looked like a tiny, female George Washington.

I remember an ice cream social out on the lawn between the church and the house, and I remember long, boring hours sitting in her living room and endless conversation about who was living where, and who was whose kin, and what those unknown-to-me people were doing now. My parents enjoyed all this local gossip because they knew everyone, but I sure didn't. Now, I know Miss Ora was a great source of genealogy and mountain stories because she knew and cared about everyone and taught most of them at one time or another, but my interest in such things came too late to take advantage of her great cache of information. And I am sure she would have delighted in sharing it all with me and having me write it down. I learned to appreciate her too late.

As in most communities, schools and churches were essential to the people who lived in Endicott during the first half of the twentieth century—their place to learn, to worship, to socialize were often one and the same.

The three churches important to our family were Long Branch Primitive Baptist Church—Eula's church; Trinity Methodist Church—Paul's church; and St. John's Episcopal Church—the Cannadays' church. Many of the ministers who served these churches were circuit riders, men who preached once a month at various mountain missions, traveling on horseback from as far away as 20 miles. The local churches cooperated by having preachings on different Sundays of the month. The Baptists held their religious services on the first Sunday, the Methodists on the third Sunday, and the Episcopalians on the second. All the churches except the Baptist had Sunday School every Sunday. Members of the congregations treated the traveling preachers to Sunday dinner—Eula and Paul Simms often fed the Methodist minister.

Each church had its own history, its own religious practices, and its own beliefs. The Long Branch Primitive Baptist Church was built on a tract of approximately five acres in a valley beside the main road between Crossroads and Endicott, on land donated by James Cannaday II before the Civil War. Long Branch Creek, a tiny rill, ran in back of the church, a natural place for Baptisms, I always thought, but there was not enough water for immersion. Primitive Baptists believed in spontaneity by their preachers and professed confessions with baptism by immersion for their congregants. They celebrated communion only once a year.

The Baptist preachers in my grandmother's day were Tom West and Jim Goode Hash. Both followed the dictates and traditions of the Primitive Baptists by allowing God to speak through them from the pulpit. They did not interfere with the Almighty by preparing a sermon or even sketching down notes about what they would say. They bravely trusted in the Lord to provide inspiration and words when it came time to preach each Sunday. Earl remembered the general lingo and lilt of most of the sermons he heard and could give a short demonstration in the same sing-song chant as the preachers of his youth. His parody of one of those sermons went something like this: "And da ma falldara I went way down yonder a rah and the dog treed a woodchuck a rah and a brush pile and they jumped up on it a rah and they stomped it a rah. And away they went a rah." Now if Earl was right, it appeared that God often only put nonsense into the mouths of his preachers. The real sermons often went on in that sing-song vein for hours.

Tom West was the head preacher at Long Branch before his assistant, Jim Goode Hash, succeeded him. And in the way of the secular world, the succession followed a scandal. It happened around 1920—Elva was about 12-years old, Earl 14. The children remembered Tom West well, prob-

Jim Goode and Nannie Hash with 3 of their children

ably because he had a distinctive, long, white beard that flowed half-way down his chest, and they wondered if he slept with it inside or outside the covers. To Elva and Earl he looked like Moses. Their memory of this old world prophet look-alike was enhanced by the photograph Elva made of him with her brand new Kodak "Brownie Hawkeye" camera, while he was standing in front of the picket fence, over by the grape arbor, one Sunday after church when he was invited to the Simms house for dinner.

From all accounts, Brother West was a good man, but he had a weakness which Baptists did not tolerate: a fondness for drink. When the members of his congregation found out about his drinking, they expelled him. He gave up drinking, returned to the church, confessed his sin, and asked his congregation to forgive him. To remain pastor of the church he had to receive the acceptance and forgiveness of the entire congregation. Everyone voted in his favor except two people, Nannie Snead Hash, (Jim Goode Hash's wife) and her sister Betty Snead Hatcher. Because West did not have a unanimous vote of confidence, he was evicted and his expulsion became the "talk of the country." Eula was furious about the injustice done to her minister. Thanks to his wife and his sister-in-law, Brother Hash became the head preacher at the Long Branch Primitive Baptist Church.

Jim Goode Hash was an interesting and complicated man, ambitious and hard-working. He was given to strange sick spells which forced him to his bed; some thought he suffered from migraine headaches, others whispered the frightening word epilepsy. He excused himself from preaching one Sunday morning by saying, "I have a bellyache, and I just can't go on." Jim Goode was not only a minister, he was also the local postman; sometimes he combined his duties by marrying a couple right beside their mailbox or by preaching a funeral while he was supposed to be on government "business." In addition to delivering the mail, he often carried packages, or food, or messages from one customer to another on his route. Jim Goode was a smart man who worked hard to improve himself; he wanted to get ahead so much that he studied his children's textbooks. This extra effort paid off. He became a notary public and was able to write deeds and to sign official papers and documents.

One of Hash's responsibilities as head of the church was to hear testimonials. The Primitive Baptists required a conversion experience by anyone who wanted to be baptized and join the church as full-fledged members. It was an essential step, they believed, on the way to a heavenly reward. Most of the Baptist conversion experiences were modest, private affairs. My Grandmother Eula, for instance, had a dream that she should join the church. That was enough to qualify her for baptism and membership. The conversion experience of Jaythiney (Ja-thi-nee) Adkins Shively was more dramatic. Jim Goode presided over a gathering of church-goers at the Shively house the evening Jaythiney gave her testimonial. Her husband Lou Shively, sweet natured and easy-going, and her brother Robert Adkins, witty and irreverent, were among the observers. She began the story of her religious change by telling of a dream she had had. In her dream she had seen an angel circling around the house, and she was sure the angel was coming to get her husband Lou. With that, her brother Robert could stay quiet no longer; he spoke up and said, "Why, Jaythiney, that was no angel, that was a buzzard." He put an end to the seriousness of the occasion and the gathering dissolved in laughter. When asked what happened after that, Brother Hash said, "Well, that broke up the meeting."

The next step toward membership in the church was a public event, a Baptism by complete and total immersion. For that, the church fathers needed a deep pool of water, some of which they found in Runnett Bag Creek, (like the natural hole near the Thomas's across from the Peters's), and some of which they created by damming up sections of the local streams and creeks. When Grandpa Rakes joined the church, they plugged up a spot on Otter Creek near his house and lowered the old man into his own stream, seated in his own chair.

Children rarely grasped the solemnity of these religious "drownings." They often got so tickled that they fell into giggling fits at the sight of grown men and women dressed in their Sunday best, wading out into waist-high water, accompanied by the preacher who pressed his hand over their faces, tipped them over backwards into the creek water, and gave them the church's blessing. The new converts emerged from the holy dunking with wet clothes stuck to their bodies, their hair plastered to their heads, and water spewing out of their mouths and noses as they gasped for breath. For obvious reasons, the preachers generally conducted baptisms in the summertime.

The normal order of worship at the Long Branch Baptist Church called for preachings once a month, on the first Sundays, congregational meetings on the first Saturdays, communion once a year, and the annual Primitive Baptist Association meeting.

Eula attended her church faithfully. She sat up front with the other baptized and full-fledged members—women on one side of the pulpit, men on the other. The members of her family sat in the regular pews. Only after her parents moved to Salem did Elva sit next to her mother in a Baptist church and hear her mother's sweet singing voice.

Not everyone who came to Long Branch Church attended the worship service; some brought their relatives but remained outside and socialized. The socializers included Charles Snead, who married Eula's sister Effie Rakes, and Johnny Bird Rakes, a distant relative who was "not quite right." To pass the time and to amuse himself and anybody else who was lolling around the church yard, Charles told Johnny Bird that he had his shoes on backwards. The pitiful, hapless fellow believed Charles and switched his shoes. Then he sure enough had them on the wrong feet. So Charles and the other "mature" grown men had themselves a laugh at poor ole Johnny Bird's expense.

In summer the Baptists often conducted services outside in the fresh air with the preacher's pulpit and the log seats for the parishioners under oak trees. One summer Sunday, the church service was under way and the preacher was well into his sing-song sermon when members of the congregation began screaming, jumping up and scattering—frightened by a snake hanging from a branch in one of the trees.

The two important annual events of Long Branch Primitive Baptist Church were the one Sunday they celebrated communion, accompanied by all-day preaching, and the yearly meeting of the Primitive Baptist Association, or "Associations" as everyone called them. Congregations from the 17 member churches of the Primitive Baptist Association in Franklin and the counties of Floyd and Patrick met at a different church each year, which meant that Long Branch hosted Associations only once every 17 years. When their turn came, everyone in the community, no matter their church affiliation, was welcome to participate and often pitched in to help. Associations went on for several days over a long weekend, with meetings and preachings and food (and lots of it)—everyone brought something from their gardens and their kitchens for the giant pot luck suppers held on the church grounds on "groaning boards" laden with food. When the Association was at Long Branch, people visiting from the other community churches stayed with friends, family, and other Primitive Baptists in Endicott. Eula and Paul filled up all the beds in their house, made pallets on the floor for others, and sent any remaining guests to the barn with straw tick mattresses. Associations were the religious and social highlights of the year.

Paul was a Methodist, but unlike his wife who only worshipped at her church, he and the children were ecumenical and attended all the local churches, depending on which one had a minister on hand to lead the service.

On the third Sunday, Preacher Craddock rode 20 miles on horseback to conduct services at Trinity Methodist Church. The beloved pastor boarded with local families— either Paul and Eula Simms, or Sam and Nanny Thomas, Elva's friend Glendola's parents who were pillars of the church, or Mr. Will Thompson, who was the Sunday School Superintendent, notable for his many gold teeth (a sign of affluence and style in those days) usually crammed with bread crumbs, (Paul also had a glow of gold teeth before he replaced them with a complete set of false ones), or with

Uncle Jim, before he "got religion" and became a member of the Holiness Church.

Around 1916 the Methodist church burned to the ground. Elva was only eight or nine years old, but she remembered that night well. She was staying with her friend Glendola Thomas whose parents, Nanny and Sam, rushed to the scene of the tragedy. By the time anyone knew about the fire, it was too late to save the church. People speculated that "some drunk" had sought shelter under the church, made a fire to stay warm, and unintentionally set the building ablaze. No one ever knew for sure what happened. The parishioners raised money to replace their house of worship, which had been a fine building with many architectural details that included lattice work around the foundation and steps to the front door. Unfortunately the congregation was unable to collect enough funds to recreate the beautiful church and had to settle for a simpler building.

Occasionally the Methodists at Trinity Church held revivals to win new converts. A highpoint of the service came when the evangelist issued an invitation to members of the congregation to come forward, kneel down on the mourners' bench, confess their sins and join the church. Nanny Thomas and other "strong" Methodists circulated among the congregants and encouraged timid souls to "go on down." Neither Earl nor Elva ever accepted the invitation from Nanny or the revivalist, and by the time they were older and at Ferrum Training School, there were no mourners' benches for such public displays of personal remorse and conversion.

Paul attended at least one revival, but he fell asleep during the sermon. The next day the visiting preacher, unaware of the man he was dealing with, reprimanded "Brother Paul" for dozing off during the preaching. Paul shot back that he had worked hard that day, that he had made a determined effort to be there that night for the service, and had the preacher had anything worth hearing he would have stayed awake. (In a pique at his admonishment, Paul withdrew his pledge to build a new Sunday School for the church.)

At this same revival, or maybe at a different church service, (I'm not sure,) Paul took his young son Edsel with him to Trinity and noticed that the boy was not joining in singing the hymns. So Paul encouraged him, "Come on, Edsel, sing." But when he heard the child's pitiful effort, he relented and said, "That's okay, son." The irony was that Edsel came by his monotone naturally; his father, Paul, was also tone deaf, but that did not stop him from singing at the top of his voice, much to the mortification and embarrassment to his older children.

The revivals at the Methodist Church were restrained compared to those at the Assembly Holiness Church, which met down the road at Laurel Bluff School. In his later years Uncle Jim joined the Holiness church. He was a serious member in good standing with the fundamentalist church when a new convert to the church asked him what he should do with his still. Jim answered the new member in no uncertain terms: "You must break up your still and destroy your moonshine operation." That reply didn't satisfy the convert who sought advice from another, more practical man in the community, Paul Simms. When he asked Paul what he should do with his still, Paul told him to "Sell it."

Elva, Russell, and Edsel attended a revival at the Holiness Church out of curiosity, and to gawk at the "holy rollers" as they were called. The three of them got their eyes full. They saw people "filled with the Spirit" get down on the floor and roll around, and others become so carried away with emotion from the music and the excitement of the meeting that they stomped their feet and danced with their eyes closed, their hands in prayer position. One woman became so overcome with religious passion that she peed all over herself. The three intruders sat in the back, quiet as mice; they didn't dare say a word or laugh out loud, no matter how much they wanted to. That was the last time the young spies ever visited a Holiness revival. They were glad to return to the relative calm of the Baptists on the first Sunday, the Methodists on the third, and St. John's Episcopal Church on the second.

It was somewhat surprising to me that the Episcopal church, known for its high-toned, emotionally reserved services managed to thrive in the unsophisticated culture of the country. Probably this Episcopal church took on a country flavor. It was also a tribute to I.T. Cannaday's powerful personality, influence, and leadership—folks attended the church because he did—and to Miss Ora's hard work in the community and to her ice cream socials which she organized to benefit St. John's.

The Cannadays held the first ice cream socials at their home. I.T. and Miss Lucy cleared out the wagons and cars from the family's large garage and turned that ordinary building into a wonderland by hanging Japanese lanterns and selling delicious hand-cranked ice cream. Elva remembered this as a magical evening. It was the first time she ever saw a Japanese lantern and the first time she ate an ice cream cone.

The Cannadays were the mainstays of St. John's. They donated the land, the funds for its construction, and they boarded Miss Ora Harrison, the teacher and Sunday School director, before she had a home of her own in "ecclesiastical" territory. They took care of the minister who often stopped by their house on his way to St. John's. Cousin Tanny, I.T.'s affectionate family nickname, was a sociable fellow and gave the weary cleric a drink or two before church. This meant that the Man of God often conducted services while inebriated, resulting in added flair to his preaching by his jumping on the church platform and slapping his fist in his palm (much to Miss Ora's disgust and disapproval) while he delivered his sermon.

Miss Ora kept St. John's going for over 30 years after the Cannadays left the country. Eventually she left too, retired to Roanoke in the 1950s. As more and more of its young citizens left Endicott, the churches and schools which had been vital to our family and their neighbors and friends, closed their doors. St. John's has been de-consecrated and is now a private residence. Trinity Methodist has not fared so well. It has fallen into disrepair, the building abandoned and almost hidden under Virginia Creeper, poison ivy, vines and brambles. Of the three, only Long Branch Primitive Baptist remains a functioning church with meetings once a month. The one- and two-room schools, Bitty Hill, Laurel Bluff, St. John's, Trinity, gave way to the Endicott School in the 1930s. Even the Endicott School has closed and is a well-maintained residence. But at one time these churches and the schools held this small Virginia community together; they were social centers, places to learn and worship, places beloved by the entire community

Notes for Chapter XII, Religion and Education Over in the Country:

1. Elva couldn't remember the boy's name, so 'Joe' is an alias.

2. I have several of the hand woven coverlets from St. John's loom.

3. Eventually the Cannadays sold their Franklin County home and Miss Jenny moved in with her niece, Jane Moore.

13
Not All Work

My grandfather Paul Simms is the protagonist of the majority of these stories, which took place between 1915 and 1950. He, like all the Simms kin, loved a good joke and a well-conceived prank, especially if he was the perpetrator.

When we reminisce about life on the Simms family farm, we sometimes get misty-eyed and sentimental about the glories of self-sufficiency and living close to the land, about growing and eating our own food, about breathing clean, clear air and drinking fresh spring water, about mountaintop views and hillsides covered with rhododendron, laurel and wildflowers, about the sheer delight in visits from neighbors and relatives and creating our own simple, non-technological pleasures. From a grandchild's point of view, it was all those things and more. So why would anyone ever want to leave such a paradise? Because it wasn't, of course. Not for the matriarch and the patriarch. For them it was relentless labor, drudgery with little letup in keeping that gerbil wheel of work in motion. But it wasn't quite that either. There was work and plenty of it, but there was well-earned fun and laughter, and plenty of that too.

Much of the fun, jokes, play, pranks, and mischief began with the patriarch himself—Mr. Paul, Daddy, Grandpa, "Taz" who had inherited that Simms chromosome with its peculiar twist.

Paul adored little children and enjoyed entertaining them with games and stories and tales he made up on the spot. He also took enormous pleasure in scaring the life out of those sweet little darlings. When the young cousins came for a visit Paul could be persuaded to be "it" in a game of blind man's bluff, a role he relished. He covered his eyes with a blindfold (which probably had a tiny peephole in it), counted to ten while the children hid, then he came after them, with his arms outstretched like a Frankenstein monster, making a frightening, growling noise as he grabbed at the youngsters. The small fry shrieked and screamed like children always do, squirmed, dodged, and scampered away.

At bedtime his children begged their father to "tell us a tale." He told original yarns which he made up as he went along, or told his own warped version of "regular" fairy tales. He often had his own "babies" sobbing over sad stories about poor little Red Riding Hood or the pitiful three little pigs. He screwed the familiar stories into pathetic renditions, adding death and destruction to the usual "happily ever after" endings. It wasn't just the stories that evoked the "desired" emotional response, but the way he told them. Part of his fun was getting children to react, either with fear or with tears.

A few of Paul's tales have stayed alive in the memories of his children and grandchildren. The most famous one, the story of family legend which I have retold in the "Over in the Country" chapter, was a yarn about a Whiffenpoo, an imaginary beast who flew onto rooftops at night, hooked sleeping boys or girls with his 20-foot-long forked tail, took them home to his den and ate them for supper. I have my own original tale which Grandpa told me about another kind of monster, a Cow-eater.

I was just a little girl, no more than eight years old, but I vividly remember crawling onto my grandfather's lap and, like my mother, uncles and aunt before me, asking him "to tell me a tale." He agreed. As we settled into one of the ladder-back chairs by the large open fireplace in the kitchen, he turned on his creative imagination and began.

He told me that a dreadful beast was roaming over all the farms on Hurd's Branch, the Griffith Hill, and as far away as Endicott, wreaking havoc. The creature was a Cow-eater, a horrible, snaggle-toothed, nasty varmint who, just as his name would suggest, was devouring farmers' prize animals at an alarming rate. The men in the community fought back; they banded together and formed a posse to track the Cow-eater. They followed the hairy beast's trail to the opening of a deep, dark cave, but none of those grown men was willing to pursue the creature any farther. They needed someone, a brave someone, to go into that dangerous animal's dungeon and run him out so they could shoot him. That's where I came in. My grandpa wanted me to save the day, to be the one who would walk into the cave with a stick and drive out the awful beast; he assured me that I had nothing to fear because this monster would not eat little girls.

The comfortable lap grew a little less so. I protested mightily that there was NO WAY (*IN HELL* although I didn't say that part, it was implied) that I was going into that Cow-eater's den. Grandpa, in his deep, slightly gruff, uncompromising, certain voice, insisted that no harm would come to me. "Oh, yes. You have to go; we need you. He won't eat you." I was equally insistent and refused outright to risk my young life on the off-chance that a ferocious, cornered monster would not eat me alive. "No, Grandpa, I am not going into that Cow-eater's den." This exchange went on for several back-and-forths until he gave up, but with a smile.

Of course, I knew it was just an imaginary story and my very own grandfather would never put me in such terrible jeopardy (if for no other reason than my grandmother would kill him if he did). Still, I was caught up in the convincing pretense. It continues to amuse me to this day when I think about the time my grandfather worked his magic, using his own brand of humor and terror to entertain me (and himself. I know he got some sort of twisted pleasure watching me squirm).

I am not the only grandchild who owns a Paul-original story. Betty Jane Simms Hagan has one too. Hers, the Fire-Headed Monster Story, proved, (in case there was any doubt), that our grandfather was the Stephen King of Hurd's Branch.

He told little Betty Jane, who was at most five years old, a tale about his frightening encounter with a fire-headed ogre. It seemed that one pitch black night he was walking through the woods when he heard a noise behind him. He spun around in time to see an amazing sight: a formless, shadowy monster with one very distinguishable feature, fire burning in the center of his forehead. Startled and scared to death, Paul began to run for his life, but the mysterious creature ran after him. The faster Paul ran, the faster It ran. The more Paul picked up speed, the more It picked up speed until, finally, our poor grandfather collapsed, exhausted and out of breath. Able to run no farther, he staggered and sat down on a nearby log. The firey-headed beast pulled up and sat right down beside him, just as if they were buddies, old friends. The Thing said, "We've had us a right good little run," and Paul replied, "And we're going to have us another as soon as I catch my breath."

Children, grandchildren, and cousins were all treated to Paul's bizarre tales, icing on the cake for youngsters staying or visiting on the Simms farm. Harold Simms, Paul's half-brother Gale's son, recalled a winter-time visit with the Simms family in 1919 when he was quite small.

Paul had been down at his father, Jim Simms', house, and invited his little nephew, Harold, who lived with his grandparents, Jim and Mary Simms, to come home with him and spend the night. The invitation was agreeable to everyone, so he brought Harold up the hill to his house. The little boy had a fine time playing at the Simms farm, especially with his cousin Edsel who was only one year younger. But then night fell and Harold began to miss his home and his bed, and started to cry. So Paul, whose idea it had been to bring the little fellow there in the first place, had to take his upset nephew home. Meanwhile, snow had fallen and covered the ground. Uncle Paul helped dress Harold for the frigid outdoors. He pulled on Harold's white rubber boots with the red stripe around the top, boosted him up on his shoulders and carried him down the road the short distance to his house. The snow had crusted over, so that every step he took made a crunching sound crunch, crunch, crunch all the way to the home-place. He was no more than five years old at the time, but Harold, (in his 80's when he told me the story), remembered that "ride" for the rest of his life, "just like it was yesterday," he said.

Paul found other ways to amuse the youngsters and himself at the same time, like taking them to see the spectacle at the Long Branch Church. Elva had a vague recollection of a show of some sort held at the church one summer's evening when she was a very little girl. Her father rounded up all the children in the neighborhood, including their young relations at his father, Jim Simms' place, piled them into his wagon, clicked, clicked to the horses, and took them off to see the production. Most of the details of the entertainment of that evening are lost, but Elva did remember a big screen set up at the church and pictures projected onto it. From her description it certainly sounded as though primitive movies had arrived in Franklin County. Of course, Paul Simms wasn't going to miss out on anything unusual or new within his purview.

He was wonderful with small children, but he was also a stern disciplinarian, especially as his children grew older. He may have thought that they would go astray if he didn't keep them in line. They remember their father being free with the switch and that "there was never a time when you couldn't get a whipping." Except when Betty came along. According to her older siblings she got away with a lot, probably because Paul realized by then that the whippings didn't do any good any way.

My grandfather loved a good joke, whether it was telling a funny story or reciting a poem, or playing a prank on some poor victim. Paul had a huge repertoire of funny stories, handed down to him by his older relatives, about idiotic Irishmen. (Those stories no doubt came from the English side of the Simms family, not from his mother's Irish kin.) For instance, there was the stupid Irishman who had a vine growing out of his thatched roof. To get rid of the noxious weed, he pushed his cow up on the roof to eat it, rather than pulling the vine down himself.

Paul's favorite poem, which Edsel loved to quote, was called *Dried Apple Pie*:

I abhor, detest and despise fried apple pies.
The farmer takes his sorry fruit;
It's wormy, bitter and hard to boot.
And on a dirty cord is strung
And in the garret window hung;
And there it serves a roost for flies
Until it is made into dried apple pies.
So tread on my corns and tell me lies,
But please don't pass me dried apple pies.

Amusing jokes and poems were the stuff of entertainment for most folks in the country, but where the Simms crowd stood out was in its practical jokes. They were creative masters; their skills ranged from harmless, simple silliness to intricate malice. In the harmless category was one of Paul's earliest pranks when he set out to frighten his young wife Eula. He had been away from home for the entire day, and by the time he returned it was dark and raining. He rode up to the house on horseback wearing a black rain cape, which covered his head and most of his face. Without dismounting he knocked on the front door, and when Eula answered, he leaned down from his horse, disguised his voice and asked for directions to a neighbor's house. She did not recognize her own husband, but their little girl Elva did, called out "daddy," and exposed his trick.

That hoax was an innocent tease compared to the most famous prank in the family—the prank of pranks, a trick so clever and devilish that it inspired me to collect stories for a family memoir. This dirty deed, which I call "malicious wounding," was played on Cousin Green Spencer.

According to my mother, you had to know Cousin Green to understand why anyone would want to play such a mean trick on him. In the community of Endicott, over on Hurd's Branch, everybody knew the man was an obnoxious, but harmless pest. Green loved to talk. He talked all the time and he talked in a loud roar. After a while, no one paid any attention to what he was saying. He had an irritating habit of showing up at Paul and Eula's house squarely at mealtimes for some of Eula's good cooking. Of course they, usually Paul, graciously invited him, as they would anyone, to "come on in and have a bite; it's on the table." Eula would scurry around opening another can, setting another place, and pulling up another chair. Green had a home of his own. In fact, he had a wife and at least ten children that we could count. He was the original double dipper, eating first at his own house and then at his neighbors'.

One of Green's nearest neighbors on Hurd's Branch was London "Skinny" Wagoner. The two men had a fractious relationship, often fussing and fighting. After one of their fallings out, Jim and Gale Simms (Paul's younger half-brothers), decided to take advantage of the quarrel and have a little fun at Green's expense. The two of them, along with Skinny Wagoner, cooked up an elaborate scheme.

One evening Jim, Gale, and another country fellow whose identity has long since been forgotten, invited the hapless Green to go along with them to Paul's, perhaps for a meal. It was an invitation he was quick to accept. By careful pre-arrangement, the men met up with London Wagoner, who began to taunt Green, picking a quarrel over one thing and another. Jim joined in, taking Green's part, egging things along, saying to London, "You aren't going to talk to Green Spencer like that while I'm here." Jim was carrying a shotgun, and when the verbal exchange continued on at a furious pace, he shouldered the weapon and fired at London at point blank range. London grabbed his chest, keeled over, and collapsed onto the ground.

Jim then turned on the stunned Green, put the gun in his hand and said, "This is all your fault, Green. If you hadn't started arguing with London, none of this would have ever happened." Green objected strenuously that it wasn't his fault at all. He hadn't been the one who fired the gun, and he certainly wasn't going to take the blame for killing London Wagoner. When the others sided with Jim, making it three against one, poor ole Green began to cry and said, "This is the worst thing that has ever happened to me. I thought losing my little child was terrible, but that wasn't anything compared to this." With that, they all fled the scene of the crime, leaving London lying "dead" on the road.

Afterwards Jim stopped by Paul's house to tell him how the trick on Cousin Green had worked slick as butter. Those two brothers must have laughed and slapped their thighs at the thought of the unsuspecting man's distress. The next morning Paul got in on the plot. He went to see Green to "find out" from him what had actually happened. Paul told Green that his brother Jim had stopped by the house with some outlandish tale about London Wagoner being shot. Not only that, he told Green, Jim had borrowed $200 and headed off to West Virginia. Green gave Paul his version of the "tragedy," declared his innocence, and once again exclaimed that this was the worst thing in the world that had ever happened to him, worse even than losing his little child. Paul offered his sympathy and wished he could help him, but insisted that he had to take his brother's side.

Green decided then and there that the best thing for him to do was to hide out in the hills for a while until things blew over. Several days later he emerged from hiding and cautiously asked the first person he met about the murder of London Wagoner. The man said, "I don't know what you are talking about, Green. London is perfectly all right." Green didn't believe a word of it and told the man, "I know damn good and well that London ain't all right; I was there and I saw the fire come from the end of the shotgun at close range." They had left London dead in the road.

It was only later when Green saw London with his own eyes, walking around fit as a fiddle, that he realized he had been duped, that the Simms boys had taken the slug out of the gun before Jim fired it. Green must have been torn between relief that he would not be arrested for murder and desire to commit a real one.

Cousin Green Spencer was not the only or the last victim of a Simms prank. One such fellowI think it was Johnny Bird Rakes, who "wasn't quite right"—stopped by the farmhouse one day. Eula was no where in sight and Paul pointed to a small dark bottle on top of the kitchen cabinet and said to Johnny Bird in a whispering, conspiratorial way, "Get yourself a drink. She's not here." So the gullible guy took a big swig of castor oil or cough medicine or some other foul-tasting medication, and promptly spewed it out all over the floor. Paul couldn't control his laughter, but pretended he had really thought the stuff was whiskey. (I can testify to this bit of mischief because I saw it with my own eyes.)

Henry Sylvadus Adkins, always called Henry Vadus, joined the dubious ranks of Paul's victims when he went with Paul to Lakeside Amusement Park in Roanoke for a ride on a roller coaster, the Mountain Speedway. Henry Vadus had spent most of his years tucked away on his small farm up on Hurd's branch and had never been to an amusement park, much less ridden or even heard of a roller coaster. When they were at the park and getting ready to board the Mountain Speedway, he believed his good friend Paul who told him that they were going to get in a little car and go for a nice ride (Paul may have even elaborated and said "in the country.") Paul did suggest to Henry Vadus as they were "boarding the train" that he might want to hold onto his hat. The next thing the innocent man knew, he was strapped into a seat, chugging up an incline, ready for a pleasant excursion, when all of a sudden the world dropped out from under him. "It liked to scared the life out of me," he said later. We all know that Paul enjoyed Henry Vadus' fearful reaction to what must have seemed to him a death plunge into the unknown.

The Simms "boys" were often the brains behind any foul play; they were the con artists, the slick operators, the last laughers on almost every fun-loving trick pulled, over in the country, except once, when they went too far and outsmarted themselves. For some reason, the brothers Paul and Jim had decided to swear off drinking for a whole year. The two of them made a pact and went so far as to sign a document which Henry Adkins, the hunchbacked Justice of the Peace notarized. Perhaps what inspired them to make the pledge official was seeing Old Man Henry Adkins, who was an intelligent man, so crippled with curvature of the spine that he couldn't straighten up, riding around in his horse and buggy which served as his office. As far as anyone knew, Paul and Jim actually drank very little, although Eula did say that on the rare occasions when her husband did drink, his nose turned so red that she thought it was going to bloom. Maybe it was out of boredom, or a dare, or maybe it was just those twisted Simms' chromosomes at work, but the brothers swore off and stuck to it for a year.

Twelve months later, to the day, Uncle Jim showed up at his bother Paul's house and insisted that the entire family come home with him. It was mid-December, bitter cold and snowing when Paul, Eula, and the children Earl and Elva rode over to Uncle Jim's on horseback. At Jim's house, his wife, Aunt Lera, (who was Old Man Henry Adkins' niece), had prepared a big supper. After they ate, Jim and Paul left the others and went out to the kitchen, a small, separate building off to the side of the main house. This was where Jim had stocked up a nice supply of moonshine whiskey, and the two brothers proceeded to "get into it." It didn't take long before they were both roaring drunk, whooping it up, and romping around outside in the snow, wishing each other "Merry Christmas." The women and children were inside the house by the fire in the living room, watching with horror as their husbands and fathers acted like idiots. Paul fell over a snow-covered box, his feet shot up in the air and buried his face in the snow. Eventually Lera and Eula persuaded their men to come in out of the cold. At this point the fun was over for everyone. Paul and Jim got sick and began to throw up. The women rushed around to protect the carpet, which was laid down in strips and fastened to the floor. They detached the rug and rolled it up, then they corralled the wayward men in one of the rooms in the main house and left them there to "pay for their sins." Aunt Lera was worried about them, but Eula wasn't. She told Lera to just lock them in and leave them alone. They were safely inside and couldn't hurt themselves nor freeze to death. That was the only time Earl and Elva ever saw their father intoxicated. He drank so little that he wasn't accustomed to the effects of alcohol. Because this was a one-time event, it stood out as a humorous memory. If it had happened more often, it would have been a disgrace.

There was a generous plenty of moonshine over in the country; it was a staple crop, the livelihood of many of the residents. When the supply outstripped local demand they "shared" their bounty with thirsty people in Roanoke and neighboring communities. Franklin County had and still has the dubious reputation as the "moonshine capital of the world."

There was a time, before Prohibition and government interference, when making and selling liquor was perfectly legal as long as the manufacturer paid the fee to produce a particular quantity of whiskey, say $10 to brew 100 gallons. Often a distiller would make an additional 100-200 gallons of moonshine off the record. This was where the profit was, or so I have been told. There were government agents who checked records of whiskey makers to be sure they were abiding by the law.

During the years when making whiskey was legal, members of our family had a hand in the lucrative business. Paul helped his cousin I.T. Cannaday with a whiskey-making venture; J.R. Simms, Paul's father, made copper worms and hogsheads for moonshiners, and he was one of their best customers.

After the Legislature made distilling a crime, our family members worked only on the fringes of the moonshine world as far as I know selling supplies such as sugar and gallon jugs. Many of the independent-minded folks in the country found it difficult to understand why the law demanded that they end a business practice which had always been legal, profitable, and to them, harmless. With the onset of Prohibition and the Depression, many of them went underground. The general opinion of most residents of Endicott toward their neighbors who were in the moonshine business was to stick together, to protect each other from the outsiders, the dreaded revenue agents, with an informal alarm system. If someone spotted a revenuer, he got on the telephone with the news, which spread faster than Kudzu, that "something's coming up the road."

Not all the revenuers were outsiders, Paul's half brother Gale was a particularly effective agent. He was a local and knew most of the men involved in the illegal business, as well as the locations of their stills. It was his job, if he caught a man operating a still, to break it up and arrest the offender. This happened to a man who was not only making liquor but was sampling his own product a bit too freely. Foolishly he said, "I just wish old Gale Simms would show up now." His wish was granted. Old Gale showed up, overheard the comment and broke up the still.

The process of making whiskey was a mystery to me, but not to my Uncle Earl, (or to my father or my grandfathers, for that matter) who tried to enlighten me with a detailed explanation of this age-old business.

This is how it distilled through my brain.

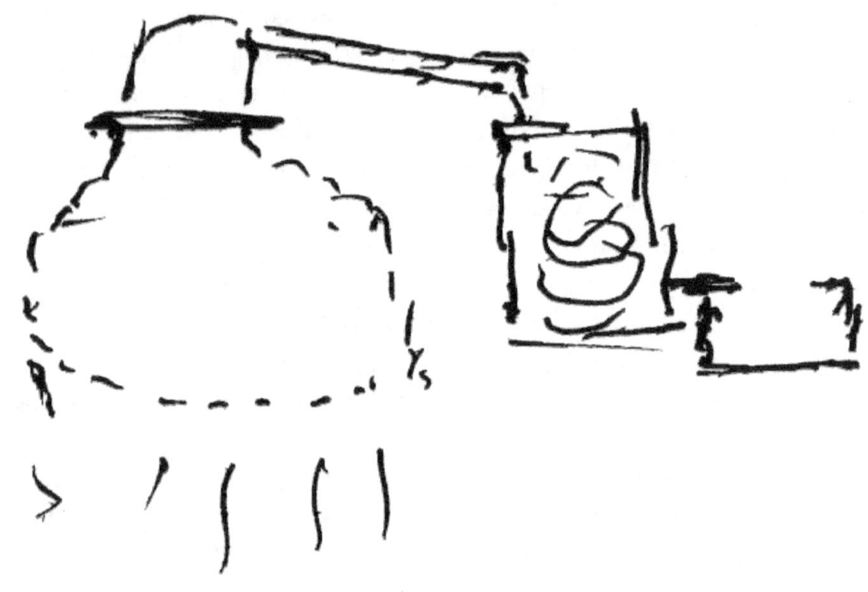

Uncle Earl's drawing of a still for my edification

To make corn whiskey, a businessman needed the right equipment: (1) a hogshead—a large, open, wooden barrel, measuring approximately 4' in diameter by 5' in height, with a capacity of 500 to 600 gallons of liquid; (2) a distillery or still—a huge copper pot with a cap to transfer the precious substance through a copper coil or worm; (3) a small barrel which held the worm as cold water passed through to create steam; (4) a tub or wash-tub to collect the distilled liquor; (5) mason jars or 5 gallon tin cans to store the finished product.

Equally essential were the right ingredients: a mixture of grains —ground cornmeal, some rye and barley, all of which were processed with sugar and yeast. The whiskey manufacturer also needed a source of water, usually with a strong downhill flow through the still; a shed to protect the operation from the elements; and the all important recipe, which according to family legend was imported from Ireland and called for approximately

80% corn, 10% rye and 10% barley. The exact proportions varied according to a secret calculation known only to the distiller.

The moonshiner combined the grains with 300 to 400 gallons of water in the hogshead and allowed the mixture to ferment for a week or so until it was ripe. He dipped the fermented grain by bucket-loads from the hogshead, which held enough mash for three runs through the still, into the copper pot and filled it two-thirds full. He built a fire under the copper pot and made sure that cold water from the creek ran into the barrel which held the worm. When the mash got hot enough, steam rose up from the still into the cap, traveled down through the coil or worm, (which was situated off to the side of the cap,) condensed by virtue of the cold water surrounding the worm, and collected in the wash tub as corn liquor. Finally the manufacturer transferred the whiskey to mason jars or tin cans, ready for distribution. He sold his goods to a bootlegger who hauled it to lucrative markets in Roanoke and elsewhere.

There was an optional process called doubling back or rerunning the whiskey, which produced a higher proof, a stronger liquor with greater alcohol content. To double back, the moonshiner removed the mash in the still and put the first-run whiskey back into the copper pot for a second processing.

The use of copper, rather than zinc or tin, was absolutely essential to avoid the unwanted side-effect of blindness. Uncle Earl did not know of anyone who was so foolish as to use any material other than copper, which not only protected customers, but also lasted longer than other less expensive metals, until revenuers busted it up.

The specialized knowledge of how to make whiskey came in handy in an unexpected way for Cousin I.T. Cannaday's son Russell. When he was a young college student at the University of Maryland (about 1927during Prohibition), his public speaking professor asked each student to make a ten-minute talk on a subject he, the student, knew well. Russell decided to talk on *How to Make Corn Liquor*, obviously something he had learned back in Franklin County. After his presentation the professor called him aside and in a very gruff voice said, "Cannaday, I want to see you after class." Russell feared he was in big trouble, but he was soon relieved and amused when the teacher wanted instead to know if Russell could get him some of that corn liquor.

Perhaps Russell was inspired by his father I.T.'s successful Maryland moonshine experience. After the Cannadays moved to Towson and their neighbors learned of the family's Franklin County, Virginia origins, the fame of which had reached the pastoral Maryland horse country, they asked him if he could procure some illegal whiskey for them. And I.T., intent on impressing the prosperous landowners in his new surroundings, did it up right. He used his connections back home to buy enough five-gallon tins of moonshine to fill a portion of a train car and had it shipped to Sparks, Maryland. The station manager in Ferrum and the manufacturers gladly cooperated, and the booze flowed easily and swiftly from Southwest Virginia to Eastern Maryland. It was even said, after the phenomenal whiskey feat, that the citizens around the Baltimore suburb wanted to run I.T. Cannaday for governor. (Perhaps his slogan could have been: "A man who can make you happy and get things done.")

Years later, long after Cousin I.T.'s successful moonshine caper, Earl Simms put on a show of his own for the home folks back in Franklin County, but his feat of daring do had nothing to do with the making, sale or distribution of corn liquor. In the late 1940s Earl, who by then was living in Salem, had gotten his pilot's license and bought a J3 Piper Cub airplane for the grand sum of $1,000. For Paul this marvelous circumstance—a son who owned an airplane—got his mischief-making juices flowing. He came up with a dazzling scheme to create a stir and terrorize his neighbors over on Hurd's Branch. These country folks had never seen or heard an airplane up close, but that would soon change. Paul "created" a landing strip on the top of his farm, "Chestnut Ridge," which was high and relatively flat, but covered with rocks. He cleared away the white flint stones to make a safer, less bumpy runway for Earl to land his plane. Just as Paul expected, the noise and sight of the aircraft caused great excitement all over Endicott, and even more excitement for Earl. He had no trouble landing the diminutive aircraft, the problem came when he tried to take off. He started the propeller by hand, hopped back in the plane, revved the motor and throttled it forward as fast as its 55 horsepower engine would allow, and made the heart-stopping discovery that the newly made runway wasn't quite long enough. The plane lifted off the mountain top, but then dropped down, for what must have been several long, frightening moments before the laws of physics took over and the Piper Cub lifted skyward and flew safely back home to Salem.

So Earl and the mountain people got their fright, and Paul, as so often was the case, got his fun. Whether it was entertaining children with games or imaginary monsters, teasing friends with mischievous pranks, or enjoying a sip or two of moonshine, Paul and the rest of the Simms crowd found a way to temper the hard days of work with moments of pure fun.

14
Kinfolk and More

Many wonderful stories and reminiscences remain which don't fit precisely into the framework of the Simms family memoir, but I couldn't let them disappear like wood smoke rising up into thin air. For one reason, the anecdotes in this chapter were a source of entertainment for the family while they sat around the fireside in the evenings or gathered for dinner on Sunday afternoons. In addition to their own stories, Paul, Eula, and their children often recounted incidents about their kinfolk, their neighbors, and life in the country.

Among the beloved Simms relatives were the Brogans. Aunt Gracie, (Paul's younger sister), her husband Uncle Bob and their six children, Elsie, Wilma, Minnie, Fred, Harris and Geneva, lived near Callaway, on Floyd and Franklin Pike, ten miles from the Simms farm. From time to time the two families visited back and forth, bringing along cousins, one of whom—Wilma—was Elva Simms' favorite, her roommate and best friend at Ferrum Training School. Wilma must have been a character all her life. I remember meeting her when I was a college student. She was an impressive woman of generous proportions, with a great smear of red lipstick across her wide mouth, and an exaggerated manner of speaking, pronouncing each word carefully and distinctly with some sort of accent that owed nothing to her Franklin County roots. At first I was bothered by what seemed to me, affectation, but I soon discovered that Wilma was a gracious woman with a heart and a sense of humor to match her size.

Wilma obviously loved to eat. Even as a child she delighted in the pleasures of the table, and, like most children, she needed instruction in table manners. Aunt Gracie told her little girl that when the family had company for dinner, she must hold back, wait her turn, and not be the first one to reach for the fried chicken. So the next time the family entertained, Wilma, following orders, announced at the table in front of everyone that, "Mother told me not to be the first one to grab the fried chicken, but I want a potato, and I want the biggest one on the plate." Thus, canceling out Aunt Gracie's effort to instill manners in her not so little girl.

Grace Simms and Bob Brogan

Unlike her brother Paul, Grace had a dark complexion with jet black hair and sharp equally black eyes set back in a low forehead. Her father, J. R. Simms, insulted Grace by telling her she looked just like Minervy (Rakes) Midkiff, a pitifully poor, unkempt, unattractive neighbor. She did, in fact, favor this woman who was a distant relative (the more distant the better, my mother said). "Aunt Grace was a good-looking woman and Minervy might have been too if she had ever washed her face," my mother said. Uncle Bob, on the other hand, was fair and round, and looked like the Irish actor who played Scarlett O'Hara's "Pa" in *Gone with the Wind.* An even more colorful member of the Brogan household was their unusual pet, a parrot named Polly. This Polly, like most parrots with the same name would say, "Polly wants a cracker." If she didn't get her cracker right away, she would follow up with, "Polly wants a damn cracker."

In the 1930s Elva and Russell Cannaday were driving on the road toward the Simms farm when they met the Brogans coming in the opposite direction. Uncle Bob, who wasn't mechanically inclined, and Aunt Gracie were in their old touring car on their way home after a visit with Paul and Eula. As they passed by, Aunt Gracie leaned out of the window,

Elsie and Wilma Brogan

while the car was still moving, and said, "We can't stop to talk because your Uncle Bob won't be able to get the car started again if we do."

Not all of the stories about Aunt Grace and Uncle Bob Brogan's family were humorous anecdotes. When they were a young couple, they suffered a cruel sadness which must have haunted them all their lives. They lost their first baby, Frank, who, according to family gossip, fell into the fire. No one was around to rescue him, and the baby burned to death. Terrible losses happened in those days and were too awful to think about, too awful to talk about, so they didn't. All we know is that it happened.

Isaac Thomas "I.T." Cannaday was Grace Simms Brogan and Paul Simms' first cousin. Family members often called one another "Cousin"—Cousin Paul, Cousin Eula, Cousin Lucy, Cousin Tanny (I.T.'s nickname). The Cannaday name and family were the most prominent in that small corner of the world. It seems odd and out-of-place that in a democratic community of struggling dirt farmers and self-sufficient men and women that a social hierarchy was alive and well. Perhaps it is just part of human nature. Over in the country there was a definite snobbery, a sliding scale of "importance" with some folks on top and some on the bottom; certain families did not "visit" with certain other families. In the Simms family, for instance, Uncle Jim revealed his feelings of inferiority to his half brother Paul: "You think you are better than I am, just because you are a Cannaday, and I am a Shively." Both men had the same father, but Paul's mother was Betty Cannaday Simms and Jim's was Mary Shively Simms.

The Cannadays or Kennadys, as their name was often written in 18th century deed books, were among the first settlers in Southwest Franklin County. The family migrated from central Virginia in the 1780s and before that from Ireland, according to family tradition. The clan laid claim to a continuous stretch of land along the Runnett Bag Creek. Over the next

150 years the Cannadays prospered, multiplied and until the 1920s settled more and more land, generally along that same stream. At that time, at the dawn of modern America, people in backwater Virginia began to flee the country. I.T. Cannaday (47-years old in 1920) and his wife Lucy (42-years old) were among the first families to "escape." An ambitious man, I.T. had gone as far as he could in Franklin County. He was as successful as he was going to be there, and he wanted more. So he bought a large dairy farm in Maryland and moved his wife, against her will, and their six children to that Yankee state. But before 1920, I.T. and Miss Lucy were "the" family of Endicott.

Isaac Thomas "Tanny" Cannaday did not inherit great wealth; in fact, he may not have inherited anything except good business sense, an enthusiasm for hard work, and a desire to succeed. As a young man, like so many others in and around Endicott, including his cousin Paul Simms, Cannaday left home for West Virginia to work in the mines. I don't know how long he stuck with that god-awful job, probably only a short while.

Once back home, his future brightened. He convinced a prosperous local farmer, Clem Snead who lived on Otter Creek, to lend him money to open a store in Endicott, and he had the great good luck to marry one of the prettiest, sweetest, and best-tempered women in Virginia, according to everyone who knew Lucy Peters.[1] Then he went about the business of growing a large family and making his fortune. By the time I.T. was ready to move on, he owned the biggest and best-supplied general store within a five mile radius; he was the local postmaster with the post office tucked into a corner of his store; he had a sawmill, a grinding mill, a blacksmith shop, all in a prime location on Route 40; he sent his children to prep schools (Virginia Episcopal School and Chatham Hall). I.T. had given land to construct an Episcopal church mission, St. John's in the Mountains; he owned an impressive brick house on a hill top near his business ventures and his church, with a view of the Blue Ridge Mountains. It was about this time that a teacher asked one of her students at the Bitty Hill School, "Who is the president of the United States?" The little boy paused, thought for a minute, brightened and said, "I.T. Cannaday." Such was the man's fame over in the country.

I.T. was no beauty—tall and lanky with a prominent, hooked nose—but his wife certainly was. Folks agreed that Lucy Peters Cannaday was one of the loveliest women anywhere around. She had delicate features, soft brown hair and wide set eyes. Miss Lucy was blessed with fair skin, but "cursed," she thought, with freckles, an affliction she fought with buttermilk facial baths and wide brimmed hats which she wore to avoid the

I.T. and Lucy Cannaday with their children Charles, Harry and Zera

sun and reduce the chance for acquiring more blemishes. Pretty of face she was, but her real beauty was her gentle disposition, her sweet nature, and her easy laugh.

Cousin Lucy was quite a fine horsewoman with a good seat, but on at least one occasion she lost control of the animal she was riding. It was Easter, and she was sitting astride her horse, dressed in her Sunday clothes topped with a fancy new bonnet when the animal, startled by a bee sting, spooked and galloped away carrying his rider under low-growing tree limbs which snatched off her hat. Instead of being upset, this fun-loving woman laughed at herself and the humor of her predicament. Another time, she had just finished milking when the ornery cow kicked over a full bucket of milk. Unlike Cousin Paul, who threw a rock at his "sorry" animal when this happened to him, she fell over laughing.

Miss Lucy was a woman of principle. In the early days of their marriage, I.T. had a sideline business of making (and no doubt) selling moonshine, an occupation she despised. She told her new husband to get out of that line of work or she would report him to the revenue agents. She prevailed.

With a large house to manage and six children to care for, Lucy Cannaday was a busy woman, always in a rush. One of Russell's early memories of his mother was watching her try to thread a needle in such a hurry that she couldn't quite get the cotton thread through the eye. She was a generous woman, willing to help her neighbors whenever possible. When requests to borrow her large copper pot became excessive, instead of saying "no," she bought a second one. So she had one to lend and one for herself. Outside of church activities, she probably did not have time for charitable or political causes, such as women's suffrage. She did, however, find time to vote in 1920, the first federal election in which women were allowed to cast ballots. At the voting booth she was so overcome by the enormity of the moment that she almost fainted.

Cannaday children - Russell, May and Ted

The Cannaday children were all boys—Harry, Ezra, called Zera, Charles, Ted, Russell—with one blessed exception, the number five child, a beautiful little girl, May, born next-to-last, in between Ted and Russell. She was the most adored, the most precious, the most spoiled child in the country, unlike the boys who were expected to work all the time (or so they thought). "Papa couldn't stand to see us idle and made work for us," my father Russell told me. Sometimes he had the boys move a pile of rocks from one place to another to keep them occupied and out of trouble. May, however, never had to turn her hand or do a lick of work. So you can imagine the family's panic when this favored child became desperately ill from an attack of appendicitis. It was around 1915, near her tenth birthday.

I.T. frantically telephoned the family's physician, Dr. Cobb, in Rocky Mount and insisted that he come and take care of his seriously ill child. The doctor, who would not have been able to say "no" to Mr. Cannaday, drove a car (if he had one) or a buggy (if he didn't) the 20 miles from his office to the Cannaday home in Endicott. He examined May, determined that the little girl was too sick to move to a hospital, and that she required an operation, which he was not qualified to perform. For that Dr. Cobb called a surgeon friend in Martinsville who took the train to Ferrum where I.T. met him. When the doctor and the father finally arrived after a ten-mile ride from the train station in Ferrum to the family farm, it was the middle of the night. Even so, the surgeon had to operate immediately. The family turned the kitchen into an operating room; they put May on the table, brought in every lamp in the house, and family members took turns holding the lanterns for the doctor to see to perform the surgery. The operation was a success, and the beloved little girl soon recovered.

May wasn't the only Cannaday child who had a close encounter with death. Her brother Charles had what must have seemed to him a near death experience. One day the young fellow was out for a walk in one of the many forested wood lots near home when he suddenly came upon a black racing snake. Both Charles and the reptile were startled by this unexpected and unwanted encounter. The snake, which could move like streaked lightning, lit out after the little boy, chasing him until he almost dropped over with fatigue. At that point Charles had had enough. Angry, he turned on the black racer and chased after him until the snake slithered away at breakneck speed, or so the story goes.

Some years later—in 1920—I.T. Cannaday uprooted his family and moved them to Sparks, Maryland, a farming community north of Baltimore. This was a reluctant transplantation for everyone except the "master." He was in search of what? Prestige, opportunity, success, greener pastures, a new challenge, an escape from a claustrophobic backwater, sophistication? For years after they left it, the Cannadays held on to their house in Endicott. Miss Jenny, I.T's mother, continued to live in the house and take care of it. In summertime Miss Lucy and some of the children, usu-

Cannaday farm in Sparks, Maryland

ally May and Russell, came back "home" for long stays. But then in 1927, in one of the saddest turn of events in the Cannaday story, Lucy died. Of what, we don't know. She was only 49. Her death was a devastating shock, and without her to hold it together the family drifted apart.

By the time Lucy died, the Cannaday children were grown and the youngest, Russell, was a student at the University of Maryland. May told me that she was studying music at Peabody Institute in downtown Baltimore. The loss of her mother was so overwhelmingly depressing that she stopped going to class. She continued to go downtown every day, but went to picture shows instead of piano lessons. The final blow to family unity came with I.T.'s hasty, and to his children, disastrous marriage to a woman half his age, Eleanor Hale. A once prominent and well-regarded man, I.T. lost the affection of his children who turned away from him, and the respect of people who had known him, looked up to him, and admired him; they now considered him a foolish old man, no longer the President of the United States in anyone's eyes. I.T. eventually sold the dairy farm in Maryland, and he and Eleanor retired in Roanoke. I only remember seeing him at the end of his days in a hospital bed, through the distortion of a crumpled oxygen tent. He died soon after, at age 80. Eleanor got all of his sizeable fortune.

I.T. Cannaday's one sibling, Florida Cannaday Moore Atkins, (or Flordy, as everyone called her), and her second husband Henry Sylvadus

I.T. and Eleanor Hale Cannaday, c1929

Atkins, (or Henry Vadus as everyone called him), lived up the hill from Paul and Eula Simms, across from the Bitty Hill School. Because they lived near my grandparents I remember them, though only vaguely. In my mind they were the epitome of a hillbilly couple, somewhat like the Clampetts—tall, skinny, with sunken jaws when their teeth were out, unsophisticated but warm, friendly and funny; living in a small white house with chickens running round everywhere, paying not much attention to yard work, the road running beside their house with a gully, a garden and a cow nearby

When Flordy's two boys, Artis and Hobart Moore, (children from her first marriage to Archer Moore), grew up, they loved to play poker. Like all gamblers, they were not always successful. After one catastrophic evening of sizeable losses, Hobart said to Artis, "I wish to God that I'd never learned to play poker." Artis replied to his brother, "You better wish that you had."

Another of the Cannaday relatives, Lucy's brother Arthur Peters, told the remarkable story of a farmer from Floyd who came to Franklin County looking to buy a cow. The farmer happened to meet Arthur and asked him if he knew someone in the community who had dairy cows for sale. Of course, Arthur did and said, "Oh, yes I know a man who has cows for sale, but he is unreliable. In fact he is the biggest liar in the world; you can't believe a word he says." So, when the farmer from Floyd met the lying farmer from Franklin and asked about buying one of his cows, the liar said, "I do have a cow for sale, but she is roguish and ornery and will kick over the milk." Aware that he was dealing with the biggest liar in the world, the Floyd farmer disregarded the warning and bought the cow. When he got his new animal home to Floyd, he found that she was roguish and ornery and kicked over the milk, just as the Franklin County farmer had told him.

Arthur Peters' wonderful story was just one of many that folks in the country loved to tell on their neighbors. One of Paul's favorites was about Minervy Midkiff. Minervy was a widow whose husband Henry had committed suicide by drinking carbolic acid, a vile method of death duplicated, some years later, by his and Minervy's son Earnest. As a result of Henry's early demise, Minervy was left with very little means to care for her passel of small children. She was pitifully poor and run ragged by her pathetic circumstances. Even so she carried on and did the best she could. One day in a pouring down rainstorm Minervy showed up at Paul's store, soaking wet and looking miserable. He asked her why in the world she was out on such a nasty, rotten day. She replied that she was there because "old have-to got ahold of me."

Another country character with an unforgettable line was Emaline Underwood. Emaline was a notoriously bad housekeeper whose house was disgustingly filthy. When a visiting neighbor suggested that she and her children would be better off if she spent a little more time scrubbing with soap and water, Emaline replied that, "I'd rather die of *jarms* than over work." Aunt Lera came to assist Emaline with the birth of one of her numerous children. When Emaline's water broke, Lera began to clean it up, but the doctor told her not to bother. "It's the only thing sterile in the house."

Emaline and Minervy were sad cases, but the same cannot be said for Mikey Thomas. The citizens of Endicott were generally neighborly people who cooperated and got along with one another, but Mikey was an outstanding exception to the "do unto others" rule. Mikey was a successful businessman with a store and a mill near his home above Otter Creek, not too far from Grandpa Rakes. But he was a mean-spirited man who was thoroughly disliked by his neighbors who eventually found a way to encourage him to leave the country. In the early 1920s Mikey worked for the school system in an administrative position which required him to visit the classrooms for inspection or oversight. During one of those tours, he purposely humiliated one of the new teachers, Delma Simms, Paul's half sister and Elva's Ferrum Training School roommate. Delma had recently completed her associate degree from Radford College and begun teaching in one of the schools in Endicott. At the time the local school administrators required that all teachers be at least 18-years old. Delma was only 17, a few months shy of her eighteenth birthday, a fact Thomas knew. That did not stop him from putting Delma on the spot by asking her her age in front of a classroom filled with students. Not knowing how to handle the situation Delma made the mistake of answering that she was 18. Mikey jumped on her response and in his hateful, whiney voice saying, "You're lying, you're the same age as my daughter, Elsie," mortifying the youthful woman.

This was just one example of his cruel behavior. There must have been many others because Mikey Thomas was "run out of town." He knew it was time to leave when his barn mysteriously burned, then his mill. He and his wife, (who was Lucy Peters Cannaday's sister), and their children moved several counties away to Buchanan.

The behavior of Mikey Thomas and his treatment by the local community was unusual. Most people in this isolated rural area were more like the Simms' friend and neighbor Arthur Snead. Arthur, his wife Elsie, their son Lawrence, and daughter Vida lived beside the road that crossed Runnett Bag Creek and led to the Simms farm and on over to Hurd's Branch. Arthur and Lawrence came to the rescue of folks like my grandfather numerous times. Before the road was paved and the bridge constructed across the creek, travelers regularly got stuck in the mire of that miserable road or in Runnett Bag Creek. Arthur was always there, with his horse if necessary, to help pull the wagons and buggies out of the mud, snow, or ice.

Snead was an intelligent but uneducated man and a bit naïve. When he first heard a radio, he did not believe the sound was actually coming over airwaves. He was convinced someone was inside the box talking or throwing his voice. He refused to accept the fact of radio waves, and when people insisted they did exist, he said it just wasn't so. Arthur had a wristwatch, but no one was sure whether or not he could tell time. Whenever anyone asked him what time it was, he would show them the watch and say, "You tell me."

Modernity began to find a its way into the backwoods of Franklin County; by the 1930s electricity, radios, and telephones had arrived, connecting people who lived in the country to the rest of the world. The telephone company first strung lines in the Endicott section of Franklin County around 1915. The early telephone was a big, brown box attached to the wall with a conical black cylinder to speak into, and a separate ear piece on a chord extending from one side of the box, and a hand crank on the other side to ring up others on their line or to call a central operator; there was also a gold bell at the bottom of the telephone box which sounded when calls came in. The telephone lines were laid out geographically. Anyone on the Hurds Branch line who wanted to call someone who wasn't on their line—in Roanoke, say—had to call a central operator who was, in this case, Sam Thomas, who lived on the Runnett Bag Creek road. Sam would switch the caller to another main or central area—the Crossroads operator—who then switched them to an operator in Ferrum, then to Rocky Mount, and finally to Roanoke. If Sam wasn't home or available, the caller just had to wait.

All lines were party lines, with 10 to 12 households on a line, each with a distinctive ring code. The Simms' ring was one long and two shorts. Everyone on a party line knew everyone else's ring and no one hesitated or thought it bad manners to listen in on their neighbors' conversations. In fact it was expected, an entertainment, an obligation—almost. One of Paul and Eula's party line members admonished herself by saying, "I've gotten so lazy lately that I haven't even been listening in on the telephone."

The major problem with this neighborly snooping was that the more people tapped into the lines and listened, the more they bled the signal which became weak and hard to hear. Weak voice signals could sometimes contribute to serious situations. Nurse Annie Barlow, the local midwife missionary from England, was having trouble delivering Macey Midkiff Gillespie's baby. She needed advice and was trying desperately to call the doctor in Roanoke, but she could not get through because too many people were doing their "duty" by eavesdropping. Finally she had to order them to "Get the hell off the line. I'm dealing with an emergency here and need the line clear to make a long distance call to the doctor." Everyone cooperated and hung up immediately. After making arrangements to take her patient to the hospital in Roanoke, Nurse Annie helped Macey into her car, and had driven as far as Boones Mill when the baby decided "it was time." She pulled off the side of the road, delivered the baby, turned the car around, and drove Macey and her newborn back home.

The Endicott area was a little later than the rest of the nation in acquiring inventions like telephones and radios due in large part to the mountainous terrain and the condition of its roadways. One of the most "notorious" of those roads was Cannaday's Gap, a precipitous two to three mile drop from the top of the Blue Ridge Mountains (not too far from the present day Smart View pull-off on the Blue Ridge Parkway) at the Floyd County line into the valley formed by Runnett Bag Creek. The very mention of the words 'Cannaday's Gap' could bring whistles to knowing peoples' lips. They would shake their heads and tell stories, both amusing and terrifying, about incidents that happened along that stretch of road, which even today remains a fright with plunging descents, steep drop offs, and blind curves. It gives brakes a work-out and drivers heartburn. But when that little "highway" was constructed in the middle of the 19th century by James Cannaday, it was a marvelous improvement, a direct passage across the mountains to the west.

The unwritten law of this one-lane mountain road was that anyone coming down the mountain had the right-of-way over anyone going up, because the ascender could stop more readily than the descender. That generally accepted rule proved to be a problem for one of the local bootleggers who was driving a car loaded with a fresh supply of moonshine. He was headed up the mountain when he met a man on a slide (a wooden sled pulled by a horse) coming down the mountain. They could not go by one another and were at an impasse, or so it seemed, until the "whiskey baron" solved the dilemma. He pulled out a roll of dollar bills, bought the other man's slide, pitched it over the side of the cliff, and continued on with business.

Russell Cannaday had a dilemma of his own coming down Cannaday's Gap. His problem also involved a vehicle, but in this case it was his own. He was returning home from work in Floyd and had Celeste Simms as a passenger. She had hitched a ride with him to go to town to renew her teacher's certificate. Half way down that treacherous mountain road, Russell's car had a flat tire, a common automotive experience in the early days of rubber manufacture, and normally not something to worry over. Russell was a pro at changing tires and was prepared to tend to this temporary inconvenience. He got out of the car, unloaded the jack and the spare tire, and began to pump up the car. But the vehicle was on too much of an incline and every time he tried to lift up the automobile, it fell off the jack. After repeated attempts to jack up the car and repeated failures, the generally sweet-natured but quick to anger Russell lost his temper. In complete disgust he hurled the jack over the side of the cliff accompanied by a long stream of creative profanity, something else he was proficient at, and drove home on the flat tire, now completely ruined. We probably have Celeste, who was much more amused by the circumstances than Russell, to thank for saving and sharing this particular family story.

Cannaday's Gap was the most dangerous road over in the country, but it was not the only one. The wicked hairpin curve around Long Branch Creek, on Route 40 between Long Branch Church and Endicott, was also hazardous and the scene of many accidents. For the Simms' neighbor Charlie Rakes, it was doubly troublesome. Charlie was a new driver in a new car when he came to the sharp horseshoe bend on Long Branch Hill; he misjudged the curve, drove off the road, and wrecked his car. Not too long after the accident, he was driving along the same road showing a friend who was riding with him the site of the unfortunate incident when he wrecked his automobile again in the exact same spot.

Elva was another victim of Long Branch Hill, although she couldn't really blame the hill for her trouble. She was driving home from teaching school with another teacher. Just as she got to the perilous hairpin curve, the brakes on her car failed. She told her passenger, Liz Scott, to jump, but Liz wisely decided to stay in the vehicle. Elva managed to drive the car into the bank of the hill and avoid a catastrophe, but she was so shaken by the accident that she could barely walk when she got out of the car.

The roadways, waterways, hills, and hollows of the mountain community of Endicott have a long list of fascinating place names. Many were named for the people associated with them—Cannaday's Gap, Stan Martin Mountain, Griffith Hill, Nowlin's Mill, Hurd's Branch, and Tharp Creek, for example; others, such as Otter Creek, Laurel Bluff, Buttermilk Creek, Turkey Branch we can only guess their origin. We do know that in the late 19th or early 20th century the local postmaster chose the name Endicott for this area of Franklin County. According to Paul's father, J. R. Simms, officials in Richmond gave the local postmaster three choices of names for the community, and he selected "Endicott." Other than Endicott the most interesting name to our family is Runnett Bag Creek, the stream

Earl Simms and Elva Simms Cannaday visit the country in 1998

along which the Cannadays settled and expanded their holdings from the first days they came to Franklin County. It is an unusual name and throughout its history, beginning in the 1780s or sooner, has had many different spellings in deed books and different explanations for its origin, including the possibility of a similarly named creek in Ireland.[2]

Today, many of Endicott's original homes are gone or overgrown with Virginia Creeper, honeysuckle, and kudzu, and are rotting away. Our ancestral Cannaday log cabin, which stood for 220 years, has given way to neglect and collapsed. For the most part the self-sufficient, industrious farmers like my grandparents have left, and their way of life has disappeared, gone up in smoke—just like the Simms farmhouse.

One of the real joys in doing the research for these stories was a trip I took back to the site of the farm with my Uncle Earl in his nineties and my mother in her eighties. We walked to the far barn, still standing though bent with age, and climbed up the Chestnut Ridge to the place where chestnut and fruit trees once flourished, where Uncle Earl landed his airplane in the 1940s and where there is a spectacular view of the Blue Ridge Mountains in the distance.

Down in the valley at the home-place site, we could see the bottom land, which had fed the family with vegetables for 50 years, now a maze of brambles, weeds and vines. The place where the farm house had stood was no better, filled with tree stumps, deteriorating fence posts, and saplings competing with honeysuckle vines for survival. Amid all that vegetation we managed to unearth the concrete walkway which had led to the side door of the house. My mother, determined to locate the spring house, trudged down to the branch through the poison ivy, red and pink multiflora rose bushes, and snakey-looking weeds with her silver-handled cane (actually a regular cane wrapped in duct tape for better gripping) to steady herself and to fend off for any unexpected or unwanted wildlife. She yelled out when she found it. Only the concrete wall and a few orange day lilies remained; the branch was still and almost dry.

In spite of the sad condition of the once glorious Simms farm, that June day the mountain laurel and rhododendron were at their peak, a riot of pink and purple blossoms covered the cliff sides from Runnett Bag Creek to the Ivy Hill, a grand salute to a brother and sister on their return to the country.

Notes for Chapter XIV, Kinfolk and More:

1. Clem Snead was father of Charles and Samp Snead who married Eula's sisters, Effie and Lillian Rakes.

2. The name for the creek—Runnett Bag or Runnett Bagh or Running Bagg—among its many spellings, may go farther back, but that is as far as I have traced the Cannaday family deeds.

Closing Note

In 1998 when I began what I called "the project," all I planned to do was collect and preserve the Simms family stories. I had heard many wonderful stories over my lifetime and even had a few of my own, but I had absolutely no idea that the family history that existed in my mother's, her brothers' and sister's memories was so rich and extensive. I didn't know what I had gotten myself into or where it was going to lead.

After several years of asking questions and listening to my relatives tell me tales about their childhoods and about their parents, stories about grandparents they knew and grandparents they didn't, legends and myths about frontier kinsmen, I began to realize that I had more than a few pranks and interesting children's tales to re-tell. I had to admit to the awesome task of writing a book, a family memoir.

I posed most of my questions to my mother Elva and my Uncle Earl. They were the oldest Simms children, had the deepest memories, and lived closest to me. The two of them continually surprised me with the details they could recollect; the more I delved, the more I woke up their past, and the more they remembered.

Uncle Earl was 92 when I started the "project." Over the next four years he was increasingly confined to his bed and died in 2002. When Mother and I went to see him for interview sessions, he would brighten, no doubt glad to have some company, but gladder to have a chance to return to his happy boyhood days over in the country, and to have the stories from his life written down, and in that way to save his life even after he was gone. One day as I was leaving and went to kiss him goodbye, he held my hand and said, "You are a good girl." A compliment I treasure.

The author and her family at a reunion held at the Rakes homeplace c1959. Standing: Becky and Kenneth. Seated: Russell and Elva Cannaday

My mother was my first editor. She read every word and gave her blessing to each chapter with an encouraging, "Very good, Sweetheart." Except when I had gotten something wrong, then it was "No, honey, it wasn't like that at all"—with the implied question, "don't you know anything at all?" She and Uncle Earl were often shocked by my ignorance about life on the farm or other important things, like how to make moonshine. He had to draw a picture of a still for me, which I have included in the "Not All Work" chapter. Once Mother began thinking about her girlhood, she was likely to remember incidents from those long-gone days at any time—usually at inconvenient moments, like when I'm driving the car with no way to write down even the gist of her latest recollection. "That's where Grandpa Rakes was struck by lightning," she told me on one of our trips over in the country. "*Grandpa Rakes was struck by lightning?*" I said. "I didn't know that; don't forget to tell me again when we are home."

When I interviewed my sweet, reticent Uncle Edsel, I encouraged him not to be intimidated by the presence of the tape recorder. He looked at it like it was a coiled snake and said, "How can I not be?" But once he got his mind back to the glory years when he was a student at Ferrum Training School, or a little boy on the farm, or a big brother installing the swing on the Ivy Hill, he relaxed and forgot about the recorder and took real pleasure in telling me his stories.

My uncles and my mother have appreciated my work and the opportunity to relive their young lives, and my Aunt Betty has enthusiastically encouraged me. She has told me on several occasions how much she has learned from the chapters she has read. That should not be surprising because she was the youngest child by 14 years. Betty has always been like a big sister to me, and the times I spent with my grandparents were better when she was there too.

I know that there are more stories floating around that nobody has told me yet, and that there are other versions of the stories I have told here; people's memories vary. I worry that writing them down freezes them and makes them "gospel" truth. An apt saying about memoirs, which I heard from my cousin Betty Jane Simms Hagan, comes to mind: "These stories are all true; some of them actually happened."

I am grateful to my uncles, to Betty, to Mother, for generously sharing their early years with me and to Harold Simms, (Paul's nephew), and Mary Elizabeth Simms Whelby, (Paul's niece) who told me stories I had never heard before which enrich the memoir, and to all my other relatives and friends who have encouraged and advised me.

I would like to thank Louis Hodges who tried to get me straight about the life cycle of bees, and Carol Karsh who helped with the maps, and most especially I want to thank my husband Holt who read and carefully edited every word of every chapter. So if it isn't any good it's his fault.

Appendix A

This Appendix contains more complete genealogies of the Cannaday, Simms, and Rakes families than appear within the text.

KENNADY/CANNADAY GENEALOGY

WILLIAM KENNADY/CANNADY SR. (b. c1715-d. c1805) M BIDDY

Their son:

WILLIAM KENNADY/CANNADAY JR. (b. c1735-d. 1801) M NANCY

Their children were:

1. **James Cannaday, Sr.** a Rev. War Soldier, (b. c1755-d. 1817) m (1775) Elizabeth Rakes, born in Buckingham County (b. c1756-d. c1853)
2. Sarah Cannaday m John Radford (moved to NC in 1802).
3. Misnier Cannaday m Samuel Underwood d.1803.
4. John Cannaday m Nancy?
5. Nancy Cannaday m James Allen

JAMES CANNADAY, SR. (b. c1755-d. 1817) M (1775) ELIZABETH RAKES (RAIKES) (b. c1756-d. c1853)Their children were:

1. **James Cannaday 2nd** (b. c1783-d. 1861) m (1813) Sarah (Sally) Young (b. c-1789-d. 1861).
2. David Cannaday (b. c1794) m (1819) Jane Walker. They moved to Raleigh Co., VA, later WV).
3. Elizabeth Cannaday m (1797) Isaiah Turner.
4. William (Patrick Billy) Cannaday (b. 1781-d. 1874)
   m [1] Martha (Patsy) Wright
   m [2] Nancy Hill.
   He had 20 children, 20 slaves, and lived in Patrick County.
5. Mary (Polly) Cannaday (b. 1781-d. 1861) m (1800) Pleasant Thomas.
6. Charles Cannaday (b. 1793-d. 1853) m (1822) Mary Ingram (b. 1805-d. 1859). He died of measles.
7. Pleasant Cannaday (b. 1801-d. 1829) m (1822) Elizabeth Young (b. 1805-d. 1907). They had four children, one of whom was:
   Isaac Young Cannaday (b. 1825-d. 1875) m (1843) Mary "Polly" Rakes (b. 1824-d. 1870). She was the sister of R.R. Rakes.Two of their 9 children were:
   A. Lucinda Elizabeth Cannaday (b. 1852-d. 1886) m (1872) James Robert Simms (b. 1844-d. 1928). They had five children:

i. Arthur Simms (b. 1873-d. 1899).
ii. Julia Mary (Mollie) Simms (b. 1875-d. 1949) m (1897) Baxter Franklin Denison (b. 1872-d. 1944).
iii. Paul Simms (b. 1878-d. 1964) m (1905) Eula Mae Rakes (b. 1886-d. 1982).
iv. Homer Harry Simms (b. 1881-d. 1904).
v. Virginia Grace Simms (b. 1883-d. 1948) m Charles Robert Brogan.

B. Charles Cannaday (b. 1849-d. 1895) m Virginia Boyd (b. 1850-d. 1933). Their children were:
i. Florida Cannaday (b. 1878) m (1) Archer Moore (2) Henry Sylvatus Akins.
ii. Isaac Thomas Cannaday (b. 1873-d.1953)
m [1] Lucy Peters (b. 1878-d. 1927) Their children were:
1. George Harry (b. 1895-d. 1966) m Inez Kelly
2. Ezra (b. 1898-d. 1957) m Emma Hancock
3. Charles Jackson (b. 1900-d. 1939) m Mammie Rakes
4. Theodore (b. 1902-d. 1975)
m [1] Mammie Marshall
m [2] Viola Stone
5. Minnie May (b. 1904-d. 1988)
m [1] Albert Ingram
m [2] James Roberson
6. Isaac Russell (b. 1907-d. 1976) m (1930) Elva Simms (b. 1907)
m [2] (c1928) Eleanor Hale.

8. John Cannaday (b. ?-d. 1830) m (1812) Martha (Susan) Winfrey
There were perhaps 3 or 4 other children for whom there are no records.

JAMES CANNADAY 2ND (b. c1783-d. 1861) M (1813) SARAH YOUNG (b. c-1789-d. 1861) Their children were:

1. Peter Cannaday (b. 1813-d. c1903) m Mildred Ann (Millie, Annie) Turner (b. 1815)
2. James B. Cannaday 3rd (b. 1815-d. ?) m (1837) Martha Turner (b. 1819-d. c1838)
3. Isaac Cannaday (b. 1817-d. 1861) m (1841) Mary Ann Shelor (b. 1815-d. 1891) He represented Franklin County in Virginia Legislature.
4. William A. Cannaday (b. c1815-d. 1900) m Sarah J. Shelor (b. 1825-d. 1922)
5. **Caroline Y. Cannaday** (b. 1820-d. 1899)m (1841) Ignatius Andrew (Andy) Jackson Simms (b. 1816-d. 1855)
6. Elizabeth Cannaday m (1847) Thomas Banks (Major)
7. Stephen H. Cannaday (never married) d. 1871
8. David Cannaday 2nd (never married) b.1830-d. 1859
9. Sarah (Sallie) Cannaday (b. 1831-d. 1855) m (1854) Valentine Harrison Byrd
10. Mary Cannaday (b. 1830, ?twin of David) m Wiley Menefee
11. Harriett Elizabeth Cannaday (b. 1826) m Thomas Moseley (b. 1830)

12. John Treadwell Cannaday (b. 1833-d. 1896)
m (1857) [1]Sarah (Sally) Banks
They were the parents of Hughes Dillard Cannaday.
m [2] Caroline Malinda Prillaman (b. 1841-d. 1917)

CAROLINE Y. CANNADAY (b. 1820-d. 1899) M (1841) IGNATIUS ANDREW JACKSON SIMMS (b. 1816-d. 1855) Their children were:
1. **James Robert Simms** (b. 1844-d. 1928)
m (1872) [1] Lucinda Elizabeth (Betty) Cannaday (b. 1851-d. 1886)
m (1887) [2] Mary Pope Shively (b. 1864-d. 1968)
2. Andrew Jackson Simms m Blanche Shelton
3. Julia Simms m Turner Griffith
4. Mary (Sally?) Simms
5. Virginia (Jennie) Simms (d. 1904) m Lewis Hancock

JAMES ROBERT SIMMS (b. 1844-d. 1928)
M (1872) [1] LUCINDA ELIZABETH CANNADAY (b. 1851-d. 1886)
Their children were:
1. Arthur Simms (b. 1873-d. 1899 in Sand Lick, WV)
2. Julia Mary (Mollie) Simms (b. 1875-d. 1949) m (1897) Baxter Franklin Denison (b. 1872-d. 1944)
3. **Paul Simms** (b. 1878-d. 1964) m (1905) Eula Mae Rakes (b. 1886-d. 1982)
4. Homer Harry Simms (b. 1881-d. 1904)
5. Virginia Grace Simms (b. 1883-d. 1948) m Charles Robert Brogan
M (1887) [2] MARY POPE SHIVELY (b. 1864-d. 1968)
Their children were:
1. Archer Gale Simms (b. 1888-d. 1970)
m [1] Nola Dudley (d. 1914)
m (1918)[2] Ruth Watson (b. 1896-d. 1968)
2. James Simms (b. 1889-d. 1975)
m [1] Lera Adkins (b. 1892-d. ?)
m [2] Ellen Carter
3. Bessie Ora Simms (b. 1896-d. 1978) m John Goode
4. Lillian Delma Simms (b. 1903-d. 1990) m Claude Lumsden (b. 1900-d. 1959)
5. Amy Simms (b. 1906-d. 2002) m (1925) Grady Thomas (b. 1906-d. 1993)

PAUL SIMMS (b. 1878-d. 1964) M (1905) EULA MAE RAKES (b. 1886-d. 1982)
Their children were:
1. Leonard Earl Simms (b. 1905-d. 2002)
m [1] Ruth Griffith (b. 1907-d. 1991)
m [2] Irene Aliff (b. 1907-d. 1988)
2. Althea Elva Simms (b. 1907) m (1930) Isaac Russell Cannaday (b. 1907-d. 1976)
3. Eron Edsel Simms (b. 1915-d. 2006)
m [1] (1940) Sylvia Shively (b. 1919-d. 1961)

m [2] (1963) Corene Martin (b. 1925)
4. Betty Iris Simms (b. 1929) m (1952) George Rodney Hayes (b. 1925)

SEMMES, SIMMS GENEALOGY

MARMADUKE SEMMES (b. c1635-d. 1692/3) M (1668) FORTUNE MILBURN (b. c1647-d. 1701), widow of [1] Bulmer Mitford (b. c1643-d.c1665) Their children were:

1. Anthony Semmes (b. 1671-d. 1709)
2. James Semmes (b. 1670-d. 1728)
3. John Semmes (d. 1718)
   He was the father of four children.
4. **Marmaduke Semmes** (b. c1675-d. 1729) m Elizabeth Clarkson (b. c1679-d. c1736)

MARMADUKE [II] (b. c1675-d. 1717) M (1707) ELIZABETH CLARKSON (b. c1679-d. c1736), widow of [1] William Smith (b. c1674-d. c1692), m (1692).
Children of Marmaduke II and Elizabeth were:

1. Ruth Semmes
2. **Francis Semmes** (b. c1711-d. c1770) m (1733) Lucretia Chapman
3. Eleanor Semmes
4. Elizabeth Semmes I (b. 1716-d. 1716)
5. Elizabeth Semmes II (b. 1717) m (1730) Abel Carrico

FRANCIS SEMMES (b. c1711-d. c1770) M (1733) LUCRETIA CHAPMAN
Their children were:

1. Elizabeth Semmes (b. 1734) m (James) Murphy
2. Jane Semmes (b. 1736)
3. Joseph Semmes (b. 1738) m Elizabeth
4. Marmaduke Semmes (b. 1741) m Susannah
5. Chloe Semmes (b. 1743)
6. **Ignatius Semmes** (b. 1745-d. 1819)
   m (c1772) [1] Sabret Hobart (b. c1749-d. 1788)
   m (1790) [2] Jane Nance
7. Francis Semmes m Mary
8. Williamson Semmes
9. Ann Semmes
10. Eleanor Semmes

IGNATIUS SEMMES/SIMMS (b. 1745-d. 1819)
M (c 1772) [1] SABRET HOBART (b. c1749-d. 1788)
M (1790) [2] Jane Nance. The children were:

1. Polly
2. Anne

3. Elender
4. Exoney
5. Marget
6. Jancee
7. John Dabney
8. William Robertson
9. **Ignatius Andrew Jackson Simms** (b. 1816-d. 1855) m (1841) Caroline Young Cannaday (b. 1820-d. 1899)
10. Marmaduke Manor

IGNATIUS ANDREW JACKSON SIMMS (b. 1816-d. 1855)
M (1841) CAROLINE Y. CANNADAY (b. 1820-d. 1899)

Their children were:

1. **James Robert Simms** (b. 1844-d. 1928)
   m (1872) [1] Lucinda Elizabeth (Betty) Cannaday (b. 1851-d. 1886)
   m (1887) [2] Mary Pope Shively (b. 1864-d. 1968)
2. Andrew Jackson Simms m Blanche Shelton
3. Julia Simms m Turner Griffith
4. Mary (Sally?) Simms
5. Virginia (Jennie) Simms (d. 1904) m Lewis Hancock

JAMES ROBERT SIMMS (b. 1844-d. 1928)
M (1872) [1] LUCINDA ELIZABETH CANNADAY (b. 1851-d. 1886)

Their children were:

1. Arthur Simms (b.1873-d. 1899 in Sand Lick, WV)
2. Julia Mary (Mollie) Simms (b. 1875-d. 1949) m (1897) Baxter Franklin Denison (b. 1872-d. 1944). Their children were:
   a. Baxter Okemah
   b. Betty Marinda
   c. Grace
   d. Paul
3. **Paul Simms** (b. 1878-d. 1964) m (1905) Eula Mae Rakes (b. 1886-d. 1982)
4. Homer Harry Simms (b. 1881-d. 1904)
5. Virginia Grace Simms (b. 1883-d. 1948) m Charles Robert Brogan.
   Their children were:
   a. Elsie
   b. Fred
   c. Wilma
   d. Harris
   e. Geneva
   f. Minnie

M (1888) [2] MARY POPE SHIVELY (b. 1864-d. 1968)

Their children were:

1. Archer Gale Simms (b. 1888-d. 1970)

m [1] Nola Dudley (b. ?-d. 1914). They had:
a. Harold Simms (b. 1914) m Elvarine Ingram (b. 1920). Their children are:
i. John
ii. Tillie
iii. Cynthia
iv. Claudia
v. James
m (1918) [2] Ruth Watson (b. 1896-d. 1968). The children of Archer Gale Sr. and Ruth were:
a. Archer Gale Jr. (b. 1919-d. 1970)
b. Celeste (b. 1921-d. c 2001)
c. Mary Elizabeth Simms Whelby (b. 1926-d. 2004). Her son is:
i. Joe Whelby
2. James Simms (b. 1889-d. 1975)
m [1] Lera Adkins (b. 1892-d. ?) Their children were:
a. Mildred (b. 1911)
b. Essie (b. 1912)
c. Mammie (b. 1914)
d. Edith (b. 1918)
e. Christine (b. 1922)
f. James Ralph (b. 1924)
m [2]Ellen Carter
3. Bessie Ora Simms (b. 1896-d. 1978) m. John Goode
4. Lillian Delma Simms (b. 1903-d. 1990) m Claude Lumsden (b. 1903-d. 1959). Their children are:
a. Russell
b. Joyce
c. Edith
d. Robert (b. 1934)
5. Amy Simms (b. 1906-d. 2002) m (1925) Grady Thomas (b. 1906-d. 1993). Their children are:
a. Jean (b. 1926)
b. Barbara (b. 1938)
c. Pat (b. 1941)
d. Bill (b. 1943)

PAUL SIMMS (b. 1878-d. 1964) M (1905) EULA MAE RAKES (b. 1886-d. 1982) Their children were:
1. Leonard Earl Simms (b. 1905-d. 2002)
m [1] Ruth Griffith (b. 1907-d.1991)
Their son was:
a. Vance Keith Simms (b. 1928-d. 2006) m (1950) Virginia Baier (b. 1930)
i. Paul Keith Simms (b. 1955)
ii. Martin Leonard Simms (b. 1956-d. 1958)

iii. Mark Eric Simms (b. 1959)
iv. Karen Ann Simms Harris (b. 1965)
m [2] Irene Aliff (b.1907-d. 1988)
2. Althea Elva Simms (b. 1907) m (1930) Isaac Russell Cannaday (b. 1907-d. 1976)
Their children are:
a. Lucy Rebecca Cannaday Merchant (b. 1941)
b. Kenneth Simms Cannaday (b 1946)
3. Eron Edsel Simms (b. 1915-d. 2006)
m (1940) [1] Sylvia Shively (b. 1919-d. 1961) Their children are:
a. Judith Simms Strawn (b. 1941)
b. Richard Edsel Simms (b 1943)
c. Betty Jane Simms Hagan (b. 1945)
m (1964) [2] Corene Martin (b. 1925)
4. Betty Iris Simms (b. 1929) m (1952) George Rodney Hayes (b. 1925)
Their children are:
a. George Rodney Hayes Jr. (b. 1952)
b. Claire Simms Hayes Brant (b. 1956)
c. Paul Thornton Hayes (b. 1960)

RAKES GENEALOGY

CHARLES RAKES (b. c1745-d. 1835/8)
m [1] JANE
Their children were:
1. **Samuel Jackson Rakes** (b. c1783-d. 1852) m (c1815) Lucinda Nowlin (b. 1801-d. 1865)
2. Dorcas Rakes (b. c1785) m (1812) Richard Reynard Winfrey (d. 1842)
3. Anna Rakes (b. c1787-d. c1836) m (1814) Joshua (Joseph) Hall
4. Mary (Bashie) Rakes (b. c1789) m (1806) Edward Cockram Jr.
5. Rhoda Rakes (b. c1791) m (1803) John Spalding
6. Elizabeth Rakes (b. c1793) m (1806) Robert Boyd (b. 1780)
7. Charles Rakes (b. c1795)
8. Sarah Rakes (b. c1797) m Isham Cockram Sr. (b. c1773-d. 1860)
9. Constant Rakes m ?Cannaday
10. Female Rakes m Fleming Plasters
11. Female Rakes m James Light
12. Female Rakes m John C. Hall
13. Janes Rakes (b. c1781-d c1880) m (1800) Brice Edwards (b. 1779-d. 1856)
m (1827)
[2] Nancy Hall Hubbard

SAMUEL JACKSON RAKES (b. c1783-d. 1852) m (1820) LUCINDA NOWLIN(b. 1801-d. c1865) Their children were:
1. Charles Rakes (b. 1821-d. ?) m (1841) Mary Ann Griffith (b. 1825 ?)

2. Judith Rakes (b. 1823-d. ?) m (1839) John F. Griffith
3. Mary "Polly" Rakes (b. 1824-d. 1870) m (1843) Isaac Young Cannaday (b. 1825-d. 1875
4. German (Jarman) Rakes (b. 1826-d. 1880) m (1850) Mary Ann (Ellen) Allen (b. c1831)
5. **Richard Randall Rakes** (b. 1827-d. 1905)
   m (1854))[1] Sarah Deborah Turner (b. c1836-d. 1887)
   m [2] Mary E. "Molly" Dent (b. 1868-d. ?)
6. Virginia Jane (Jennie) Rakes (b. 1829-d. c1930) m (1847) David Hall (b. 1826-d. 1862)
7. Malinda E. "Linda" Rakes (b. 1830-d. 1924)m (1848) John Isaac Snuffer (b. c1827)
8. Samuel Jackson Rakes (b. 1832-d. 1864) m (1852) Ruth Ann Thomas (b. 1830-d. ?)
9. John Rakes (b. 1934)
10. Nancy Rakes (b. 1836-d. ?) m (1852) Fleming Turner (b. 1832-d.?)
11. Alexander Rakes (b. 1838 d. 1928)
   m (1858) [1] Violet Annie Turner (b. 1841-d. 1885)
   m (1886) [2] Sarah A. Bennett (Burnett) (b. 1842-d. 1900)
   m (1901) [3] Priscilla "Pearl" Lucinda Harris (b. 1880-d. 1936)
12. Christopher (or Clyde) Columbus Rakes (b. 1840-d. 1928/32?) m (1865) Martha V. Nowlin (Nolen) (b. 1845-d. 1920)
13. Lucinda Elizabeth "Betsey" Rakes (b. 1846-d. 1928/32?) m (1862) James M. Spencer (b. 1839-d. ?)

RICHARD RANDALL RAKES (b. 1827-d. 1905)
m (1854) [1] SARAH DEBORAH TURNER (b. c1836-d. 1887)
Their children were:
1. Charles Jefferson Rakes (b. 1854-d. 1896) m (1876) Honey (Exoney)(Martha) Ellen Ross (b. c1857-d. ?)
2. Judith A. Rakes (b. 1855?-d. 1949) m (1873) Charles P. Nolen (b. 1850-d. c1948)
3. Nancy A. (Ida Bell) Rakes (b. 1859-d. 1930) m (1875) Sparrell Wood (b. 1847-d. 1937)
4. William E. Rakes (b. 1866-d. 1946) m (1890) Lilly Alice Nolen (b. 1873-d. 1944)
5. Gooley Rakes (probably Columbus McGruder)
6. Israel G. "Is" Rakes (b. 1868-d. 1943) m Truly E.(b. 1871-d. 1945)
7. Susan A. Rakes (b. 1872-d. c1895) m (1891) Robert E. Lee Sr. (b. 1866)
8. **Columbus McGruder Rakes** (b. 1864-d. 1952)
   m (1885) [1] Ophelia A. Thomas (b. 1867-d. 1920)
   m (1922) [2] Sallie Willie Sigmon (b. 1887-d. ?)
9. Samuel Tyrone Rakes (b. 1877-d. 1907) m Cinderella Nolen (b. 1879-d. 1968)
   m (1892) [2] Mollie Dent (b. 1868). Their children were:
   a. Richard H. Rakes (b. 1893)
   b. John M. Rakes (b. 1896)
   c. George Robert Rakes (b. 1901-d. 1990)
      m (1920) [1] Maude Lillian Shough (b. 1902)

m (1945) [2] Minnie Alice Foley

COLUMBUS McGRUDER RAKES (b. 1864-d. 1952) m [1] (1885) OPHELIA A. THOMAS (b. 1867-d. 1920) Their children were:

1. **Eula Mae Rakes** (b. 1886-d. 1982) m (1905) Paul Simms (b. 1878-d. 1964)
2. Iva Nora Rakes (b. 1888-d. 1977) m (1908) John Will Bowling (b. 1886-d ?)Their children were:
   - a.Reuben Eldridge (b. 1907-d. 1970)
   - b. Leonard Harold (b. 1909-d. 2003)
   - c. Lena Elisabeth (b. 1910-d. 1978)
   - d. Noel Ned (Dick) (b. 1912-d. c2006)
   - e. Vivian (b. 1913)
   - f. Thelma (b. 1914-d. 2006)
   - g. Muriel (b. 1916-d. 2005)
   - h. Lawrence (b. 1918)
   - i. Sylvia (b. 1920)
   - j. Hallie Mae (b. 1922-d. 1978)
3. Pearl Rakes (b. 1893-d. 1896)
4. Effie Beulah Rakes (b. 1898-d. 1999) m Charles Snead (b. 1887-d. 1963) Their children are:
   - a. Rubye Snead Slayton Nixon (b. 1918)
   - b. Charles Hubert Snead (b. 1924)
5. Lillian Lena Rakes (b. 1903-d. 1995) m Samp Snead (Charles' brother) Their children are:
   - a. Warren Snead (b. 1922)
   - b. Neza Snead Jolly Woolwine (b. 1927)

m[2] (1922) Sally Willie Sigmon (b. 1887-d. ?)

EULA MAE RAKES (b. 1886-d. 1982) m (1905) PAUL SIMMS (b. 1878-d. 1964) Their children were:

1. Leonard Earl Simms (b. 1905-d. 2002)
   m [1] Ruth Griffith (b. 1907-d. 1991)
   m [2] Irene (b. 1907-d. 1988)
2. Althea Elva Simms (b. 1907) m (1930) Isaac Russell Cannaday (b. 1907-d. 1976)
3. Eron Edsel Simms (b. 1915-d. 2006)
   m (1940) [1] Sylvia Shively (b. 1919-d. 1961)
   m (1964) [2] Corene Martin
4. Betty Iris Simms (b. 1929) m (1952) George Rodney Hayes (b. 1925)

Appendix B

This appendix reports the sources for the transfers of land by the Cannaday, Simms, and Rakes families from Chapter I, Settling the Ancestors.

Cannaday Family Land Acquisitions And Dispositions:

8. Deed References for William Cannaday Sr. Franklin County, VA Courthouse: 1786, purchase of 140 acres for 10 pounds, Deed book 1, p. 124; 1790, purchase of 134 acres for 5 pounds, Deed book 2, p. 354; purchase of 180 acres for 44 pounds, Deed book 2, pp. 283-4.

In 1792 he kept clerks busy recording the sale of six different pieces of property. The list from Franklin County, VA Courthouse follows: sale of 180 acres for 10 pounds, Deed book 2, pp. 342-3; sale of 106 acres for 10 pounds, Deed book 2, p. 344; sale of 60 acres for 10 pounds, Deed book 4?—probably book 2, pp. 351-2; sale of 135 acres for 10 pounds, Deed book 2, p. 359; sale of 129 acres for 30 pounds, Deed book 2, pp. 436-7; sale of 93 acres for 10 pounds, Deed book 2, p. 436-7. In 1801, he sold 145 acres for 60 pounds, Deed book 4, pp. 248-9 and 30 acres for 15 pounds, Deed book 4, p. 242. In 1802, he purchased 60 acres for 10 pounds, Deed book 4, p. 441, and in 1804 sold 100 acres for $50, Deed book 4, pp. 569-570.

9. Deed Reference for William Cannaday Jr. Franklin County, VA Courthouse: Deed book 2, p. 363; Deed book 2, p. 542; Plat Book #1, p. 56.

11. Deed Reference for William Cannaday, Sr. Franklin County, VA Courthouse: Deed book 4, p.243.

12. Deed References for John Cannaday; Franklin County, VA: Deed book 2, pp. 399-400; Deed book 2, pp. 435-6.

17. Deed References for James Cannaday I, Franklin County, VA, Courthouse. In 1790, he purchased 300 acres for 25 pounds, Deed book 2, pp. 285-6; 1792, he added 129 acres for 30 pounds, Deed book 2, p. 363 and the same year sold 105 acres for 5 pounds, Deed book 2, p. 547; in 1801 he purchased 145 acres for 60 pounds, Deed book 4, p. 248-9; 1804, he added 180 acres for 50 pounds, Deed book, p. 529; and in 1804 another 100 acres for $50, Deed book 4, pp. 569-570.

23. Deed References for James Cannaday II's land purchases, Franklin, County, VA, Courthouse: Deed Book 5, p. 464; Deed Book 6, p. 285; Deed Book 7, pp. 48, 598; Deed Book 8, p. 579(?); Deed Book 11, p. 56 (1819 purchase of 140 acres and premises from William and Martha Cannaday); Deed Book 13, pp. 208, 260, 378, 382; Deed Book 14, pp. 115, 346, 427; Deed Book 16, pp. 39, 209; Deed Book 17, p. 156 (1841 purchase of Hairston estate for $5400); Deed Book 21, p. 206; Deed Book 23, 418(?; Deed Book 24, p. 24; Deed Book 25, p. 156; Deed Book 26, p. 389.

Deed References for James Cannaday II's land sales on record, Franklin County, VA, Courthouse: Deed Book 12, p. 572; Deed Book 18, p. 194; Deed Book 19, p. 494; Deed Book 19, p. 495 (Sale of 30 acres to William Martin in 1847, probably a portion of the land that Paul Simms purchased from his father in 1903.); Deed Book 20, p.40; Deed Book 22, pp. 13, 15; Deed Book 24, pp. 25, 187; Deed Book 26, pp. 276, 390; Deed Book 27, p. 67 (Sale of 442 acres and premises for $5000 to John Treadwell Cannaday in 1860, probably Hairston Estate).

Simms Family Land Acquisitions And Dispositions

44. Deed References for Francis Semmes. Stoney Hill sold to William Clarkson. June 1, 1736, Prince George's County, Md; November 11, 1736 purchased 103 acres. Charles County, MD, Deed book 02:174; 1747 or 8 sold 103 acres of St. Georges to Hudson Wathen. Charles County, MD. ChD 22:333. The deed was signed "Francis [×] Simms; 1764, purchased 100 acres near "Zachiah Swamp" ChD L3:460; 1767 sold 103 acres St. Georges to Bennett Wathen. ChD 03:288.

48. Deed References for Ignatius Simms. Henry County, VA Courthouse: Deed book 1, p.162, Deed book 2, p. 66; Survey Book l, part 2, p. 298; Deed book 3, p. 397, Deed book 1, p. 72; Deed book 2, p. 191.

50. Deed Reference for Ignatiues Simms. Henry County, VA Courthouse: Deed Book 7, Page 614.

52. Deed References for Andrew Jackson Simms. Patrick County, VA Courthouse: Deed book 10, p. 1; Deed book 10, p. 73, Deed book 13, p. 383, Deed book 15, p. 219; Deed book 15, p. 221.

54. Deed References for Caroline Simms. Franklin County, VA Courthouse: Deed Book 27, page 284, Deed book 56, p. 468.

Rakes Family Land Transfers

58. Deed References for Charles Rakes. Henry County, VA Courthouse; Deed book 3, pp. 390-391; Patrick County, VA Courthouse: Deed Book 1, p. 201, Deed book 1, p. 514, Deed book 2, p. 549; Deed book 9, p. 220.

61. Samuel Rakes land purchases: Deed book 4, p.217, Patrick County; Deed book 8,

p. 19, Patrick County; Deed book 9, p. 78, Patrick County; Deed book 9, p. 326, p. 340, Patrick County; Deed book 9, p. 535; Deed book 11, p. 226; Deed book 13, p. 192, p. 194, Patrick County.

65. Richard Randall Rakes land transfer references: Deed book 15, p. 90, Patrick County; Deed book 18, p. 103; Deed book 19, p. 50, p. 399; Deed book 20, p. 5, p. 67; Deed book 24, p.54; Patrick County.

68. Land transfers for C. M. Rakes: Deed book 25, p. 389, Patrick County. Deed book 43, p. 598, Franklin County.

Appendix C

This appendix records the sources for wills of the Cannaday, Simms and Rakes Families.

Chapter I

Cannaday Family Will References:

19. Will regarding Elizabeth Cannaday, James Cannaday Sr.'s widow. Will Book 4, p.169, Franklin County.

20. Will for James Cannaday Sr. Will Book 2, pp.169-171, pp. 211-213. Rocky Mount, VA Courthouse.

27. Will for James Cannaday II. Will Book 13, p. 140, Franklin County Courthouse in Rocky Mount.

Simms Family Will References:

With the benefits of modern technology I was able to find copies of Marmaduke and Fortune Semmes' wills on the internet, documents which are on file at the Maryland Archives. In this way I was able to reach across 300 years to read the last wishes of my earliest American grand-parents' at home on my laptop computer.

33. Fortune Semmes will reference: St. Mary's County, Volume 11, pp. 200-201, Hall of Records, Maryland State Archives, Anapolis, MD.

35. Marmaduke Semmes' will: As noted in his will, Marmaduke had purchased the Middle Plantation tract from Andrew Woodberry. Will of Marmaduke Semmes, St. Mary's County, Volume 6, p. 33, Hall of Records, Maryland State Archives, Annapolis, MD.

39. Marmaduke Semmes' will.

40. Fortune Semmes' will.

41. Marmaduke Semmes II will. I have two references to his will. Prerog Ct. of MD Will Book (PCW) 14:518 and Will Book, Annapolis, MD, Charles County wills A. B. #3, folio 118.

45. Reference source for Francis Semmes' will. Charles County Will Book (ChW) AE6:0; also Prerog Ct of MD Will Bk 38:196.

51. Will reference for Ignatius Simms. Will Book 1, pp.118-120, pp.304-5, Patrick County.

Rakes Family Will References:

59. Reference for Charles Rakes' will: Will Book 3, p. 2, Patrick County.

60. Charles Rakes' will. Will Book 3, p.34, Patrick County.

62. Samuel Rakes will reference. Will Book 4, p. 159, Patrick County.

63. Samuel Rakes will reference: Will Book 4, pp. 257-259, Patrick County.

66. Reference to will for Richard Randall Rakes. Will Book 9, pp. 107-109, Patrick County.

Appendix D

On July 26, 1997 the descendents of Revolutionary War soldier, James Cannaday Sr. gathered at his gravesite, above his home-place in Franklin County, to place a marker provided by the Daughters of the American Revolution (DAR) to honor his service to America.

George R. Hayes, Betty Simms Hayes' husband, presided at the ceremony. George thanked Frieda Clark Cannaday for her work in securing the marker from the DAR.

Becky Cannaday Merchant's husband, J. Holt Merchant, Ph.D. in American History from University of Virginia, made the following remarks:

> *It is easy to forget how much we owe this man James Cannaday and a relative handful of others, a few thousand others. It is hard to imagine now how different the world might be if he had not participated in the Revolutionary War. Many said 'I have to work my farm; I have to go out and find land; I want to stay with my family; I can't be bothered.' But he was bothered and he did take part in the war and in his way he made the world a very different place for those of us who live in it now. It is also very easy to forget how much he sacrificed, he and the thousands of others who made the American Republic possible. Looked at from one point of view, this was not a great war, not many men participated in it. Certainly it was not fought on the scale of the Civil War or WWII. But it was not one of our small wars; it lasted a long time, eight years—longer than any of our other wars. It began in Lexington and Concord in 1774 and it didn't end until Yorktown in 1781. And even after 1781 the armies couldn't disband, if only because the diplomats in Paris had to have some creditable threat behind them. So the army was in existence for closer to ten years. It wasn't a small war; it stretched all the way from Montreal in Quebec, at least as far south as Savannah, as*

far west as we are today here in the mountains of Franklin County, and as far east—at least for a few participants—as the British Isles. Of course not any one soldier fought everywhere. Some soldiers, and perhaps James Cannaday was one of them, fought Indians. Some soldiers fought Tories and some soldiers fought British regulars. They may have done it in and around New York City, Staten Island, across the Delaware to Princeton and Trenton, and later in the famous battlefields in the north—Germantown, Brandywine Creek, Monmouth Courthouse, or he may have fought in the South, in the Waxhaws, Cowpens, Kings Mountain, Camden, Guilford Courthouse, and perhaps he was at Yorktown with Washington and the great surrender. But wherever he was and whatever he did, he sacrificed greatly. The central government, the Continental Congress was weak, and found it very difficult to support the war adequately. The state governments were small; some of them couldn't support the war; some of them wouldn't support the war. Certainly one of the shocking things was the reluctance of ordinary Americans to make the sacrifices to pay the taxes, to join the army. But we know he did. If he was like most other American soldiers he had too little food, too little corn, too little pork, too few weapons, too little ammunition, too few boots, too few uniforms, too few horses. And yet somehow he and they persevered; they stood up to the British. They took the worst the British had to hand out to them. And they not only persevered, they won. They made possible the formation of the American Republic. And so it is entirely appropriate that we are here today on this wonderful hillside looking out over this wonderful little valley. It is entirely appropriate that we remember James Cannaday and his sacrifices and his perseverance and finally his success.

At the conclusion of the ceremony, George read a prayer written by Elva S. Cannaday, James Cannaday's great, great, great granddaughter.

Remember, Oh Lord, our ancestors, Elizabeth and James Cannaday, who came to this land and established a home and a heritage for us, who stand here today. Make us thankful for their courage and their strength. Bless this memorial to James Cannaday's memory and make us, his descendents, worthy of our heritage. Bless this great country and grant that the course of this world may be such that we will know peace in our time, and we leave this place and go forth inspired by the examples that our ancestors set for us. In Christ we pray. Amen.

Appendix E

Remembrances of the Cannaday Family

By Hughes Cannaday c. 1920

My grandfather James Cannaday, Jr. (1786-1861) lived at the place now known as the Mat Spencer place on Runnet Bag Creek... My grandfather owned over fifty negros (*sic*) and raised twelve children (one of whom represented Franklin County in the Virginia Legislature—Isaac Cannaday). James Cannaday owned all of the land on Runnet Bag Creek for five miles...

My grandfather made the road up the mountain between Franklin and Floyd and it was named Cannaday's Gap in his honor.

They said they kept two women weaving in looms they used in those days making the twelve children and fifty negros (*sic*) clothes. He owned the mill that is now operated by I.T. Cannaday and the farm that I.T. Cannaday now ownes (*sic*), since it has been owned by I.T. Cannaday he has been doing extensive business. He has a handsome dwelling and runs a large store and post office. He has turned the old James Cannaday mill into a rolling mill. There is a splendid Episcopalian Church and school building on the same place, which runs winter and summer by two of the very best teachers: Miss Ora Harrison from Franklin County and Miss Newland from New York. I.T. Cannaday has a family of six children: Harry, Zera, Charles, May, Theddie and Russell. All of them are people for their county to be proud of, __they having been raised in it. Harry, their oldest son is now operating a big farm in Maryland. Zera is Cashier (*sic*) of a bank in Martinsville. Charles is his father's clerk in store and post master. While the others are in school. The farm on Runnet Bag Creek that I own now and inherited from my father John Treadwell Cannaday, ___859 acres was my grandfather's negro (*sic*) quarters. So he kept negros (*sic*) there at work, and negros (*sic*) to cook all the time. He use (*sic*) to make eight hundred barrels of corn and other grain in proportion. When Christmas came it was said he invited all of his children and grandchildren, his miller and wife and all the fifty negros (*sic*) to take dinner, and white laborers too. His grandson James Simms lives on part of the James Cannaday farm on Runnet Bag Creek.

He was an old Confederate soldier and a mechanic by trade. He raised a family of ten children, who will be an honor to the generation. Some of them are living on part of the James Cannaday farm on Runnet Bag Creek.

They have an advantage of living near a Methodist School and Church and from which they have taken the advantage, and working in their Master's Vinyard (*sic*) as well as for themselves.

The farm of 869 acres that I inherited from my father is on Runnet Bag Creek and Otter Creek, which run together on the farm. This farm is now run by myself Hughes D. Cannaday and Leroy Ross, my son-in-law.

The Methodist Church and school which has been built on Runnet Bag Creek was first started up by Miss Ruth Watson, a graduate of Blackstone College. With the help of W.A. Thompson Jr. (on whose land the school was built) she has tought (*sic*) very successfully there for several years with Sallie Cannaday Ross assisting apart (*sic*)of the time. Gail Simms a son of James Simms and a great-grandson of James Cannaday married Miss Watson. The school is still running by the Methodist people, as it is a branch of the big Ferrum Training School run by Dr. Beckham. The school on Runnet Bag is known as the Trinity School and Church. It has done a great and lasting good in the way of teaching children their books as well as teaching the Way of Truth and Life.

Respectfully H. D. Cannaday

James Cannaday the father of the above mentioned James Cannaday, who was the settler lived at the Nancy Jane Martin place. His wife, who was Elizabeth Raikes lived to be 105 old.

Bibliography

Books

Cannaday, Frieda Clark. *The Cannaday Family of Virginia and West Virginia*. St. Petersburg, FL: Published by Author, 1988.

Clifton, Nettie S. *Rakes History and Rakes Miscellaneous*. Catonsville, MD: Published by Author, 1997.

Dabney, Virginius. *Virginia: The New Dominion*. New York: Doubleday & Co., Inc., 1971.

Hurt, Frank Benjamin. *A History of Ferrum College: An Uncommon Challenge, 1914-1974*. Roanoke, VA: The Stone Printing Co., 1977.

Scott, J.L. *36th and 37th Battalions Virginia Cavalry*. Lynchburg, VA: H.E. Howard, 1986.

Stillman, Peter R. *Families Writing*. Cincinnati: Writers' Book Digest,1989.

Pubic Documents

Annapolis, MD: Maryland Historical Society. Revolutionary War, Militia List.

Annapolis, MD. St. Mary's Archives. Hall of Records. Volumes #2 and 6.

Charles County, MD. Courthouse. Deed Books 2:174, 22:333, L3:460, 3:288.

___________. Will Book A, B, #3, Folio A8; A. E. 6:0.

Franklin County, VA. Courthouse. Deed Books #1, 2 ,4 ,5, 6, 7, 8, 11, 12, 13, 14, 16, 17, 18, 19, 20, 21, 22, 23, 24, 25, 26, 27, 43.

___________, Plat Book #1.

___________. Will Books #2,4,13.

Henry County, VA. Courthouse. Deed Books #1, 2, 3, 7.

___________. Survey Book #1.

Patrick County, VA. Courthouse. Deed Books #1, 2, 4, 8, 9, 10, 11, 13, 15, 18, 19, 20, 24, 25.

___________. Will Books #1, 3, 4, 9.

Richmond, VA: Library of Virginia. Archives. Land Office Grants.

Washington, D.C.: National Archives. Historical Register of Virginia in the Revolution.

Unpublished Interviews, Essay, and Genealogy

Cannaday, Elva S. and L. Earl Simms. Interviews (19) by Becky Cannaday Merchant, April 5, 1998—March 3, 2001, Salem, VA. Tape recordings.

Cannaday, Elva S. Interview by Becky Cannaday Merchant, June 22, 1998, Salem, VA. Tape recording.

Cannaday, Elva S., L. Earl Simms, Edsel Simms. Interview by Becky Cannaday Merchant, July 6, 1999, Salem, VA. Tape recording.

Cannaday, Elva S., Edsel Simms, Betty Simms Hayes. Interview by Becky Cannaday Merchant, January 16, 1999, Salem, VA. Tape recording.

Cannaday, Hughes. *Cannaday's Gap and Runnet Bag Creek. Endicott, VA, c1920.* Typed essay.

Cannaday, James II. Memorial Service for placement of Revolutionary War Marker at gravesite, July 26, 1997, Endicott, VA. Tape recording.

Corse, Thomas. Bowyer/Semmes Genealogical Chart. 1988.

Hayes, Betty Simms. Interview by Becky Cannaday Merchant, October 11, 1998, Salem, VA. Tape recording.

Simms, Edsel. Interview by Becky Cannaday Merchant, September 13, 1998, Salem, VA. Tape recording.

Simms, Harold. Interview by Becky Cannaday Merchant, April 6, 2002, Ferrum. VA. Tape recording.

Whelby, Mary Elizabeth Simms. Interview by Becky Cannaday Merchant, April 3, 1999, Salem, VA. Tape recording.

About the Author

After more than 20 years working for the Historic Lexington Foundation and the Stonewall Jackson House Museum, Becky Merchant now spends much of her time as a freelance writer. She has several projects going, or at least in mind; one is a study of land acquisition and settlement by early American yeoman farmers, like her own ancestors; the other is publishing the journal and photographs from her "tour of duty" as a National Park Service volunteer at the Petrified Forest in Arizona in 2002. The remainder of her free time she spends walking in the woods, searching out birds and wildflowers, and paddling her kayak on lakes, inlets, and other gentle waters.

Becky grew up in Martinsville, Virginia and Charlotte, North Carolina, graduated from Mary Baldwin College, and married her college sweetheart, Holt Merchant. They settled in Lexington, Virginia after a two-year stint in Germany on government business and the completion of Holt's graduate studies. They have two sons and two grandsons.

www.ingramcontent.com/pod-product-compliance
Lightning Source LLC
LaVergne TN
LVHW091034080826
845145LV00002B/483

* 9 7 8 0 9 8 0 0 0 7 7 2 5 *